HOW TO
SET UP AND
IMPLEMENT
A RECORDS
MANAGEMENT
SYSTEM

HOW TO
SET UP AND
IMPLEMENT
A RECORDS
MANAGEMENT
SYSTEM

GLORIA GOLD

American Management Association

New York • Atlanta • Boston • Chicago • Kansas City • San Francisco • Washington, D.C.
Brussels • Mexico City • Tokyo • Toronto

This publication is designed to provide accurate and authoritative
information in regard to the subject matter covered. It is sold with
the understanding that the publisher is not engaged in rendering
legal, accounting, or other professional service. If legal advice or
other expert assistance is required, the services of a competent
professional person should be sought.

Library of Congress Cataloging-in-Publication Data

Gold, Gloria.
    How to set up and implement a records management system / Gloria
    Gold.
        p.   cm.
    Includes index.
    ISBN 0-8144-0292-5
    1. Business records—Management.   2. Filing systems.   I. Title.
HF5736.G647   1995
651.5—dc20   95-15015
                                                                              CIP

Printing number

10 9 8 7 6 5 4 3 2 1

This book is dedicated
to my lifetime companion
my husband
Norman.

Contents

Foreword

It is so refreshing to have a records management publication that is not a textbook or a tedious manual. *How to Set Up and Implement a Records Management System* is a truly practical guide to implementing a comprehensive records management program that will result in cost savings for the organization and recognition for the implementer. As the owner of a consulting firm, I can appreciate how challenging it is to elevate records management to a higher priority than it now occupies. This book shows how to secure management support and how to incorporate that commitment in a full implementation strategy.

Because I consider Gloria Gold my mentor, I am pleased that others will learn from her pragmatic approach. It is remarkable to have *one* publication encompassing the process, from selling the program within the organization to designing and installing the system components. For those individuals who are charged with the records management responsibility, there is now a tried-and-true resource to guide you through your endeavor.

Patricia A. Zimmerman, CRM
President, Info Logic

Acknowledgments

In appreciation:

To all those who shared their time, wisdom, support, and resources over all the years, how do I love thee and thank you? Let me count the ways.

To whose who contributed specific items, thank you:

- *Clo Ross-Kilkelly,* SPHR, Administrative Vice President, Clairson International, Ocala, Florida—in-house newsletters
- *Jan Tutt,* Assistant City Manager, City of Ocala, Florida—records management evaluation
- *Marilyn Jordan,* City Clerk, City of Ocala, Florida—retention schedules
- *Lee Barnard,* President, Records Management, Inc., Ocala, Florida—forms relating to evaluation, inventory, and records information and disposal system (RIDS) manual (Lee is my current partner)
- *Patti Zimmerman,* CRM, President, Info Tech, Minneapolis—file management forms and other contributions above and beyond the call of duty
- *Mary Lord,* Director Human Resources, Dairyland Power Company, La Cross, Wisconsin—Optical Disk Feasibility Study
- *Jeffrey Gold,* Roanoke, Virginia—author's photograph
- The many great editors at AMACOM who held my hand

And to those whose support was critical, thank you:

- *George Kieffer,* my boss at the State of Minnesota
- *Dr. Elaine Parent,* who nagged me unmercifully
- *Sally Anderson,* CRM, who made me proud

- *Regina Ryan*, President, Regina Ryan Publishing Enterprises, Inc., my friend and capable agent
- *Susan Ayers*, Vice President, David Toushin and Associates, Inc., Minneapolis—whose dynamite brochure for my new consulting firm opened doors to large companies all over this county

And for eight marvelous years, much love and many thanks to my partner and the Vice President of The Bottom Line, Inc., *Nancy Freeman*—oh, didn't we ramble!

HOW TO
SET UP AND
IMPLEMENT
A RECORDS
MANAGEMENT
SYSTEM

Introduction

Why Your Company Should Start a Records Management Program

Records management is corporate America's secret weapon. More than any piece of high-tech equipment, records management can save hundreds of thousands of dollars, year after year, with practically no expenditure. Why? Records management is made up of tasks designed to do the following:

- Improve office productivity.
- Eliminate errors.
- Reduce liability.
- Preserve vital records.
- Facilitate the exchange of information among, between, and within departments.

and thereby:

- Cut the costs of doing business.

No matter what it's called, you have to love a program that can do all that.

Effective information retrieval is the name of the game, and records management is the winning strategy. It's not the records themselves—their bulk or their spiffy filing arrangement in modern cabinets—that give an organization its competitive edge. Files themselves do not improve a company's services or products. They do not cement customer-client relationships. But the retrieval and delivery of accurate information to the right people, at the right time, and in the right format is where it's at. This main task of records management relates directly to the mission of your company.

Even though the idea sounds like magic, realizing an effective records management program is a matter of taking these simple steps, each building upon the preceding one:

1. Determine the current cost of handling the company's records and find out what impediments there currently are to the efficient retrieval and transfer of information within the company.
2. Inventory all the company's records.
3. Assign retention periods to the data—how long the company will keep each particular record based on legal and administrative needs. These retention periods apply whether the record is on paper, computer, optical disk, microfilm, or legal steno tapes. This is called a *retention schedule.*
4. Provide a system of documentation to monitor that inventory; it should be kept up-to-date, and obsolete records should *routinely* be disposed of.

How to Set Up and Implement a Records Management System covers what every records manager needs to know. It details the two basics of records management systems: how to develop and implement a records management program and, as far as possible, what the attendant costs should be.

The Benefits of Records Management

Companies benefit from records management in diverse financial ways. Let me explain:

• The average records inventory and retention schedule determines that 30 percent of all records in offices could and *should* be destroyed. Furthermore, 40 percent of all records in storage* should be destroyed. For every file cabinet emptied and removed, the company saves an average of $1,300 a year. In addition, a file cabinet can be recycled. If the inventory and retention schedule is to empty twelve file cabinets, the annual savings amount to $15,600. In contrast, if a company operates on a 6 percent profit margin, a salesperson must achieve $260,000 in new sales to add the same amount to the company's profit line.

*In my personal experience, this figure is 70 percent, and often 100 percent.

- With 70 percent of the files disposed of or sent to long-term storage, the office staff has only the remaining 30 percent to deal with. Filing and retrieving will be improved by an average of 35 percent, and filing errors will be cut from 5 percent to practically nil. If four people are filing and retrieving at $10 an hour, savings amount to $14 a day, or more than $3,000 a year. Again, a salesperson must achieve $50,000 in sales to add $3,000 to the company's profit.

- The mere fact that a company follows an *official, routine,* and *documented* retention schedule could (and does) save it hundred of thousands of dollars in litigation. No longer are obsolete documents, often taken out of context, used as evidence against a company.

- When a company's vital records are adequately protected, thus ensuring a speedy return to business in the event of a disaster or business interruption, most insurance companies will grant a substantial reduction on premiums.

So it's no wonder that records management is such a powerful weapon. It belongs in every company's arsenal for competing in the marketplace and for public or private funding.

The Scope of Records Management

The basic tasks of records management are as follows:

- To install uniform, standard filing systems throughout the company, with indexes clearly understandable and available to those employees authorized to use the files
- To provide limited access to an in-house records storage room maintaining private or confidential records
- To establish an off-site records storage center with controlled access, which will follow a designated retention and disposal schedule
- To install a forms-management program that provides improved quality of forms, reduces overall printing costs, and eliminates the collection of redundant data
- To implement an image-reduction program such as optical disk or CD-ROM, which compact stored records, e.g., micrographics and electronic imaging systems (although newer technology will probably be developed)

- To create computerized programs that manage any or all of the above systems
- To provide written documentation describing all the records systems and procedures for maintaining them, as well as for the training of new employees in the use of records management systems
- To maintain report management programs, especially in governmental agencies, that standardize size, format, use of names, covers, binders, and paper stock
- To implement correspondence management programs that track information flow throughout an organization, ensuring that such information is available to those who need it
- To establish resource libraries containing audio and video materials, periodicals, copies of studies, reports, and archival and historical documents

In addition, some records management programs may also include voice mail, e-mail, meeting coordination, internal mailing lists, and internal newsletters. We each bring different skills and predispositions to our jobs, so different areas of interest fall into our laps as records managers.

It's important that records managers not think of themselves as merely librarians. *You are not a librarian.* That doesn't mean that the file room and the storage centers cannot be run as efficiently as a major library. But records managers simply have different goals from those of librarians.

Likewise, the demarcation between computer management and records management has blurred. Remember, mainframe computers are for recording transactions; sending statements; tracking payroll; issuing checks, licenses, certificates, credits, and refunds; and filling orders. Personal computers are for forecasting results or trends, word processing, and communications between branches, to customers, and among internal staff.

For records managers, then, the goal is not merely to store and retrieve information, and to dispose of records, but to provide information from those records in the most effective manner.

A case in point: You are storing records for an airline that has merged with two other airlines. Federal regulations require that no records from the absorbed airline may be disposed of until all phases of the merger have been completed. At that point, the retention schedule kicks in. But management needs to know which records fall into this "hold" category. Are there flight logs, maintenance records, or in-flight sales records that may be in dispute? A "hold" on the automated retention schedule will recognize these records and allow the records manager to identify them easily.

Opportunities for Records Managers

Every company needs someone to do the following:

- Organize records.
- Tell staff how to file, store, and retrieve records.
- Provide security for valuable records.
- Dispose of records when they have fulfilled their legal and administrative needs.

As the company's records manager, you are the keeper, transporter, and disposer of information. You are not a historian or an archivist. You deal in today's news and tomorrow's decisions.

Most companies are willing to pay for this service, provided it results in quantifiable savings. But most companies do not have a records manager. The field is wide open. Thus, once positive results are demonstrated, the position of the records manager is respected and considered an integral part of the information-management process.

This book will teach you, step by step, how you can become not just a records manager for your company or governmental unit but a *world-class* records manager. You will be capable of carrying out specific assignments as well as managing an entire records management program.

In short, you will have a whole new profession that you can market for a substantial annual salary.

- Entry-level salaries for records managers usually start between $20,000 and $26,000 a year.
- Experienced records managers earn from $25,000 to $40,000 a year.
- Senior records managers at the corporate level are paid from $40,000 to $60,000.
- Records management consultants often earn from $80,000 to more than $500,000 annually.

I have been a consultant for nine years, with twenty-eight years' experience in the records management business. But the important point is that my skills were learned on the job. This book describes mistakes I have made as well as what I have found works. In easy, nontechnical stages, you can go from being a nice, bright, enthusiastic person to becoming all that *plus* a world-class records manager.

Remember, when a company looks at its records manager as a good insurance policy, the salary is peanuts and the savings are megabucks. And since it is dollars and cents that get management's attention, that's how you will sell records management. All of the instructions and admonishments in this book are tied to the dollar figure. That's the bottom line.

Note: Readers of this book may be employees of private industry, non-profit organizations, units of government, or combinations of these. For practical purposes, we will call those entities "the company" and the persons who approve projects and sign checks for it, "the management."

Part One

The Way to Get Management's Attention

Sandy Koufax, a baseball great, once said that every time he went to the pitcher's mound to start a game, he was determined to pitch a no-hit, no-run game. After the opposition got a hit, he concentrated on a shutout. If the other team scored, he believed with all his heart that he would still win the game. Records managers need that same sharp focus, concentration, and dedication.

You will need to be in the most positive frame of mind because, even though you may have been employed by the company for many years, until you are its records manager, you will barely know how it works. The good news is that a perfect game is within reach every time. You can score big and establish credibility in the front office if you are properly prepared.

Chapter 1
Getting Started

So you have just been given the job of "doing something about all those records."

Or you have just finished school with a records management (or some other) major and this is your first job. Perhaps you have the responsibility of supervising a new position dealing with records management. Or maybe you will be liaison to a consultant hired to deal with "all those records." Suppose you've been looking for a new and exciting career. Doing something about "all those records" may be Opportunity that's knockin'.

If you are wondering, "How am I going to get this show on the road? What do I do first? Will I look professional, be confident, and know for sure that what I propose is the appropriate, money-saving path the company should take?"

The first thing to do is your homework. You need to organize what you know about the company and get an overview of its operations. Then you can assess your skills and bring them up-to-date.

Research

You will need several essential documents, which should all be found within the company, although it may take some digging. But persevere; the search is half the fun.

Mission Statement

Find, read, and understand your organization's mission. Somewhere in the company (governmental units and nonprofit agencies as well) will be its mission statement.

The mission statement is the basis for the establishment of the company.

You may find it in your company's library, in the attorney's office, in the state statutes, or all the way at the top, with the CEO's assistant or secretary. This statement tells the world what the organization is about: why it was created, what its goals are, and what its objectives are. It may be a simple sentence such as:

> The MRS. WEINBERG COOKIE FACTORY has been formed to produce, distribute, and make a profit from the very best oatmeal-raisin cookies in the world.

Or it may consist of several pages of goals and objectives that outline in detail the products and services that the company intends to offer to its selected market.

A mission statement may include, as well, references to providing returns for stockholders. It may even contain a resolution to return a percentage of profits back to the community in which it is headquartered. For example:

> The HIGH-TECH CORPORATION has been formed to build the world's fastest computer to handle genetic research; to market and deliver unique products and services to our customers; and to ensure ongoing profits to our founders and investors. Five percent of the annual net profit will be earmarked to support high school science projects, selected from national entries and approved by the Hennepin County Board of Education.

Such a mission statement immediately tells the records manager to be watchful for records dealing with that 5 percent distribution, stockholders' records, customer complaint records, and winners lists, plus annual auditors' reports.

Perhaps the best mission statement is to be found in the

Preamble to the Constitution of the United States of America

> We, the people of the United States, in order to form a more perfect Union, establish justice, insure domestic tranquility, provide for the common defense, promote the general welfare, and secure the blessings of liberty to ourselves and our posterity, do ordain and establish this Constitution for the United States of America.

After careful consideration, any records manager should be able to use this last mission statement to make decisions concerning the necessity of keeping, storing, and/or disposing of thousands of federal records. For example, when trying to determine the importance of keeping a particular record—say, the annual budget—measure it against the Preamble. Ask yourself, "Does this document contribute to the stated objectives? Does it help to establish justice, ensure domestic tranquility, provide for common defense, promote the general welfare, or secure liberty?" It doesn't have to be any more complicated than that.

What do you do if after all your detective work and cajoling, you cannot find anything that even vaguely resembles a mission statement? Go back to the person who hired you and suggest that one be developed. Meanwhile, you may have to make do by using your own initiative and drafting a working statement.

Go over the most recent annual reports to see if you can extract enough information for a "working" mission statement. Even if this statement exists only for your own benefit, you will need it as your centerpost: You will be able to test your retention practices against the statement.

Once you know your company's mission, you may find that little, incorrect procedures have crept into its various systems. These are often based on one-time experiences that have nothing to do with the company's mission. These procedures may, in fact, hinder or even thwart the company's mission.

Keep in mind always that the mission of the company, and the accomplishment of its stated goals and objectives, is what keeps the company in business and pays your salary or fee. Thus, the success with which the mission's goals are attained directly affects your job security. And, to close the loop, it directly affects how management regards you professionally.

To accomplish its mission, the company must make the best possible use of its resources. Typically, these are its people, its information, and its fixed and consumable assets.

Clearly, people come first (or most often they come first). Information, however, is a very close second. In a recent survey of information systems directors throughout the country, managers responded that delivering information to the front office in real time was what they believed will give their companies the competitive edge into the late 1990s and beyond.

Organization Chart

I have worked as a consultant to only one major company that did not have an organization chart (at least the top officers said there was none). Management may have thought to keep a loose rein; chaos reigned instead. For example, there was a complete lack of communication. Multiple, tiny, self-enclosed "kingdoms" were erected within the company. Lots of time was lost to fighting and scratching to protect territory. And workers often did not know to whom they reported; eventually they didn't care and left. Once, during a meeting with the management information systems (MIS) director of this company, the conference room telephone rang. The director said, "If that's my boss, get his name." It was, and we got *her* name.

The bottom line is that key people departed this company as soon as they were able. Since this was a company whose products were complex and highly regulated by the federal government, newly hired staff required significant training before they could be effective, let alone proficient.

An organization chart is a company's chain of command. It lays out responsibilities for each manager and lets those who report within a unit know how they relate to other organizational units for the purpose of—let's hear it, class—*accomplishing our company's mission!*

Exhibits 1-1 to 1-3 are examples of organization charts. As you draw up an organization chart for your own records management unit, keep these standards in mind:

1. Always include the two positions above the unit you are charting (see Exhibits 1-1 and 1-2).
2. Use proper titles for each position and names of those people holding the positions. If the position is unfilled, write *vacant* where the employee name would go.
3. It is useful to include functions on the organization chart, particularly in the planning stages (see Exhibit 1-2). When the chart is prepared for publication, however, functions are usually omitted.

Exhibit 1-3 is an example of a municipal organization chart. Services such as central services and records management (not shown on this chart) report to the assistant to the city manager.

You may wish to organize your unit differently. Records management functions lend themselves nicely to quality circles or teams of staff that may be formed to address a specific problem, on an ad hoc basis. For example, if your company has never taken a forms inventory, your team to do this might look like the one shown in Exhibit 1-4.

Preparing an organization chart for your own records management unit will force you to think through the functions the unit will be performing. The chart becomes a blueprint for changes as you request new positions and larger budgets.

Exhibit 1-1. A simple organization chart.

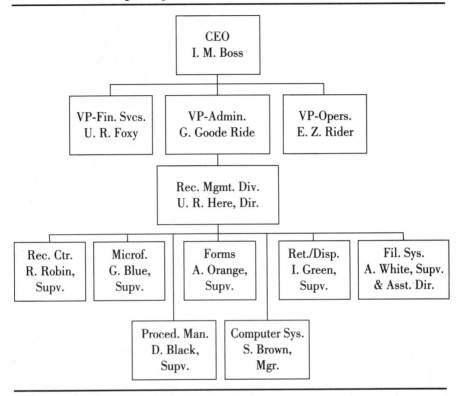

Telephone List

Now that you have some idea how your company is structured, take a good look at the company's telephone book. If personnel are listed by unit (as opposed to strictly by alphabet) review the names so you can see who belongs to which department, division, section, or unit.

Annual Report

Gather copies of the annual report issued by your company. Or, for those of you in local government, this might be the governor's state-of-the-state address or the city manager's report to the city council at the end of the fiscal year.

Private industry's annual reports are often glossy, attractive publications

(Text continues on page 16.)

Exhibit 1-2. A typical function-oriented organization chart.

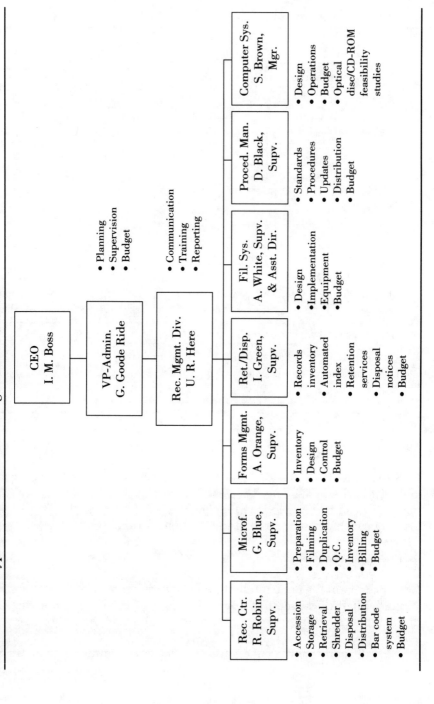

Exhibit 1-3. City of Ocala organization chart.

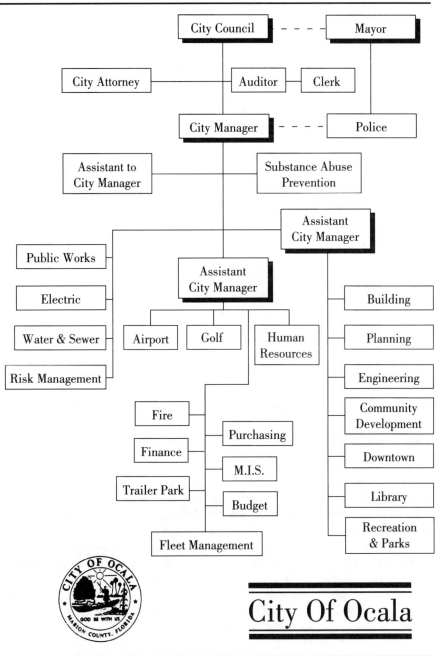

Exhibit 1-4. Forms inventory project.

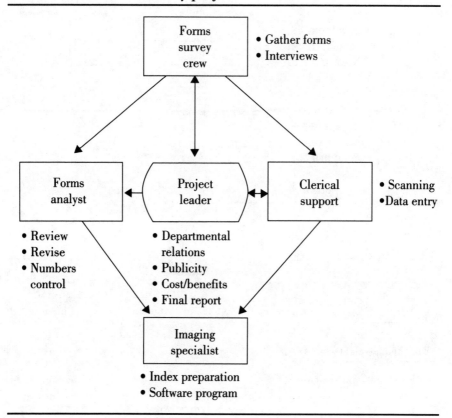

put out for the benefit of stockholders and would-be investors. Usually, they tell a good deal about the company, its plans and aspirations, and have pictures of the officers. You'll be able to start putting faces to the names in the telephone listing and on the organization chart.

Also, by going back a few years in the reports, you might get some idea of whether the company is able to fulfill its annual plans put forth so proudly, or if these continually fall by the wayside. What you read in the annual reports is, of course, probably not the whole story. Companies don't usually come out in print explaining that the reason this or that plan failed is that the key person left and took the design with him. Nevertheless, patterns begin to emerge that you may find enlightening.

Budget

The company's current budget is another eye-opening document. Digest what you can regarding planned expenditures for your department, division, or unit.* Compare these with the items listed for other departments and divisions (see Exhibit 1-5). You will begin to get a strong sense of priorities within the company, some of which may come as a surprise to you.

Remember, what you see in print regarding the dollars allocated for your records management activities is often cast in concrete. You will probably not be able to increase those funds during the current fiscal year. And if you expect to increase them in future years, you will have to justify every nickel in the clearest, most indisputable terms possible. So knowing what the budgeted expenditures are for other nonrevenue-producing units won't hurt.

For some reason I am not entirely sure of, state governments usually are organized with the department as the larger unit, subdivided into divisions, which in turn are subdivided into sections and then units. In private industry, most often the larger unit is the division, which is subdivided into departments. I mention this here because in reviewing Exhibit 1-5 you might otherwise miss the allocation for a filing system in the budget for the county engineer!

Newsletters, House Organs, Catalogs

Get copies of everything the organization publishes. Of course, if the company is a hundred years old, you don't need every published scrap of paper. But use your judgment to compile a current library and reference index so that you are up-to-date on company activities.

In the newsletter and house organs you will begin to see certain names over and over. This will give you an idea of who is most active in promoting the company's welfare; these people take part in company events and causes. Don't assume that just because a person's name appears frequently, it is a self-seeking ploy. I have found that such people really care about their company, its good name, and its products. They stand up and bear the brunt of remarks in order to fulfill the difficult assignments heaped on them by management.

Also, company publications reach a wide audience in the organization.

---

*As the keeper of company records, you should receive at least two copies of the current budget plus those for the previous two years.

Exhibit 1-5. Budget for a department of administration.

MARION COUNTY BOARD OF COUNTY COMMISSIONERS
PROPOSED BUDGET
FISCAL YEAR 1993–94
Printed: 9/28/93

105 Fund
411 Dept

County Transportation Maintenance Fund
County Engineer

Priority	Description of Item(s) Requested	Unit Cost	Proposed Quantity	Proposed Cost	Revised Quantity	Revised Cost	
1)	One ton diesel truck and bed (sign shop replacement over)	30,000	1	30,000	—	—	8-23
1)	One ton diesel truck and bed	25,000	—	—	2	50,000	8-23
2)	Asphalt testing equipment (E.P.A. banning chemical now)	7,100	1	7,100	1	7,100	
3)	Vacuum pump (replacement for sign machine)	1,400	1	1,400	1	1,400	
4)	Acid storage cabinets (required by HRS rules)	700	2	1,400	2	1,400	
5)	Air cylinder conversion kit for sign maker	550	1	550	1	550	
6)	Soldering/de-soldering station (traffic signal repairs)	850	1	850	1	850	
7)	Misc. soil testing equipment (replacements)	425	1	425	1	425	
8)	Generator - for arrow board & emergency traffic signal	400	1	400	1	400	
9)	Hand-held radios (for traffic employees that don't have)	750	2	1,500	2	1,500	
10)	Polaroid camera (for inspection employee that doesn't have)	100	1	100	1	100	
10)	Measuring wheels (replacements for worn out)	125	4	500	4	500	
11)	Desk chairs (replacements - inspection - worn out)	225	5	1,125	5	1,125	
12)	HP 425 programmable calculators (for engineering technicians that don't have)	175	2	350	2	350	
13)	35 mm camera for inspection (don't have)	500	1	500	—	—	8-23
13)	35 mm camera for inspection (don't have)	250	—	—	1	250	8-23
14)	Water coolers (replacements for inspectors)	35	5	175	5	175	
15)	Mobile radio (replacement for traffic signal bucket truck)	800	1	800	1	800	
16)	Drafting work stations	2,600	—	—	3	7,800	7-28
16)	Archival filing system	49,000	—	—	1	49,000	7-28
	Total Equipment Cost			47,175		123,725	
				Balanced		Balanced	

One company ran a contest through its newsletter. Of the total 750 employees, there were more than 700 entries.

So you begin to see the power of the press. Consider, for a moment, how you will take advantage of this as you announce the various phases of your records management program. New systems, new equipment, new employees, proposed projects, due dates, seminars, speakers—all these should be announced in the company newsletter or house organ. If your company doesn't have a newsletter or house organ, think seriously about starting one to advertise your activities, triumphs, and most important, bottom-line savings.

Exhibit 1-6 shows two pages of a newsletter I particularly like, from Clairson International, a large manufacturing company. Note the concern for the employees' well-being. Yet information is provided about the company as well.

Retention Schedule

If the company has any sort of records retention schedule, get a copy and study it. Ascertain that what you have is the most recent version.

A proper records retention schedule describes a specific records series (a collection of documents relating to a single topic) and specifies how long the series should be kept, as well as the legal citation upon which the retention period is based (see Exhibit 1-7).

Additional information that should be on a records retention schedule is as follows:

- [ ] A description of the records
- [ ] Who has possession of the records (custodian)
- [ ] Division, department, or building where records are located
- [ ] Whether or not these are vital records (necessary to company's recovery following a disaster)
- [ ] Volume of the records
- [ ] Date(s) of the records
- [ ] Whether these are records of a private or confidential nature; if so, whether the records are filed in a secured area or cabinet
- [ ] How frequently the records are produced
- [ ] How long the records should be kept in the office, central file, or storage
- [ ] When (usually the year) the records may be destroyed

The existing schedule may help you to become familiar with records series titles. Then again, if it is a generic schedule, it is probably worse than no schedule at all. Remember, if the schedule was official, the instructions

(Text continues on page 22.)

Exhibit 1-6. Example of a good company newsletter.

1994 Hardware Show

By Mary Mills

What's new at ClosetMaid!

Power Merchandising:

Our interactive system now includes a Design Idea module which enables customers to preview full color, action video concepts of storage solutions in the kitchen, bath, closet, garage, home office, children's room and laundry area, and to visualize what it would look like in their home and answer any questions they may have.

Available are Design Instructions, Installation & Product Selection guides, Hardware Selector guides and Storage Solutions. These are to help Consumers learn how to maximize the storage capacity of their home and provide a variety of project ideas.

1, 2, 3 Storage:

Packaging and merchandising clearly communicate to the consumer how to build their ideal closet from the components presented. Each component is a successful stand alone product and works as a component of the "1, 2, 3" system!

Lightning Hardware:

The strongest, most durable system on the market, aesthetically pleasing appearance, preloaded, fast and easy to install, and a cost savings from our current hardware.

Super Slide Accessories:

Our customer wanted a continuous slide rail and we gave them Super Slide, which gives them more hanging space. Now we have six Super Slide Accessories to add to the program.

Book Shelf (Profile Shelf System):

A flexible, versatile shelving with the warmth and beauty of wood. Profile shelving is designed to work with ClosetMaid Shelf Track Standards and Brackets system.

Standard & Brackets (Shelf Track):

The totally adjustable shelf mounting system, it has strength, good looks, versatility, and is easy to install. Brackets are specially designed for use with all ClosetMaid 12" and 16" deep ventilated wire shelving.

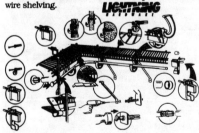

Emerson Electric Takes the Worry Out of How to Pay for School

No one can place a price tag on the value of education to one's career and family, but everyone can calculate the costs. It's a weighty sum, even for those who earn a good income.

That's why Emerson Electric sponsors U.S. Chamber so you have all the help you need. Emerson Electric employees and their family members (i.e. a spouse, children, grandchildren, siblings, aunts/uncles, cousins, etc.) can apply for financing from the program, which includes low interest, long-term ConSern: Loans for Education and federally-guaranteed student loans (Stafford, PLUS, SLS). In the case of ConSern: Loans for Education, a non-profit, privately-funded loan program, you can borrow up to $25,000 a year for tuition and related expenses, including a computer to use at school. Borrowers need to earn at least $15,000 to apply for ConSern: Loans for Education, but those who don't may add a co-signer to the application. Unlike other programs of its kind, ConSern: Loans for Education bases approval on an applicant's creditworthiness, not on need.

Applying for either ConSern: Loans for Education or the federal programs is easy and fast. Simply by calling **1-800-SOS-LOAN (1-800-767-5626)**, Emerson Electric employees and their families can talk to a knowledgeable Loan Service Specialist who will match their needs and family budget with loan programs and loan amounts. He or she will also make sure you have all the application forms you need to complete the application process for ConSern: Loans for Education or federal loans, including the Free Application for Federal Student Aid (FAFSA), which is required for federally-guaranteed student loans. There are no application deadlines, and once all the paperwork is complete, loan disbursements are made fast, typically within seven days.

A benefit of Emerson Electric's membership in the U.S. Chamber of Commerce, U.S. Chamber ConSern, The Complete Source for Financing Education, has provided $1.5 million in educational loans to Emerson Electric employees and families. For more information, Emerson Electric employees and their families are encouraged to call **1-800-SOS-LOAN**. Loan Service Specialists are available until 10 p.m. on weeknights and 6 p.m. on weekends eastern time.

Reproduced with permission.

Exhibit 1-7. A records retention schedule.

```
Run Date:  1/17/95                    Master Listing—Tagged                        Page
Run Time:  12:11AM                   Alphabetical by Record Title

===================================================================================================

Id#:  0000700
ADMINISTRATIVE SUPPORT FILES, 1976 TO 1990        Div:          Dept: CC
CITY CLERK'S MISCELLANEOUS FILES                  Cust Name:    JORDAN, M.
Media:   1-                              Privacy:  N    Vital:  N  Backup: N
Date Range On-Site:    /  /    thru    /  /
Date Range Off-Site:   /  /    thru    /  /
Storage Location: OFFIC-
--------------------------------------- Retention ------------------------------------------
Years:    3  Instructions: AUD-
Office:   1      Storage: 2      Offsite:          Dispose: 1994    Disposed: N
Governing Authority:  GRSLG # 4

===================================================================================================

Id#:  0000703
PROCLAMATIONS, CIT OF INVERNESS, 1970 TO 1990     Div:          Dept: CC
OFFICIAL PUBLIC ANNOUNCEMENTS                     Cust Name:    JORDAN, M.
Media:   1-                              Privacy:  N    Vital:  N  Backup: N
Date Range On-Site:    /  /    thru    /  /
Date Range Off-Site:   /  /    thru    /  /
Storage Location: OFFIC-
--------------------------------------- Retention ------------------------------------------
Years:    99 Instructions: PER-
Office:   PER   Storage: PER     Offsite: PER    Dispose:   0    Disposed: N
Governing Authority:  GRSLG #99, PERMANENT

===================================================================================================

Id#:  0000701
PURCHASING RECORDS, 1987 TO 1990                  Div:          Dept: CC
COPIES OF PURCHASE ORDERS                         Cust Name:    JORDAN, M.
Media:   1-                              Privacy:  N    Vital:  N  Backup: N
Date Range On-Site:    /  /    thru    /  /
Date Range Off-Site:   /  /    thru    /  /
Storage Location: OFFIC-
--------------------------------------- Retention ------------------------------------------
Years:    3  Instructions:  -
Office:   1      Storage: 2      Offsite:          Dispose: 1994    Disposed: N
Governing Authority:  GRSLG #106

===================================================================================================

Id#:  0000702
TELEPHONE MESSAGES, 1990 TO 1992                  Div:          Dept: CC
LOG OF LONG DISTANCE CALLS                        Cust Name:    JORDAN, M.
Media:   1-                              Privacy:  N    Vital:  N  Backup: N
Date Range On-Site:    /  /    thru    /  /
Date Range Off-Site   /  /    thru    /  /
Storgage Location: OFFIC-
--------------------------------------- Retention ------------------------------------------
Years:    1  Instruction: AUD-
Office:   1      Storage:        Offsite:          Dispose: 1994    Disposed: N
Governing Authority:  GRSLG #77

===================================================================================================
```

were detailed, and the schedule was being followed, management wouldn't have selected you for the records management assignment.

Physical Conditions

In your efforts to obtain your background documents, you probably had an opportunity to walk through many parts of the company. Make the most of these walks. Take a good look at the files you can see, particularly filing cabinets that are open. Are the file folders raggedy or dog-eared? Are they spilling out over the sides? Are the papers in disarray? Are files stacked on the floor beside the cabinets or on top of them? Are the cabinets all of a standard type, vertical or lateral in style, color, or condition? Can you observe anything about the company's overall filing practices?

And while you're about it, notice how much space is given over to the filing equipment and nonfiled papers, and what this is doing to the working space left to the staff.

Peek into offices as you go by. Who are the pack rats? Every company has at least one individual who is pathological about throwing things away. But don't be too quick to scoff; most pack rats got that way because of some terrifying experience. It will be your job to solve these problems—to win the confidence of all staff members so that routine disposals can begin.

So as you are making the rounds to collect your documentation, pay special attention to the central storage areas. These may be file rooms, records centers, or simply a massive collection of file cabinets in the center or at the back of a room. The files may be closet- or hallway-based. I have seen files stored in the oddest places: above the rafters of the men's room; in the boiler room; in the attic next to electrical and mechanical boxes; in the print shop and in the paint shop; in the airplane hanger next to the stored gasoline (honest!); in rooms aptly named "the spider room," "the pit," "the tunnel," and the "outhouse."

Your job is to bring about a change for the better. The worse it is now, the better you and your program will look as things improve. Warning: As you make the rounds, do not giggle, gasp, or make sarcastic remarks.

You will also want to visit any off-site storage areas during this orientation period. These areas may be in rented spaces, in other buildings owned by the company, or in a commercial records center. I have found off-site storage of records in the tank of an abandoned milk truck; in condemned outbuildings in a pasture; in an abandoned town hall with only the mice to keep them company; and in the basement of a building standing on the bank of a river famous for flooding every spring.

Take some pictures if you can so that you will remember how things were when the decision was made to hire you. Look for:

☐ Wet records and/or watermarks on walls
☐ Records stored near exposed wiring, steam pipes, paint, or other inflammables such as gasoline, kerosene, trash, or propane gas
☐ Records stored closer than eighteen inches from electrical fixtures
☐ Records spilled from boxes, covered with dust, or buried in mounds of boxes too heavy to lift

You will need this evidence for your "before" and "after" documentation. It also may be useful for your initial presentation to management.

Your homework will make you a budding expert on the company. Let's review four of the things you have learned:

1. You know what the organization is all about: its purpose, products, services, plans, past failures, and accomplishments.
2. You know who some of the key players are, where they are located, and how they relate organizationally to you.
3. You know what your budget is for the coming year and how it compares in size and apparent priority to other functions within your department or division and to other departments and divisions in the company.
4. You know what some of the records problems might be in terms of space, equipment and filing arrangement, accessibility, and security.

This may not sound like a great deal, but let me assure you, you probably know more at this moment about your company than 85 percent of the people who are working there. In fact, you may be one of only two or three people who know what most everyone in the company does.

Tools of the Trade

It's time to take stock of some specific skills you will need. You may already possess some or all of these skills; if you are proficient, you may skip this section. But if you feel the need to brush up on using flowcharts, personal computers, calculators, and telephones, then the remainder of this chapter will be useful to you.

Exhibit 1-8. Rough sketch of a flowchart.

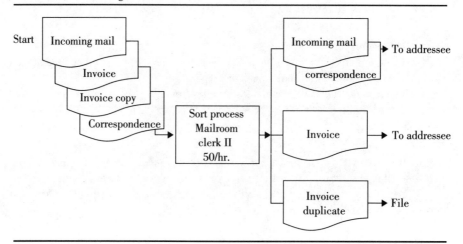

Flowcharts

Remember shorthand? Probably not. Remembering shorthand seems to be a lot like remembering Kay Kayser. Shorthand was invented so that secretaries could take down the boss's words practically as fast as he (hardly any *she* bosses in those days) uttered them. Billy Rose, a famous showman, art collector, and onetime husband of comedienne Fanny Brice, once held world titles for his speed in shorthand. He perfected his talent as assistant to financier Bernard Baruch. Obviously shorthand is not all he learned.

Shorthand was a shortcut. The same kind of shortcut is used by systems analysts. It's called flowcharting, and like shorthand, it condenses a lot of data rapidly so that it can be studied at a later time.

Instead of writing a lengthy description of a system, as in "The documents that start this process include incoming mail, invoices, duplicate copies of invoices, and miscellaneous correspondence," the analyst draws a flowchart as in Exhibit 1-8, describing, in about ten seconds, an entire day's work performed by the mail clerk. By adding brief words or phrases, the analyst can make the flowchart very specific. The chart can, for example, provide details about the operation such as the volume of transactions per day, hour, week; estimated time to complete transactions; salary or title of person(s) performing the task; and forms and their form numbers used in transactions.

The amount of information that can be captured on a flowchart seems to be almost limitless. In fact, it is that very capability that analysts must guard against. It is easy to get bogged down when flowcharting a system, detailing every aspect of the work or every responsibility. Or the opposite may take place: Key data may be left out, rendering the flowchart simplistic.

If you are called upon to chart the flow of documents in a department or division, concentrate on the essentials. Interview the people involved and sort through their responses for the critical data. And question their procedures. Why, for instance, in Exhibit 1-8, does the mail room keep the invoice duplicates?

Several years ago the manager of a state's computer division received a complaint that the daily patient count in the state's mental hospitals never tallied with the month-end count. This continually threw off the billing process, and I was asked to flowchart the documents feeding into the systems. After interviewing all the necessary parties and producing what looked like a wiring diagram for the Empire State Building, I returned to verify my chart with each interviewee.

I received sign-offs all along the line until I came to the last clerk. She looked at my mass of blocks and squares, and then looked at me with innocent blue eyes and asked, "Where do you have the part where I manually adjust the daily figures if I hear that a patient has checked himself out for the night?"

For flowcharting I use the template issued years ago by IBM, but stationery and business supply houses have a variety on hand. You may want to try out several styles until you find the one that fits you best. Aim for three things: consistency, accuracy, and complete documentation in your use of flowcharting:

1. *Consistency.* Always use the same symbol for the same function. For example, use the document block for all manner of paper documents. Don't try to draw a check one time and a notebook another; this will only slow you down. Instead, use the document block and letter in "check" or "3-ring binder," if you wish to be more precise.

2. *Accuracy.* Review your chart several times. I try to do this at least once while I'm sitting with the interviewee and then again when I go back for sign-off. You can't overdo this because you will find discrepancies, certainly among people who do the same tasks at the same time, and probably even with the person who supplied the original data.

3. *Complete documentation.* Get the numbers. When checks are processed, for example, pick up the daily volume, number of persons involved, salary data, and elapsed time. This documentation helps you analyze the

cost per transaction. Since you're going to need this data sooner or later, it's easier to get it when you do the initial interviews.

Flowcharting is not art with a capital *A*, but rather an art as opposed to a science. You have a great leeway in how you personalize your work. Your flowchart needs only to be instantly understandable to you and sufficiently complete to be understandable to those who are making the decisions. It goes without saying (but I'll say it anyway) that your flowcharts should be as unbiased as you can possibly make them.

As you grow accustomed to this tool, it will become so much a part of you that you can converse with the interviewees while you complete the flowchart, hardly needing to look at the drawing at all. I often draw the symbols freehand and then use a template for the final version. Alternatively, several personal computer software packages will produce the flowchart symbols in the sizes you select, and this creates an attractive finished product.

If you have been asking yourself the question, "As a records manager, not a computer systems analyst, when will I ever use flowcharting?" the answer is *practically every day.*

Suppose you want to install a central file on the third floor of your building and convert the current central file, which is located in the basement, to a records center for inactive storage. How would you justify the cost of such a project?

You could go to your boss and say, "A lot of time is being wasted by people running down to the basement to pull files." Or you could send her a memo reporting that three people have quit in the last year because they didn't like working in the basement. Or you could call a meeting to display brochures and layouts of new shelving, and tell everyone how nice it would be to have a central file on the third floor.

Alternatively, you could flowchart the current practice, wherein Accounting, Legal, Human Resources, and Purchasing send nine clerical support people and three managers to the basement on a daily basis in order to pull an average of forty-two file folders. The average cost per year is $84,603, which is broken down into costs for space, labor, equipment, and overhead. Then you could point out the available appropriate space on the third floor, flowchart the proposed system to be used by the four departments, and document the cost of a manned and controlled central file with secured basement storage (see Exhibit 1-9).

You can also detail the one-time cost of equipment and the ongoing cost of maintaining the operation. If the bottom line showed that costs can be recovered through labor savings in the first year or so, you would proba-

Exhibit 1-9. Flowcharts of current and proposed systems.

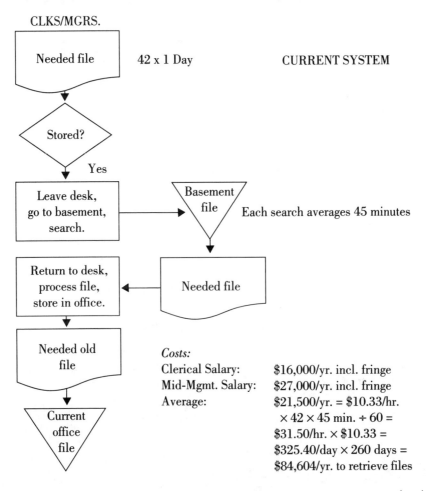

CLKS/MGRS.

Needed file   42 x 1 Day   CURRENT SYSTEM

Stored?   Yes

Leave desk, go to basement, search. → Basement file   Each search averages 45 minutes

Return to desk, process file, store in office. ← Needed file

Needed old file

Current office file

Costs:
Clerical Salary: $16,000/yr. incl. fringe
Mid-Mgmt. Salary: $27,000/yr. incl. fringe
Average: $21,500/yr. = $10.33/hr.
$\times$ 42 $\times$ 45 min. ÷ 60 =
$31.50/hr. $\times$ $10.33 =
$325.40/day $\times$ 260 days =
$84,604/yr. to retrieve files

(continues)

bly get a yes answer. In my experience this is what works (see Exhibit 1-10).

Because flowcharts are not always easily read by most managers, I recommend including a legend that explains to readers what the various symbols represent.

The symbols I use most frequently are shown in Exhibit 1-11. As you can see, most manual processes can incorporate these symbols. To denote a

Exhibit 1-9. (*continued*)

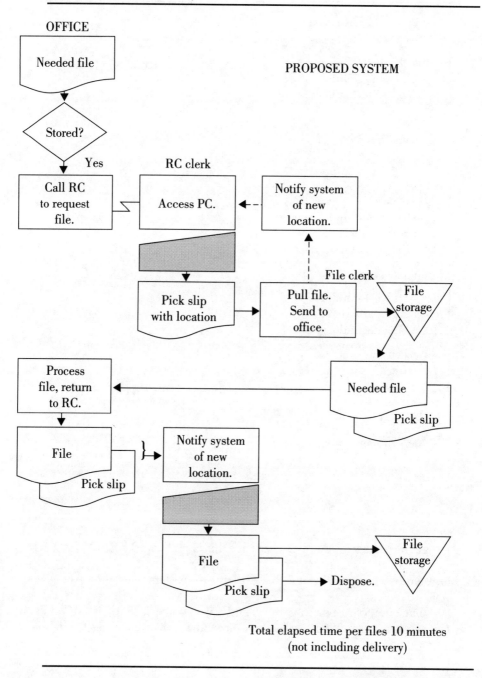

OFFICE

PROPOSED SYSTEM

Total elapsed time per files 10 minutes
(not including delivery)

Exhibit 1-10. Comparison of two records systems.

Current System	*Proposed System*

Comparison of Costs

42 files/day @ $7.75/file/		42 files/day, 7 hours/day	
45 minutes/file = $325/day		@ 10 minutes/file	
		Delivery	1 hour/day
		One full-time clerk	8 hours/day
Total	$84,603/year		$16,000/year

Comparison of Systems

• Files are messed up in storage.	• All files are delivered same day or may be picked up at file room counter.
• No record of where retrieved record goes, is stored, or who has it.	
• No security.	• Files are secured by limited access to file room, plus record of where file is.
• Key staff leaves desk for forty-five minutes at a time.	
• Hearty dislike of the system, causing labor turnover.	• Basement space is available for other uses.

Annual Costs

		One-time move/shelving	$ 8,000
		Computer/printer	3,500
		Software	1,500
		Labor	16,000
CY	$ 84,603		$ 29,000
CY+1	84,603		16,000
CY+2	84,603		16,000
CY+3	84,603		16,000
CY+4	84,603		16,000
CY+5	84,603		16,000
Total	$507,618		$109,000

PC or mainframe computer system, I use a combination of the same symbols. The newer templates contain symbols for all state-of-the-art technologies, and these are the types you should use.

Let's do a simple exercise. How would you flowchart a system where the incoming documents are accounts payable statements that need to be matched against the temporarily stored receiving memos before payment can be made?

If your flowchart looks something like the one in Exhibit 1-12, you have passed Flowcharting 101 and are ready to go forth into the world, template at the ready. But if your diagram doesn't look exactly like mine, not to worry. Flowcharting gets easier each time you do it. Remember the first time you picked up a pool cue and how awkward it felt? All you need is a little practice.

Speaking of practice, I generally flowchart from the top left of the page down to the bottom and then either go back up to the top using the next clear available space, or go to the next page. But some analysts flowchart from left to right across the page, using large computer paper for their work. It's a matter of preference. The important thing is that the flowchart enables you to do the following:

- Understand the current system and see weak spots.
- Analyze the procedures and their costs so that you can propose necessary changes to improve the bottom line.
- Think about the system in terms of your company's mission.

Can you be a records manager without doing flowcharts? Possibly. Can you be a world-class records manager without flowcharting? Nope.

Personal Computers

I am not a computer programmer. I couldn't write a line of code on a double dare. But like you, I came of age in the computer era. The computer is here to stay—maybe not in its present form, but certainly some form of automated transcription and calculation will be with us for the foreseeable future. It's foolish to try to ignore it or to avoid using its many benefits. Records managers who refuse to learn computer operations do so at their own peril.

If you are not yet PC literate, take steps to correct this condition at once. Remember, a record is a record is a record, regardless of the medium upon which it has been created. And records exist today on computers, both mainframe and personal, on e-mail, optical disk, microfilm, cassette tapes, and

Exhibit 1-11. Flowchart symbols.

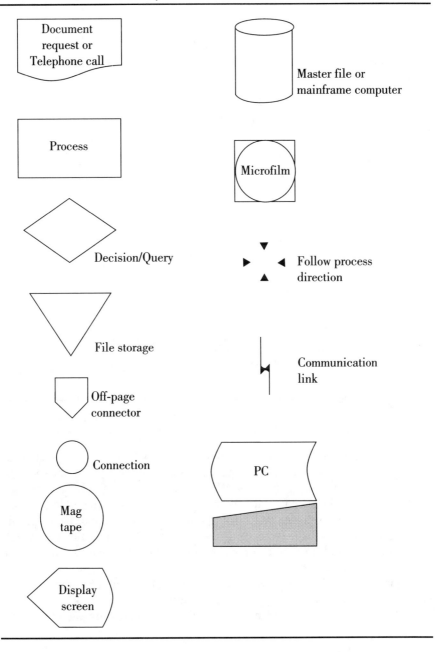

Exhibit 1-12. Flowchart for accounts payable statements.

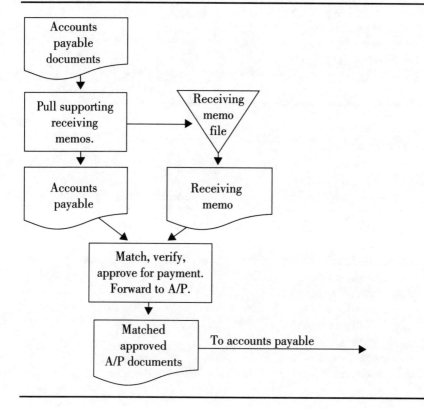

several dozen other media in addition to 8-½-by-11-inch paper. It is essential you become familiar with all the media your company utilizes, especially the personal computer.

At the very least, you will need to do your own work using a basic word-processing program. In addition you should be able to use a spreadsheet, a graphics package (you want your reports to look terrific, don't you?), a forms design program, and a records management program. Find a software package that will perform several functions for you.

Don't waste time reinventing the wheel. Your mainframe dataprocessing staff will thank you; in fact, they will probably kiss your feet when they hear you aren't going to bother them about your needs.

Telephones

I know you are muttering, "Hey, lady, I've been talking on the phone since I was three years old."

However, there's "talking on the phone" and there's using the telephone to extend your reach. Good telephone skills can help you be in two places at the same time. Two instances come immediately to mind:

1. Recalcitrant interviewees
2. Vendors and peers

Many records managers bite the dust because they allowed fellow employees to keep them from finishing assignments and/or meeting deadlines and schedules. Don't be one of them.

Keep saying to yourself: "I am, by strict adherence to the practice of good records management, saving the company many thousands of dollars a year. My methods and procedures often keep us out of court, save us from fines and legal judgments, prepare us for disaster, and protect us from chaos. Management wants me to continue doing my job. So I will not allow fellow employees to dissuade me from my course. I may be momentarily delayed, but I will not be derailed."

I know, that's a lot to keep saying to yourself, but you get the idea. World-class records managers have backbone. To give you an idea of how to handle recalcitrant interviewees, this is a style that has worked:

How to Get an Appointment With
Ms. Vera Busy, Office Manager:

Ms. V. Busy: Ms. Busy speaking.

You, Intrepid RM: Hello, Vera. This is Gloria Gold. I am the new corporate records manager and I have been told that you can help our program enormously. I wonder if I could stop by to see you for about twenty minutes this afternoon. Would 2 P.M. be OK?

Vera: Well, I'm very busy this afternoon. I really don't have time. And I'm leaving for vacation tomorrow for three weeks. Why don't you call me after that?

You: Well, I'm afraid then it will have to be this afternoon—anytime you say. You see, Mr. [president's name] has given me a very short deadline, and since he assured me you were a key player . . . well, I wonder if we could do it the last thing this afternoon. I'm usually here until six or six-thirty. How about five-thirty?

Vera: I see. Well, all right. If you're sure about the twenty minutes. Let's do it at two. But I have a meeting at two-thirty and I need a few minutes to get ready.

You: Oh, that's terrific! Thank you, Vera. See you at two then.

Then hang up. Try to be a few minutes early. Vera will probably be on the phone when you arrive and keep you waiting for several minutes just to prove she is as important as she says. But that's OK. Let her win, too. The best deal is when everyone is a winner. And of course, stick to the twenty minutes unless Vera keeps the conversation going longer. Nine times out of ten, if you are well prepared and act professional, you will make an ally and Vera truly will be of enormous help.

Use the telephone to verify and reverify numbers, dates, and facts you may have picked up during your interviews. If something doesn't jibe, telephone. If you can't read your writing, telephone. If the dog ate the last page when you were working at home, telephone. Don't be shy. Remember our flowchart example? Call the mailroom and ask, "Why do you file duplicate copies of invoices?"

You have the right to the correct data, and your professional career hangs in the balance. When in doubt, telephone. I often telephone my interviewee when I have no doubt, just to say, "I thought you'd like to know how those numbers added up. Does that total surprise you? No? Good. I just didn't want you to be surprised in our presentation meeting."

Vendors

Vendors have a special place in my heart. Living and working in Minnesota was a tremendous boost to my professional education as a records manager. Our very proximity to 3M (Minnesota Mining and Manufacturing), which has corporate headquarters in St. Paul; IBM, which has a large installation in Rochester; Unisys, with a large installation in St. Paul; and Control Data, located in Bloomington, meant that State of Minnesota departments were prime targets for new products and services. Kodak, Bell & Howell, Minolta, and Canon also had vigorous marketing representatives in Minnesota. They, in turn, attracted many other excellent independent organizations devoted to marketing information tools.

As a result, vendors with the "newest," "improved," or "tomorrow's" products were eager to share information. These vendors were the best sources for understanding current technology, and working with them provided the best practical experience. Let me explain.

A vendor calls on you with his company's new widget. You listen to the whole spiel. It's interesting, to be sure, but your current needs are being met by current products. Now comes the stretch: What situations can you envision where this product would be useful? *Think* (as IBM says)! What problems do you have that this product might help solve in any way? Could it help you do new wonderful things?

Even if nothing comes to mind, file the literature or make an appointment to see the new product in action. If 3M or IBM thought enough about it to bring it to market, someday you may find it's the perfect solution to your next problem.

Play fair with the vendors who call on you. Keep appointments you make. Listen attentively and, need I add, politely. The time will come—trust me—when you need that friendly vendor. You will need price quotes, shelving layouts, or equipment specifications—and here is a perfect use for the telephone.

Say to each vendor you call, "You know our company goes out on bid for this type of product. I will ensure that you are on the bid list. But in the meantime, would you please give me a price quote? I will not hold you to this price, nor should it be your bid price."

I also inform the vendor by telephone when I am about to make the proposal and suggest that she may call me on the following day. I describe how the presentation went and the status of her item. That seems fair, doesn't it? I follow up immediately with a telephone call to my purchasing unit to be sure the vendor is, in fact, on the bid list. If not, I take the necessary steps to see that the vendor is added.

When the item does go out on bid, I make another telephone call to Purchasing to be sure that the vendor was included. In some instances when I have received an enormous amount of help, I even call the vendor to be sure the bid was received.

This may seem like a lot of monkey business for a vendor who is trying to sell to you, but remember that the vendor is also providing information, a distinctly different service. In my experience, this routine saves a lot of headaches and misunderstandings. Then when you need another favor, you will probably get it. Pronto.

Another important use of the telephone is your own network of peers. Most of us are not only happy to pass on information and help but positively flattered to be asked.

One caution: Remember that those friends of yours, who may also be records management consultants, make their living giving advice. While most of them are delighted to assist in solving small problems, you can hardly expect them to welcome being asked to solve a major problem for no charge. The reasonable thing to do in such cases is to invite the consultant to come to your office to discuss the problem and to give you a proposal. Usually there is no charge for the proposal, which will be a cost estimate to recommend the solution and costs to implement the changes. You can then decide if the fee is worthwhile or if you need to seek other means to solve your problem.

At the same time, there is an awful lot of bad information out there. Bad information costs money—more money than doing nothing. Beware of advice from people who have not been in the business very long, or who work for organizations that are different from yours. What works for one company may not be the answer for you. You have different legal and administrative needs. You have different staff capabilities. And in all likelihood you have different equipment.

Calculators

The calculator is your friend. The calculator is your lifeguard. The calculator is your mother reminding you to eat breakfast, your dentist telling you to floss, and your stockbroker advising you to buy low and sell high. You absolutely *must* check and recheck every set of numbers you ever use for the rest of your life. Period.

Pencils and Erasers

Use an automatic pencil with a .05 lead. Get used to carrying a soft eraser with you. The one on the pencil just doesn't last more than a few times.

Try to make your corrections in your notes and in your flowcharting as you go along. This keeps your notes more logical and cuts down on revision time when you study them later. In the long run, striving for accuracy the first time around may well save you time and effort.

In regard to note-taking and flowcharting, if you can get used to printing in capital letters, you will be amazed at how much easier your notes are to read, particularly if several days have elapsed from the initial meeting.

As a consultant with as many as fifteen jobs going at one time, I have found that any tool which saves time and contributes to accuracy is dear to my heart. Certainly, as a grown-up you are free to take longhand notes in purple ink and never, never use the telephone or calculator. But I warn you, you will feel guilty about it.

Chapter 2

The
Records Management
Evaluation

The ancient Chinese had a most reassuring thought: "A journey of a thousand miles begins with a single step." So don't be daunted by the seemingly insurmountable tasks before you. Shortly, you will be:

- Designing, implementing, and maintaining a first-class records management program for your company
- Becoming a world-class records manager in the process

The good news is that you've already started. Look at what you already know about the company:

- You know what the company is all about, why it was founded, what its goals and aspirations are.
- You know who some of the key players are and how their work interrelates with other divisions or departments. You know their budgets and some of their contributions to the company.
- You know where most of the records are stored and are probably aware of some of the storage and retrieval problems facing you.

In short you have begun to scope out the program you must implement. The next step is for your eyes only: developing your private plan to show where you are today and where you want to be in five years. This plan will be your blueprint for progress—something to clutch on those dark days when everything looks hopeless.

Your Private Five-Year Plan

Using the same kind of research you have just completed in Chapter 1, I developed my own plan when I formed the records management division for the state of Minnesota. Using the organization chart format, I laid out the three units, their staffing, and the budgets I thought I would need to deal with more than 110 state agencies, 50 boards and commissions, and 750 units of local government—all of which the Minnesota Statutes declared would be my territory. Five years later I had a division of twenty-six people in three sections of records and records storage, forms design and management, and micrographics.

Your five-year plan may be as simple as an organization chart, or even more basic. For example, it could be a listing of the objectives you wish to accomplish, such as:

- Install an official automated inventory, retention, and disposal system.
- Implement a vital records protection system.
- Complete a forms inventory and install the control system.
- Develop an in-house records center for short-term storage.
- Establish a long-term records storage center in a secure, low-cost site out of the building.
- Research and develop the optimum image-reduction program for company records.
- Complete miscellaneous programs as assigned by management and as determined by the records management evaluation.

If you have had experience in budgeting and staffing (or even if you haven't, what the heck—have a go at it anyway!), draw up a plan for all of the above that includes your estimates of staffing and budget. Don't worry if you haven't sufficient information now for such an exercise. Your first major task—preparing a records management evaluation, described later in this chapter—is going to provide the data you need for your five-year plan. A word of caution: Don't try to plan for more than five years. The world moves too swiftly. New technologies appear to solve problems you didn't even know you would have.

The above list of tasks reflects those that normally fall within the realm of records management. However, every company is different. I have worked in companies where records management included operations of the in-plant print shop, while at others the reverse was the case. Records management may be part of the facilities management function or the legal department, may operate as part of purchasing or be in the controller's office. All these units bring different alliances to your program, making it easier in some cases to accomplish goals and more difficult in others. In one company for which I was a consultant, the records management department reported to the personnel director, who had the disturbing habit of falling asleep during records management meetings.

In any event, your supervisors will undoubtedly have some miscellaneous assignments for you. Do tackle these with good cheer and utmost skill. These side tasks have two benefits:

1. You will get to know more people in your company.

2. You will build on your reputation to solve a problem, handle a sticky situation, or relieve your boss's workload. She will come to rely on you to complete an assignment on time and under budget, using skill and creativity. That image will predispose her to back your plans even more enthusiastically than you might have reason to expect.

At any rate, keep your five-year plan to yourself. There is no point in letting anyone think you are "empire building" when what you really are doing is preparing your own blueprint. If brought out into the open, it may well scare the daylights out of your boss.

But how do you know where you are today? What do you use for comparison? Where are your benchmarks? The point is that although you have a pretty good idea of why you were given the records management responsibilities (with or without a budget), you don't have any idea of what Walter Winchell used to call the "true facts of the case." You don't know what information handling is costing your company. You don't know where the bottlenecks are in the information flow and what is causing them. Ta-dah! Enter the *records management evaluation.*

The Records Management Evaluation

In our experience, it is a waste of time—and in most instances, downright foolhardy—to try to sell management on any program not based on fact and dollars. There may be in this world some silver-tongued devils who can convince a tightfisted management committee that the benefits of "intangibles," the awesome results of "what if's," or the civic accolades due to munificent acts of recycling are worthy bases for substantial investments in space, equipment, and personnel. But you probably are not such a silver-tongued devil, and such gullible committees rarely exist.

Fortunately, you don't have to depend on charm or guesswork. You can use the tried-and-true, never-fail method to win over even the most intransigent management, the most nitpicking controller, the hardest-headed attorney. Just remember that there is no substitute for facts and numbers. And facts are exactly what the records management evaluation gives you.

Over the years, I developed a formal structure for determining the costs of handling information in any organization. Costs are based on these three tangibles:

1. Space
2. Equipment and supplies
3. Personnel (or labor)

These specifics represent actual dollars. Fortunately, the figures are fairly easy to come by. And because they are generated within the organization, they are understandable and, most important, believable to management.

You may be saying to yourself: "But I already know the problems. Why should I go through the evaluation steps? I was told to solve certain problems. Won't the evaluation just point out these problems again and won't my boss wonder why I have spent so much time retelling what he already knows?"

Yes . . . and no. Most of the problems are recognizable, although it is likely that several more will surface during the process. The problems may be more serious or widespread than management suspects. Or what management perceives to be the problem may be a symptom of a much deeper illness. Your boss may understand the problem, but does he know what the problem is costing in dollars? How can you justify any new program, or even make the simplest changes, if you don't know how to calculate the savings generated by the improvements? But when your facts and numbers are organized through the evaluation process, the potential savings are so astounding that it will be almost embarrassing to speak about them in public. And you will want to document those savings, but you can't unless you know what your current costs are.

Therefore, the records management evaluation provides threefold results:

1. The evaluation takes a snapshot of current costs and projects such costs for the next five years. If the decision is made not to implement your recommendations, those are the costs the company can expect to pay.

2. The evaluation defines existing problems in information handling, transferring, and storing of records. It raises additional records issues that are frustrating staff members, and it gives a voice to their own ideas for solving some of these issues. Do not underestimate the value of staff input.

3. Once issues, problems, or challenges are defined, you are able to formulate reliable estimates of time and dollars to effect solutions.

This is the bottom line of your presentation to management: item 1 minus item 3 equals *savings*.

With this documentation in hand, you can graphically lay out your improvement program, describing both its one-time costs and its ongoing costs. Based upon current costs determined by the evaluation, the dollar savings are laid out in black and white. You will have management's attention; can its heart be far behind?

Several times in the past nine years a client has said, "I need the program, not the evaluation. Just come in and fix the problem." When I could not dissuade the client, I have been very sorry. For some reason the fix was OK, but I was always waiting for the other shoe to drop. What did I miss? The client was satisfied, but I was not.

You, on the other hand, live in a better world. It is up to you to convince your boss that you are proceeding correctly. If you need more ammunition, Exhibit 2-1 is a sample rationale for the evaluation that you may modify or elaborate upon to assure your boss that it is the only way to go.

How to Do a Records Management Evaluation

Now that I have you convinced, and you have your boss convinced, let's proceed with the evaluation. The following is a step-by-step process. Follow it as you would a recipe. If you get into trouble, refer to the sample evaluation included in Appendix A.

The Interview Form

The evaluation format is designed to gather a lot of information in a very short time, by a very small staff, with minimum disruption to employees. Even though you have your boss convinced, you don't want to give the impression that this is going to be your Sistine Chapel. You want to be through with the project inside of four weeks—three weeks, if possible.

(Text continues on page 44.)

Exhibit 2-1. The records management evaluation rationale.

Objectives

The evaluation develops two figures: (1) the cost of managing records at the present time and (2) the investment required to bring the records management program to the following point:

- Vital records are secure.
- Records are disposed of routinely and in legal compliance.
- Stored information can be retrieved accurately and on a timely basis.
- Records volume may be reduced, where appropriate, through the use of imaging systems and database indexing.
- Maintenance of an ongoing records program can be accurately determined and *budgeted*.
- The *feasibility* of implementing information management technologies can be evaluated and justified.

Method

The study will take place over a two- or three-day period* with the final presentation being made within ten days.

You will survey all records produced on all types of media. All storerooms, vaults, basements, attics, fan and boiler rooms, stairwells, cabinets and countertops, floor corners, and spaces under desks are surveyed as well as all standard filing equipment.

Key personnel in each unit will be interviewed. You will observe workflow, working space, and all work tools. Issues of concern to employees interviewed will be recorded and analyzed.

Final Report

All data gathered are organized so that they will serve as a planning tool for the company not only in the near future but during long-range planning and budgeting. These are the typical units within the report:

- Introduction: purpose, scope, background
- Evaluation method and staff
- Executive summary of findings: record volume, vital records security, information retrieval, current management issues
- Details of findings
- Cost of current methods of storing records: space, personnel, equipment

- Projected costs over a five-year period
- Recommendations in chronological sequence for achieving a comprehensive records program—list of recommendations, estimated hours and cost, equipment and facilities needed, and conversion cost estimates as understood at the time of survey
- Detailed steps of each recommendation/company commitment in hours
- Five-year projected records management costs following implementation of recommendations and anticipated savings
- Potential image processing applications—those record series that could be reduced in volume through the use of either microfilm or electronic imaging
- Proposed action plan and qualifications of study team players

Presentation

At the presentation, you will distribute the report and review significant items. The presentation should be made to those who have the decision-making power to support an ongoing records management program. The attendees list—those who should hear the report—can be developed by you on the second day of the survey.

The evaluation will address all questions, as well as any findings that may not have been pertinent to the survey topic. It should be your intention to explain clearly and completely the findings and recommendations of the report. Your presentation must cover not only current costs but potential dollar savings possible through a comprehensive records management program. You will identify each area where savings appear to be reachable within the first year of the program as well as those that have long-range potential.

The evaluation serves the company as a budgeting tool for future planning.

Benefits

The benefits of having the records management evaluation made prior to taking an inventory or dealing with other issues are as follows:

- The evaluation calculates current costs so that succeeding activities can be compared on a cost-effective basis.
- Organizing the activities in a sequential manner, together with the hourly commitments required by each, allows management to select items according to priority and need.

(continues)

Exhibit 2-1. (*continued*)

- There is an opportunity to raise issues about which management has been only slightly aware.
- The recommendations allow for elimination or substantial reduction of expenditures.
- The action plan, an integral part of the evaluation, allows management to accurately schedule those activities selected for implementation.

---

*With adequate help, two to three days are sufficient. If one person is working alone, the evaluation will probably take ten to fifteen working days. In companies employing more than 950 people, I add more staff to the project in order to finish within five working days.

In my experience, the quickest way to gather information is through the survey sheet and with in-person interviews. You ask, "Why not just send out the sheets to everyone and ask each person to return the completed sheets?" Because some key people won't respond; because you will get answers only to the items on the survey sheets and not the information that comes from one-on-one encounters; because your due dates and timetables will fall by the wayside; because you will miss the opportunity to get to know which of your fellow staff members are enthusiastic supporters of your program and which you have yet to convince.

In other words, you'll get less valuable data through the mail and spend more time doing it. There is just no comparison in the quality of data gathered.

When you use the interview process in conjunction with survey sheets, you want to select those people who handle large series of records. In general, these people are in:

- Accounting   • Purchasing
- Personnel   • Marketing
- Finance   • Quality control

You do not have to interview people who do not work with records, such as assembly-line personnel or warehouse staff, although supervisors of such units should be included. Also, in units where many staff members are working with the same records or the same types of records, you will interview only one or two people. You can interview several of these people at the same time, keeping track, of course, of all those who have contributed to the project. Accounts Payable and Accounts Receivable are two divisions that fall into this category.

The next step is to determine precisely what you want to find out, in addition to costs. A sample evaluation interview form is provided for you to modify as you see fit (see Exhibit 2-2). Often management has a need to know:

• *What are people keeping in their file cabinets?* In one company, the answer resulted in a five-year ban on the purchase of new filing equipment and saved the company $500,000 over the five-year period. Not bad for an evaluation.

• *Is the microfilm program effective or is it time to consider electronic imaging?* And if so, what are some of the records series that should have priority? In one company, the answers to this had a twofold effect: They eliminated the need for a costly microfilm laboratory refurbishing and also fit in nicely with the company's in-process disaster recovery plan.

• *Why can't anybody in this company find anything? Don't our people know how to file?* The problem one client had was not that people couldn't file. There were just too many individual filing systems with no written procedures for any of them. Newly hired employees, not being able to decode the previous incumbent's system, set up new systems. So the only material that could be found was the most recent. They might as well not have filed anything at all.

• *We are reorganizing or moving some offices. Which groups use the same records and should be near each other?*

You can begin to see the ramifications and far-reaching effects of this investigation.

Determining the Interview Schedule

With the form finalized, take out your organization chart to select the persons you will want to interview.

Be realistic. You should be able to interview and complete the evaluation form for about five people in the morning and about five people in the afternoon. The more help you have—that is, other people to conduct interviews—the more staff members you can interview in a day. However, this may be a mixed blessing. It's harder to work alone, but unless you are

(Text continues on page 48.)

Exhibit 2-2. The records management evaluation form.

Person Interviewed

Name(s): _____

Title(s): _____

Department: _____

Analyst: _____

Records Inventory and Retention

Do you have an official records retention schedule:	yes	no	
Have you ever destroyed records:	yes	no	
Do you have a list of records destroyed?	yes	no	n/a

Vital Records

Are any of your records vital [*define "vital"*]?	yes	no
Are these routinely back up off-site?	yes	no

Records Volume

Is your records volume increasing annually?	yes	no	same
If volume is increasing, by what percentage?	_____%		

Information Retrieval

Do you file and/or retrieve files?	yes	no
Percentage of time spent seeking information	_____%	
Who else handles files for you?		

Title	% of time

Image Reduction

Do you currently use an image-reduction process?   yes   no
Type/comments: _____
Do you have record series that you would like to
    see on an image-reduction system?   yes   no
List series: _____

_____

Forms

Are you satisfied with the flow and processing of
forms in the company?   yes   no

Satisfaction With Information

Would you say that the way in which records and other information are
filed, stored, and retrieved in your organization is satisfactory,
unsatisfactory, or something in between (circle one)?

Suggestions and Comments

What would you like to see happen to improve information handling or
records management in the company?

Other Comments by Interviewee

Analyst's Comments and Observations

Desktops, floors, cabinet tops, hallways, stairwells, heaters, safety, file
security, checks/money secured, optical disk potential

Volume Calculations

Filing Equipment

Number	Cabinets/Units	Linear Feet Each	Square Feet Each	Total Linear Feet	Total Square Feet
_____	2-drawer vertical	4	9	_____	_____
_____	3-drawer vertical	6	9	_____	_____
_____	4-drawer vertical	8	9	_____	_____
_____	5-drawer vertical	10	9	_____	_____
_____	2-drawer lateral	6	7.5	_____	_____
_____	3-drawer lateral	9	7.5	_____	_____

(continues)

Exhibit 2-2. (*continued*)

Number	Cabinets/Units	Linear Feet Each	Square Feet Each	Total Linear Feet	Total Square Feet
_____	4-drawer lateral	12	7.5	_____	_____
_____	5-drawer lateral	15	7.5	_____	_____
_____	Shelving units	_____	2.5 × __ ft.	_____	_____
_____	Shelving units	_____	2.5 × __ ft.	_____	_____
_____	Shelving units	_____	2.5 × __ ft.	_____	_____
_____	_____	_____	_____	_____	_____
_____	_____	_____	_____	_____	_____
_____	_____	_____	_____	_____	_____
_____	_____	_____	_____	_____	_____
_____	_____	_____	_____	_____	_____
_____	_____	_____	_____	_____	_____
_____	_____	_____	_____	_____	_____
	Loose records	_____	_____	_____	_____
	Totals			_____	_____

Averages

Shelving	2.5 square feet × linear feet of *one* shelf (3-foot-long shelf unit = 7.5 square feet)
Bankers' boxes, large	2 linear feet
Records boxes, standard	15 linear inches, may use 12 linear inches
Check boxes	Measure, 2 to 3 linear feet
Map cabinets	16 square feet
Stacks-on-steel	Same as vertical cabinets
Tubs	3 square feet

confident of the quality of work others will produce, it is better to go it alone. Remember, the feedback from the interviewees is especially important, and you want to use people who will get more than just the answers on the sheets.

In organizing your schedule, the following is a rule of thumb, though every organization is unique:

Total Number of Company Employees	Number of People You Will Need to See
250	30
750	55–70
1,500	90–110
2,500+	10% of the records-handling staff, excluding assembly-line workers and all but one or two sales representatives

Where you have one person performing a unique task, such as risk management, he will have to be on your list.

Let's say that you decide you will interview seventy people. Working alone, you will need about ten days for the interviews and another five or six days to analyze the data and prepare the report. Since this is the first time for you, you might want to allow as many as ten days for the analysis and report preparation.

Before preparing a sample listing, consider the need to interview the CEO. If you can get to her, it will be extremely beneficial to have top-management comments for your own consideration. For example, how does the top executive feel about records management in general, and what problems does she perceive? What priority does she give to their solution? But if the CEO is not available, the CEO's secretary should be on your list. For one thing, you already know him, having asked for the company's mission statement. CEO secretaries usually come in one of two varieties:

1. *The person who says that everything is peachy and no changes are necessary.* Just smile and nod cheerfully. You know you were hired because things are definitely not peachy.

2. *The person who tells it like it is and is willing to help you push your program forward.* If you are lucky enough to have this person in your organization, treasure him. There may be a filing system problem you can solve for the secretary when you are a world-class records manager. Do so without hesitation; allies like this are hard to come by.

Typically, in an organization of about 750 employees, your selection will look something like the one shown in Exhibit 2-3. Or your company may be so organized that this list is barely recognizable. I have been in many compa-

Exhibit 2-3. Interview selection for a typical company.

Department	Titles/Position	Number to Be Interviewed
CEO	CEO, secretary	2
Human resources	Director, 2 personnel managers, file clerk	4
Controller	Controller, 2 unit managers, file clerk	4
Treasurer	Treasurer, budget director, risk manager, file clerk	4
Chief of operations	COO, 1 department head, 1 department head if located out of city, file clerk	4
Information systems	Director, 2 managers, librarian	4
Legal	Chief counsel, administrative assistant, file clerk	3
Facilities management	Manager, assistant	2
Security	Manager	1
Engineering	Director, 2 department heads, file clerk, director's secretary	5
Research and development	Director, secretary, file clerk, 2 researchers	5
Purchasing	Director, administrative assistant, 2 buyers, file clerk	5
Accounts payable	Manager, 2 accountants, file clerk	4
Accounts receivable	Manager, 2 accountants, file clerk	4
Credit	Manager, 2 clerks	3
Marketing	Manager, 2 account executives, file clerk	4
Advertising, sales promotion	Manager, file clerk	2
Training and development	Manager, file clerk	2
Labor	Chief negotiator, file clerk	2

Department	Titles/Position	Number to Be Interviewed
Customer relations	Manager, file clerk	2
Print shop	Manager	1
Microfilm	Manager	1
Stores/warehousing	Manager	1
Shipping, freight handling	Manager	1
Vehicles/maintenance	Manager	1
Retail/wholesale sales	Manager, file clerk for each if separate	4
Total		75

nies where the position of file clerk simply did not exist. Regardless of labels, it is critical that you pick full representation, including the key people who do have the filing and retrieving responsibilities. Also, be sure to interview some of those people known to be antagonistic to change in general and who regard "their" records as sacred. Probably they didn't get their reputations by accident. By obtaining their input you will avoid making the same mistakes that upset these people in the first place.

As you can see, the example in Exhibit 2-3 targets seventy-five people for interviews. Most companies will not have all these departments, nevertheless yours may well total seventy-plus people. At this figure, it is possible for one person to accomplish the interviews in less than three weeks. The accounting staff may respond well to a group interview; the only problem is that subordinates often are loath to speak up in front of their supervisors. If you suspect such might be the case, stick to one-on-one interviews.

If staff is spread out in more than one building, allow additional time for travel. Plot out the locations, and try to schedule interviews to keep travel time to a minimum. No, you do not want people to come to you. You will get much better results if you interview them at their desks, for these reasons:

- You are causing much less disruption in their daily routine.
- You will have an opportunity to observe the working area—the clutter or lack of it.
- You may observe problems or observe problems that come up as interruptions to your interview.

- You will need to be on-site to measure the volume of records.
- If you finish an interview early, you can go right on to the next without wasting time waiting for your next appointment to arrive.

There are exceptions, of course. There may be individuals whose offices are out of town. Management may not deem it advisable for you to travel abroad or even out of state for your interviews. These interviews may certainly be done on the telephone or when such people visit headquarters.

When drawing up your interview itinerary, prepare a rough draft so you know the time slot to request from each interviewee. You will want to give each person sufficient time to get ready. Regardless of level, office workers generally do not take kindly to surprises. Never surprise someone by just showing up at his desk for an interview. That's where paranoia dwells—yours and theirs.

The Notification Letter or Memo

Let's face it: Even though management may have said many pleasant things to you at the time of your appointment, your fellow workers don't necessarily share management's enthusiasm. Many will more than likely resent a letter or memo from you requesting an interview to discuss "their" records, taking up "their" time, and interrupting "their" business.

First, get the notification letter or memo signed by the boss. That is, the CEO. This will indicate to one and all that management has made this project a priority, and that you are carrying out management's instructions.

Second, accompany the letter or memo with the interview schedule, or the portion of the schedule that relates to the addressee. That way you don't need two separate mailings and the entire project appears professional.

Third, you may want to include a list of people who will be interviewed. This helps create a feeling of exclusivity among those chosen. On the other hand, depending upon the politics in your company, this may be a bad idea. Ask your boss.

Exhibit 2-4 gives an example of a memo that works for me. Give your boss something to sign or revise; don't wait for her to write it unless you have received word that this method is the preferred one.

I prefer to give people about a week's notice. More than that and they forget, less than that and the calendars are full. Even so, you will find people who are out ill, attending meetings, on vacation, taking classes, going to conferences, sales meetings, etc. Things you can do nothing about. So plan to have some mop-up time available. You may also need to build in some alternative interviews as well if you simply cannot catch up with your first choice.

Exhibit 2-4. Sample memo to precede interviews.

[*Date*]

INTEROFFICE MEMO

TO: Those Listed Below

FROM: The Boss

SUBJECT: Records Management Evaluation

One of management's most important responsibilities is to improve working conditions for all employees. To that end we invest in tools to enable staff members to do their jobs better. One such tool is an active records management program.

[*Your name*] has been engaged to take the very first step in such a program: the record management evaluation. Ms./Mr. [*your last name*] will contact you shortly to confirm a 20-minute meeting. Please give [him/her] your cooperation, not only in responding to survey questions but in sharing your own ideas for improving our records-handling procedures.

Thank you.

The Boss

Att: Schedule of Interview

The average interview takes about twenty minutes. If you should finish sooner, just go on to the next one. If staff is available, try to get someone to help you to confirm interview dates. After confirming your schedule by telephone, and assuring each interviewee that the clock time is approximate, you are ready to do the final draft of the interview schedule. It should look something like the one shown in Exhibit 2-5.

Scheduling

Suppose that, as you look at the list, you can see it would be nice if you could interview both Labor people in the morning. If you finish with the

Exhibit 2-5. Typical interview schedule.

Time	Department	Name/Title	Location
8:30	CEO/secretary	Joe Brown, Secretary	7th Fl. Bldg A
9:00	Human resources	James Adams, Director	601 E
9:30	Human resources	Sue Smith, Training Manager	601 E
10:00	Human resources	Barb Burns, Administrative Assistant	601 E
10:30	Labor	Ann Parker, Chief Negotiator	604 E
12:30	Human resources	Tom Miller, File Clerk	601 E
1:00	Human resources	Pam Parker, Manager	601 E
1:30	Human resources	Bob Thomas, Manager	601 E
2:00	Treasurer	Dale Parsons, Treasurer	609 E
2:30	Labor relations	Addy Baker, Administrative Assistant	604 E

chief negotiator before lunchtime, call Addy Baker to see if she is available. If so, you will have an hour or so in the afternoon to go over your notes, perhaps do some early calculations, or even pick up an interview or two that might have been suggested by someone earlier in the day. Personally, I like to leave an hour or so at the end of the day to catch up and get organized for the next day.

If you have help doing the interviews, try to have the same interviewer do everyone scheduled in a department. This gives the interviewer a sense of the issues facing that department as well as knowledge of concurring or conflicting opinions.

Always try to interview the department head first. This is simply good manners. Also, never go into a private office unescorted, nor open a file cabinet without a department employee standing close by. Even then, ask permission to open a drawer. This simple courtesy lets the staff know you are not here to pry but to collect data.

Finally, if you have any doubt about your schedule or about your schedule holding up, telephone a few days, hours, or minutes ahead to your next interviewee to announce that you will be x minutes or days late. Or, if you think a great deal of time has elapsed since you made the appointment with the interviewee, telephone to say, "Just to remind you that I'll be there to meet with you about 10 A.M. on Wednesday, the nineteenth. Looking forward to it. See you then."

Don't wait for objections or alternative suggestions, if possible. Just keep moving ahead, cheerfully and confidently. After all, who could help but look forward to meeting you?

The Evaluation Interview

As you arrive at your interview, introduce yourself and then sit down. Comfortably arrange yourself and your survey sheets so that the interviewee knows you are businesslike and are going to give your full attention to everything he says. One analyst always stacks her interview sheets on a clipboard. She has already written in all the appropriate names, a department name, and her initials ahead of time. I use a notebook for backing and making a big show of filling in all the top data before the interviewee's eyes. You will have to decide which method is more comfortable for you.

Briefly go over the reason for your visit, referring to the boss's letter. I try to approach this in nonthreatening terms, such as, "We are looking for ways to improve our records handling. Your responses will help to formulate recommendations that we hope will do just that" (instead of "Management thinks nobody around here knows how to file!").

I also try to provide a glimpse into the future: "This part of the process will take about four weeks, at which time I will make a report to Management. [If the report date has already been set, by all means announce it.] Then monies can be budgeted for the approved changes. To make recommendations that are realistic, I need your input. I have here a very short two-page survey. Ready?"

Try to keep the tone friendly, not adversarial, and assume an air of mutual cooperation. In a pleasant voice ask for an explanation of anything that should come up which you do not understand. An example would be:

Interviewee: I only keep DDX records in there.
You: Oh, DDX. Please, what does that mean?
Interviewee: DDX letters are the customer complaint letters on our lawn spray DDX. There is always the possibility that these letters may need to be sent to Legal to respond to litigation.

Now you have real information, not to mention several questions:

You: Do these letters require special security?
Are there copies floating about and if so, who has them?
Is there a routing procedure for alerting Marketing, R&D, and Legal under various conditions?
What about Credit?
Who responds to these letters, and who does the follow-up?

Make a note to ask some of these questions when you get to the other departments. Ask the appropriate questions *right then*, during your interview. If you don't have the opportunity or the time just then, make a note to follow up by telephone.

Completing the Records Management Evaluation Form

Refer back to Exhibit 2-2 as you go through each item with the interviewee.

Name(s):	The name or names of the person you are interviewing.
Title(s):	Use a standard set of abbreviations—e.g., VP for vice-president, Dir for director, CEO for chief executive officer. This list of standard abbreviations can be prepared ahead of time from the organization chart.
Dept/Div:	In many state agencies, the department is the larger entity subdivided into divisions. In many private businesses, the division is the larger entity and its subdivisions are departments. Your organization chart should tell you how such breakdowns are created in your company.
Analyst:	That's you. Put your initials here.

Now for the questions. Try to ask questions in a consistent manner and tone. Try not to lead the interviewee into giving the response you may want to hear. The sentences in quotes are suggestions for your own use.

Records Inventory and Retention. In asking about the next item, add some explanations of your own, such as: "Do you have an official, printed records retention schedule? By *official* I mean is it printed, kept up-to-date, and abided by everyone?" If the answer is yes, politely ask if you may have a copy.

The last two items under "records inventory and retention" refer to records destroyed. A simple yes or no to each will do. If the interviewee is new in the job, use N/A for Not Able to answer.

Vital Records. Vital records were mentioned briefly in Chapter 1 as those necessary to a company's ability to be back in business within x hours, days, or minutes following a disaster or business interruption. (I use twenty-four hours as a benchmark.)

I once posed the question to the director of a theatrical company: "Are any of your records vital?" He replied, *"All* of my records are precious!"

Here are the types of records for which you should be on the lookout. All vital records are equal in priority. There are no degrees of "vitalness."

> *Type A.* Necessary to reestablishing the company within twenty-four hours: contracts, accounts receivable, payroll, incorporation documents, formulas, engineering drawings of products, board minutes, inventories, patents, procedure manuals for word processing, data processing, programs (current), order processing, vendor lists, current litigation files. This list is by no means complete. If you don't see those records, what do you do? *Ask!*

> *Type B.* Costly, one-of-a-kind records: original maps, drawings, presentations, surveys, studies (benchmark).

> *Type C.* Archival/historical records: planning documents, awards, ceremonial documentation, annual reports, articles, newsletters, house organs, photographs, advertisements of company's products.

Many companies have taken the time and trouble to secure properly some of the type A records—for example, payroll—but most prefer to take their chances with other vital records.

You will find that in many companies, computer tapes are backed up, but very often the backups are kept in the same building, often in the same area, as the originals. The backups in the computer area are considered vital in case of computer failure, power failure, and the resulting loss of data. The idea that an entire building may be lost or uninhabitable often is not even a consideration.

Moreover, computer tapes too often are not kept for a lengthy period—from six weeks to a year in most instances—for the same reasons. So it falls on the paper printout to be the copy of record, as in payroll registers or year-end financial statements. This is a practical procedure because even if the old tapes are kept, changes in computer configurations will probably make those tapes obsolete unless they have been converted to the new system.

> It is a recognized national statistic, arrived at by risk insurance advisors, that those companies hit by a total disaster must be fully reestablished within three weeks if they are to regain their market share. Of the recovering companies that are out of business for more than three weeks, 75 percent will ultimately fail.

So the questions on vital records are essential to the welfare of the organization—as is the question, "Have you ever disposed of records?" If the answer is yes, and the company has never taken a records inventory and assigned retention schedules, this employee may have been disposing of vital documents. The person may have honestly thought that others had copies or believed the myth of a storage basement in another city. But often the individual will be fuzzy on the facts, and it is up to you to determine the reality. Which are the vital records and what care is being taken to ensure that they are available in the event of disaster? So you'll want to ask, "Now, do you think you have any records which fit any of these descriptions? Are they backed up off-site? That is, are your vital records duplicated on a routine basis and either the duplicates or the originals kept in a separate building?"

Disaster Recovery. Ask, "Is your disaster recovery plan completed, tested, and routinely kept up-to-date? You know, a plan to help you evacuate the building and set up shop at another location? Do you have one of these?"

Records Volume. First, a few words of advice. When computing volume, include all the records stored in storage, file rooms, and records centers. In computing square footage, count both the actual amount of space occupied by the equipment—the footprint—as well as the area required for standing, sitting, or kneeling to access the files. You also must include the space required to extend the drawer or movable shelf. In our sample form (Exhibit 2-2), the nationally accepted number of square feet is given for the space occupied by vertical, lateral, and open-shelf files. For example, a two-drawer file cabinet occupies the same square footage as a three-, four-, five- or six-drawer cabinet. Lateral files usually contain about 15 percent more filing space than vertical cabinets (see Exhibit 2-6).

Most facilities engineers allow a total of 9 square feet occupied space, pullout space, and standing room for vertical files, and about 7½ square feet for lateral files. And a four-drawer lateral file cabinet has a capacity of 136 filing inches, whereas a four-drawer vertical file's capacity is about 92 inches. As you can see, this makes a very strong case for lateral files. And an even stronger case can be made for four-, five- and six-drawer files as opposed to two-drawer files. Fixed, open (that is, having no shelf cover that must be lifted and rolled back) lateral shelving is even more efficient. This is the type of shelving usually found in file rooms, records centers, and storage areas. No pull-out room is required and standing room for access is immediately in front of the files to be retrieved. For example, a three-foot-long, six-shelf-

Exhibit 2-6. Two types of file cabinets.

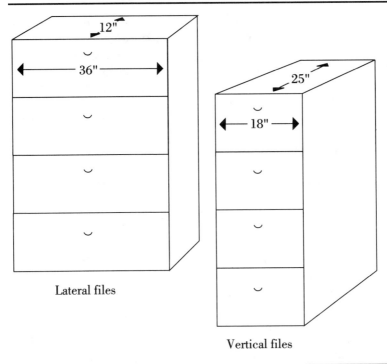

Lateral files

Vertical files

high section occupies only 6 square feet and holds about 18 linear feet of records.

Power rotating files are a very efficient use of space as well, often compacting almost 100 linear feet of records into 24 square feet of space. Does this mean that you should hasten to recommend that all office files be scrapped in favor of open shelving or that you go out on bid immediately for power files? No. You will let the system dictate the most efficient combination of equipment.

Now you are prepared to measure all filing and storage volume belonging to the interviewee and his department. Do this measuring at the end of the interview. In the meantime, ask the question, "Would you say that the volume of records in your area is increasing, decreasing, or staying the same? Increasing? Would you give me an idea as to the annual percent of increase? For example, the national average is about 15 percent. That means that the volume of records in the average American office doubles every four years or so. Do you think you are above or below that average?"

Try very hard to get an answer here. Only if the interviewee has worked in the job less than one year can you take "I don't know" for an answer. All of your figuring will be based on this set of numbers, as well as your planning. So don't let the interviewee off the hook. Suggest, "Norm, in Accounting, has estimated that the volume of his records is almost 30 percent greater this year over last. Does that seem about right to you?" Or, "Several of those I've talked to in this unit think that it's 10 to 15 percent greater each year. What do you think, judging from your own work?"

Let's take a moment here to discuss this records volume figure because it is partly the basis for many of your calculations. In the more than a hundred organizations for which I have performed records management evaluations, only one manager thought company employees were not qualified to determine if their records volume was increasing, decreasing, or staying the same. My feeling is that if the workers don't know, who does?

Information Retrieval. This series of questions is designed to help you estimate the cost of filing and retrieving records. Pick up the job levels of staff handling records so that you can attach a dollar figure to the time each person spends in pursuit of records. Beforehand you will have established three (or more if you wish) major categories and affixed a median hourly wage to each: senior management, middle management, and clerical support.

Generally speaking, these categories cover the following positions:

- *Senior management*—front-office officials, professionals, such as doctors, engineers, attorneys; division directors; branch managers; department heads
- *Middle management*—unit managers; professional trades, such as electricians or mechanics; supervisors; specialists; technicians
- *Clerical support*—administrative assistants, secretaries, file clerks, data entry operators, maintenance staff

You may want to do an even greater breakdown. The more detailed you get, of course, the more accurate your data will be. Because I was an "outsider" to the companies I worked for as a consultant, I counted myself lucky to get the mid-range for the three categories used. As you know, this sort of information is considered confidential by most companies.

Occasionally, I would receive zero salary data. For these few situations I made educated guesses. For example, for one Midwestern company, I used the following estimated salaries, including fringe benefits, which alone ran to almost 30 percent.

	Yearly	Hourly
Senior management	$80,000	$38.50
Middle management	$45,000	$21.60
Clerical support	$22,000	$10.50

Suppose the interviewee says, "I don't file myself, but three other people on the staff spend about 10 percent of their time filing. We really need a file clerk around here." Be sure to find out the categories of these three people. They could be middle managers or they could be clerical staff, or a mixture.

As you are conducting the interviews, you will find that topics surface that may sound to you like problems, bottlenecks, or symptoms of something serious relating to work flow, transfer of information, and so on. On the back of your interview sheets, using the flowchart technique, sketch out the situation. Then during the analysis portion of the evaluation, you can gather more data to see if this is an issue that has a records management solution. Some remarks that should alert you to start flowcharting are:

"We need more space."

"I spend 50 percent of my time filing"—a middle management staff member.

"It takes forty-five days to get a vendor paid."

"I can't wait eleven days to get a record from Central Files [or Storage, or the File Room]."

Image Reduction. "Image reduction" refers to microfilm, optical disk, or other image reduction methods that significantly reduce the volume of space required by the original paper. If your interviewee says, "Tell me more about optical disk," do so. Make a convert. You will be glad you did because you will learn more about the company's records in such conversations and discover excellent, cost-benefit applications in the process. Don't forget to list the records series about which your interviewee is concerned.

If you feel you are totally unprepared to discourse for ten minutes or so on the virtues of optical disk, or any other subject which may come up in the interview, respond, "We won't take the time right now, but let me make a date with you so that I can bring you literature and we can talk about possible applications—records series that might benefit from going on to optical disk. Then if you like, I can schedule a demonstration for you and any others who might be interested. OK?"

Then make a date. As soon as you are back in your office, call the vendor nearest and dearest. If all else fails, call long distance to Kodak or Bell and Howell in your nearest metropolis. Let me assure you, help will be on the way.

Checklist for Learning About New Technology

- ☐ Call vendors.
- ☐ Collect literature and read every word.
- ☐ Visit an on-site operation either at the vendor's showroom or at a company that has installed the equipment. Note: The danger here is that you may let the customer's application limit your vision in solving your own problems. It's better to understand what the equipment can do in the broadest sense than to know how it was used to deal with a specific situation somewhere else.
- ☐ Arrange to have key people visit the showroom site and bring samples of record series that may be considered for transfer to the new output.
- ☐ Discuss with key people and vendors the possibility of a pilot test on the company's premises:

  - What will vendor contribute?
  - Which records are best test material?
  - How long is the test period?
  - What are the ramifications? (Job reclassifications, effect on other department, standards for test evaluation, etc.)
  - What is the cost-benefit analysis?
  - How would we implement the system?

Forms. Be prepared to hear some real horror stories. You will learn about forms developed for no known purpose; forms without company name, logo, address, telephone number, or with no visible means of identification; and redundant, obsolete and incomprehensible forms. The most frequent complaint is, "Nobody is in charge of forms!" Collect samples of the "world's worst" that you can use in your recommendations. (See Chapter 10.)

Satisfaction With Information. Be especially alert when you ask the question, "Is the handling, transmittal, storage, and retrieval of information satisfactory, unsatisfactory, or something in between?" Most often you will get an answer of satisfactory. This is natural. People generally dislike telling others about defects within their area of expertise; nor do they wish to describe defects or bottlenecks as problems. If we like our jobs, we tend to cope with the ungainly and less-than-smooth operations. Nevertheless, you need to get to the nitty-gritty. This is how you do it: Be prepared to flow-chart—fast!

"I understand that you feel information handling is satisfactory. But look. Suppose your boss suddenly said, 'You can have anything you need, regardless of staff, cost, space, or equipment.' What would you like to see happen?" Be prepared to write as fast as you can and have extra paper handy. (I usually use the backs of the survey sheets.)

Sometimes you will also get "unsatisfactory" as a response, and several "so-so"s. These are from the articulate and brave people. They are risking something in speaking to you. They are also expecting you to follow through and effect some of the improvements they are suggesting. Do not betray their trust.

Interviewee Comments. Use this space to ask questions that management has suggested. Be careful to ask each person the same question in the same tone of voice, with the same attitude. Try to keep any personal bias out of the process.

Analyst Comments. Note here if the work area is crowded, messy, dark, dirty, and a fire hazard or if it is neat and well organized. Always give credit where credit is due. Besides, it's not always the worker's fault if the place is overflowing with records, since no filing equipment may be available. You want to establish that you are not here to poke fun or to conduct a witch-hunt.

Circle those applicable items on the sheet (desktops, floors, tops of cabinets, etc.) where records are to be found. The circled items and your notes will refresh your memory when you do your analysis. For example,

1. Do we have fire hazards?
2. Is there a need for more or different filing equipment?
3. Does anyone have time to file?
4. Is there a daily production of computer printouts that only graduates of a speed-reading course could absorb?

Volume. This item on the sheet is critical to the entire operation. Here you pick up actual square footage and linear footage currently occupied by the records. Most of your future calculations will be based upon these figures. Take your time and do a thorough job. After you've done a hundred or so of these evaluations, it will go a lot faster. Just kidding—unless you turn into a world-class records management *consultant*. There are worse things that you could do with your life.

Walk through the entire area when you do the calculations, not just the offices and areas where you have interviewed staff. Your purpose is to determine how much space is being occupied by records, in offices and in central areas, in and out of cabinets. You will need the total figure for the entire company, even though you are interviewing only a small percentage of the employees. Be sure to make this clear to the interviewee as he takes you around the area to collect this data. At the same time, be sure that you don't do an area twice. Storerooms and file rooms are easy to do more than once, especially if more than one department stores in a basement or attic. It's easy to count a pallet twice. So be scrupulous in gathering the data; you don't want it inflated or you will be suspected, however unfairly, of "manufacturing numbers."

It seems to me to be much more meaningful to deal with real-life situations, so I have created two make-believe companies that serve as examples in the next chapters of this book.

> THE AMERICAN BAGEL COMPANY (ABC) in which we study three departments—the chief executive office (CEO), the human resources office (Personnel), and Engineering. ABC Company is used chiefly to explain the evaluation report process.

> THE TERRIFIC LOTION COMPANY (TLC), which is what I imagine the circumstances will be like in *your* company. TLC Company is used chiefly to help you prepare estimates of time and staff required to implement *your* proposals.

In addition, I have included two real examples in the Appendix: evaluation performed for a small city and an optical disk feasibility study completed for a Midwestern power company. The names and identifying data have been removed.

Chapter 3
Analysis of the Data

When you have completed the interviews, you are ready for the truly exciting part of the process: analyzing the data and making recommendations. What do the data tell you and what should you do about it?

At this point you are concerned with optimum solutions—the very best system or systems to deal with the situations that surfaced during the evaluation. Not that you should avoid thinking about eventual costs, but now is the time to focus on what is best for the company in the short run as well as the long run.

A very simple computer program can be developed for your PC to help you compute the responses from your interviews. On the other hand, there is merit in the manual process, which I have always used. I need time to consider each response, and I find I do this better if I painstakingly transcribe every bit of data by hand.

Sometime while you are poring over your numbers and reading staff comments, the light bulb in your brain will click on, and solutions will pour forth in a veritable waterfall of ideas. There is no predicting when this will happen. Sometimes after only a few interviews you might say, "These people really need a central file on the third floor." And the answer is as simple as that. Other times it slowly dawns on you that any solution will fail because the problem is that the wrong people are in the jobs. Those are the worst of times.

Never doubt yourself, though. The solutions to problems will come. And with them comes the exhilaration, the high five that keeps us all slaves to our profession. You will be making proposals for staffing, equipment, or new procedures that no one has thought of before or, having considered, discarded. Systems analysis, which is what you'll be doing, is the perfect example of how one person can make a difference.

Once accepted, your proposals will change forever how the company does business. You will be affecting how people do their present jobs or how new people will do new jobs you create with your proposals. An awesome responsibility goes with making your recommendations.

Throughout this chapter and the next, I have used three departments in our first fictitious company, the American Bagel Company (ABC), to stand as examples of what documentation collected during the evaluation process will look like. It is unlikely, though certainly possible, that you will be confined to three departments. So your grid will be several pages long, your space or volume, equipment costs, and personnel costs much more extensive.

If you are comfortable with the examples, they can be your guideposts for each step in the evaluation process. Do not pay as much attention to specific numbers as to the process itself. As you do the evaluation for your company, use the ABC example as your recipe. Then you can follow the text and the example, step by step. Now, let's see what you've netted in the records management evaluation.

The Grid

Exhibit 3-1 is your basic tool for analysis. I call it the *grid*, even though it is really a spreadsheet capturing all the data from all the people you have interviewed. When completed, it lists by company unit the responses given to your survey questions, plus it provides an abstract of the comments, suggestions, and frustrations expressed by staff members. It is not a scientific sampling. You offer the comments section to management saying, "This is what the people we interviewed told us." (Often the comments are so gripping, so fundamental, so frightening that management ignores them at its own peril.)

When preparing your own grid, lay it out according to your survey form and leave plenty of room for transcribing the comments. I like to use either legal-size paper positioned sideways or computer printout paper. Keep in mind that you will be tabulating many of the columns, so don't crowd your data. After the tons of paper you have just assembled, using seven or eight more sheets is not going to matter.

Exhibit 3-2 is a completed grid from ABC—our example—depicting three departments: the CEO (front office), Human Resources (personnel), and Engineering. And Exhibit 3-3 is the department worksheet. It shows the compilation of data for the ABC company.

Match the grid headings with the sections of the evaluation survey form; you have the option to include more or less detail than I've shown in the example. Keeping in mind that three departments do not an evaluation make, look at what you have learned from your interviews:

(*Text continues on page 70.*)

Exhibit 3-1. The survey grid.

Summary of Interviews Worksheet

Department	Retention Schedule	Records Disposition	Vital Records	Backup Off-site	Volume Increase %	Retrieval: Salary Class %	Want or Have Image Reduction	Forms Satisfactory/Unsatisfactory	Overall Satisfactory/Unsatisfactory	Records Volume: Ln. Ft. Sq. Ft.	Staff Comments

Exhibit 3-2. Survey grid for American Bagel Company (ABC).

Department	Retention Schedule	Records Disposition	Vital Records	Backup off-site	DRP*	Linear Feet Volume Records	Percentage of Increase	Filing Cost Annual	Have Image Reduction	Forms Satisfactory	Overall Satisfaction	Comments
CEO	N	Y	N	N	N	1,237	15%	$1,250 - S 2,200 - C 1,029 - S 11,000 - C 11,000 - C 4,500 - MM	N	Y	S	"Would like optical disk system for corporate docs."
Human Resources	N	Y	N	N	N	896	20%		N	N	U	"Running out of filing space." "Have no security for confidential records." "Forms need total revisions. We are out of compliance with EEO on many forms." "People have no work space, areas filled with boxes of old personnel files." "Need a new system for tracking people from recruiting through hiring process. People falling through the cracks."
Engineering	Y	Y	Y/N	N	N	1,704 (Computer systems backed up, not key drawings)	15%	30,000 - S** 22,000 - C 11,000 - C 5,000 - M 5,000 - M 5,000 - M	N	N	so-so	"When drawer is full, we throw out the back stuff, put new stuff in front." "Need two more file clerks and several more filing cabinets." "We need a backup system for old drawings. If these get lost, and they do, we might as well lock up shop."
Totals:						3,837 linear feet		$108,979				

* Disaster recovery plan.

** S = senior; C = clerical support; M = middle management.

Exhibit 3-3. ABC department worksheet.

Filing Equipment Space Needs/Costs = Current

Department	Number of Filing Units	Description	Linear Feet Each	Square Feet Each	Total Linear Feet	Total Square Feet	Annual Cost @ $25 per Square Foot	Department Total Filing Floor Space Cost
CEO	16	5-D vertical	10	9	160	144	$ 3,600	
	8	4-D lateral	12	7.5	96	60	1,500	
	10	2-D lateral	6	7.5	60	75	1,875	
	25	Shelving units, 6 high, 6 feet long	36	15	900	375	9,375	
	21	Loose records	1	1	21	21	525	
					1,237	675		$ 16,875
Human Resources	40	5-D vertical	10	9	400	360	9,000	
	24	4-D lateral	12	7.5	288	180	4,500	
	12	2-D lateral	6	7.5	72	90	2,250	
	50	2 foot boxes	2	2	100	125	3,125	
	36'	Loose records	36	36	36	36	900	
					896	791		19,775
Engineering	12	Blueprint cabinets	4	16	48	192	4,800	
	36	5-D vertical	10	9	360	324	8,100	
	24	2-D vertical	6	7.5	144	180	4,500	
	30	Shelving units, 6 high, 6 feet long	36	15	1,080	450	11,250	
	72	Loose records	72	72	72	72	1,800	
					1,704	1,218		30,450
Totals:						2,684 square feet @ $25 per square foot		$ 67,100

• The volume of records for these three departments is increasing at about 17 percent a year.

• Two of the three departments have no retention schedule. The unit that says it has a retention schedule still throws out records indiscriminately when file drawers are full.

• There is no backup plan for vital records such as corporate documents, critical engineering drawings, or benefit plans; nor is a disaster recovery plan even in the works.

• Senior and middle management staffs are doing what seems to be a heavy amount of filing. (In a recent Minnesota study, it was found that engineers were spending about 45 percent of their time filing their own records. Computer-assisted design and drafting equipment totally eliminated this wasteful practice.)

• You can see that a detailed forms inventory and forms analysis is certain to be recommended.

• A feasibility study for an image-reduction system is called for to aid the Human Resources and Engineering departments. This could also tie in with the need to protect vital records.

• The storage situation definitely needs to be reviewed. Conditions in Human Resources are dangerous, not only in terms of the physical workplace (not to speak of potential fire concerns) but also legally. Keeping all those old personnel files, subjecting the company to possible legal action from terminated employees, is clearly an emergency situation.

A note of caution here: When writing your report, don't give the impression that Human Resources people don't know how explosive their situation is. For one thing, the director of the unit undoubtedly does know (and probably doesn't sleep nights knowing it). For another, you are not trying to make them look bad. That's not your job. Your job is to help carry their message to management so everyone can be more productive and the company is protected.

Always strive for the positive approach, even when you are certain you are pulling somebody's fat out of the fire. There is no gain in being Ms. Know-It-All.

Computing the Data

You will calculate the volume of records first because very often this is the most meaningful figure to management. Boxes of records, rows of filing cabinets, costs for storage space—these are tangibles that management can relate to at once. Using your grid, total the volume of records currently on hand in all locations and the square footage they occupy.

Use linear feet first. You have already picked that up in your measurements. You have made the assumption that any records seen stacked in foot-high piles on desks, chairs, or office floors are records that would be filed if time and filing equipment permitted. Obviously, some of these "loose" records would be tossed if one had time to go through them and make decisions. But the same could be said for 40 to 50 percent of the documents in the file cabinets.

Increases in Volume, Cost of Space

Now that you have your current volume of records, look at what people said about the potential increase in records coming across their desks. Is the volume increasing, decreasing, or staying the same? Total the responses of those who said it was increasing, then divide that total by the total number of respondents. Thus, if you have some who do not believe the volume is increasing, or some who say it is staying the same, you have given equal weight to their opinions. In fact, this averaging tends to offset those who claim an increase of 200 to 300 percent. If you feel that such an answer— say, of a 200 percent increase—is one given in frustration or off-handedness, you may decide to eliminate the response altogether. As an insider, you will probably be able to tell if the figure is realistic. If in doubt, leave it out of your calculations, but make a note to mention it during your presentation or as a footnote in your report.

Now, keeping storage figures and office figures separate, you can predict what the total records volume increase will be for each of the next five years. Likewise, you'll be able to determine what the requirements for filing equipment and space will be. Let's see how this works out, using our example company: The three departments in the American Bagel Company totaled an increase of 17 percent. Having recorded the figures, you have the totals as shown in Exhibit 3-4.

Look at Exhibit 3-3 carefully. What items of interest can you deduce from it? For example, did you note that two-drawer files are very uneconomical? Also, in a secured area, open-shelf filing is the most practical and economical. But when it is in the high-cost space of the CEO's office and in the Engineering Department, unsupervised access defeats the security aspect. Additionally, if the shelving is to be relocated in an enclosed room with controlled access, it may as well be placed in less costly space.

Exhibit 3-4. ABC Department space costs, current plus next five years.

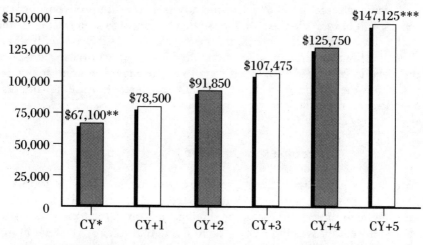

* Current Year
** 2,684 sq. ft. × $25/sq. ft., based on 17 percent increase.
*** Cost doubles between fourth and fifth year.

If approximately 30 percent of the records could be disposed of immediately, and another 40 percent could be removed to secured low-cost storage, the annual savings would amount to almost $47,250. Subtracting the cost of the low-cost storage space, say $7,000, the annual net savings would still be about $40,000, or $200,000 over a five-year period.

For example, your figures would look like this:

Current cost of space	$67,100
Subtract 30% (now eligible for disposal)	$20,130
Remove 40% (to low-cost storage approx. 1,000 boxes)	$26,840
Annual savings	$46,970
Minus annual cost of low-cost storage (@$.30 box/mo.)*	−3,600
Total annual NET savings on office space	$43,370

*Storage costs will vary from community to community. The same is true for prime office costs. One-time costs of moving should also be included.

Also, you are looking at almost 2,000 square feet of prime office space that could be freed up for other programs. Granted, this space is not contiguous. But with modern-day modules, most of it could be converted easily into offices for ten to twenty workers. It may take some "churning," as the facilities managers are wont to say. Even so, disjointed areas could mean avoiding outside space rental and all the attendant costs of communication and distribution and travel.

While we are talking about savings, remember your own company's budget? You looked that up as part of the discussion in the first chapter? How does it compare with the possibility of saving $40,000 a year in space? And that's just ABC's three departments, using very conservative figures. You begin to get an idea of your worth.

You can see that we've made some assumptions in discussing ABC. Your evaluation in your company will not have to depend upon assumptions; it will be based on fact.

For example, the ABC sample assumes that Human Resources people have not stored any records outside the office area. (Actually, I have found this to be true in about 80 percent of client companies.) The ABC sample also declares that the director's concern over confidentiality has prevented sending records to an unsecured location. My sympathies are with the director. She is playing with dynamite and knows it. Better to store the boxes under desks and along the wall, where authorized personnel can keep an eye on them.

A few years ago we needed to access the storeroom of a major American company. We were looking at operations records, but personnel records were also kept in that storeroom. So we were escorted into the storeroom by a member of the administrative staff, a secretary to a director. As we entered the storeroom, the secretary turned on the lights, gestured to us that we were on our own, and marched purposefully to a corner cabinet. He pulled out a drawer, found the file he was hunting for, and spent the next hour reading a file that was obviously none of his business. Why "obviously"? Because he said "I've been waiting two years for a chance to get my hands on that file."

So much for security. But your immediate problem is to project the cost of space for storing records in three mythical departments for each of the next five years. How do you do this? Actually, you can attack the problem in one of two ways:

1. You could take a 17 percent increase in volume of office records, and then a separate 17 percent increase in volume for storage records. You would then calculate the square footage costs separately (that is, the cost of the

Exhibit 3-5. Drawing showing number of records currently in existence.

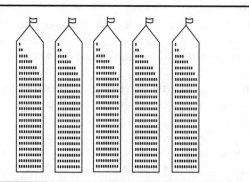

space actually occupied by the records, plus the cost of space required to access the records. The formula for computing square footage costs is part of the evaluation form).

2. You could take your total square footage costs (office space and storage space) and, using this figure, calculate the annual 17 percent increase.

Experience has shown me that the difference is so slight it is really a matter of preference. Suppose for the ABC Company we use the second formula: $95,925 × 1.17%.

A note here: The first method, slightly more complex to calculate, is often misleading and distracting. Try not to include anything that will distract from your main analysis and recommendations. Remember, the audience for your calculations would rather be back at their desks, doing "their" work.

Your PC skills will produce a graph similar to the one shown in Exhibit 3-5. When looking for a way to graphically portray the astonishing volume of company records, you may wish to use a device that has worked well for me. Compare the current volume of records to the height of a well-known structure or landmark building in the community. Then draw the number of buildings that would be filled by the current volume if the records were piled one on top of the other. The next drawing would be the additional buildings that would be filled at the end of five years if nothing were done to reduce and control the volume.

As you can see from the grid for the American Bagel Company, the current volume of records, 3,837 linear feet, would fill five skyscrapers 760 feet tall. The display would look like the drawing in Exhibit 3-5.

In five years, with volume increasing at 17 percent a year, the total would amount to 8,412 linear feet, or eleven skyscrapers!

Be prepared for some gasps and a good deal of head-shaking. Such drawings prove to be terrifyingly effective because they graphically portray something out of control. No manager wants to be responsible for filling that much space with paper. If you are in a community without tall buildings, use a map showing the distance to the nearest highway or to City Hall. Chances are your company's records won't girdle the earth, but they might make it to the county line.

Cost of Equipment

During your analysis of the records data, separate the bare cost of filing equipment from the personnel cost in filing and retrieving records. You want to do this because management should know that senior staff members spend a certain percentage of their time filing. Also, *many* records are not in cabinets, but are on chairs, floors, on top of cabinets, and so on.

There is also some generic data available on this matter and you may be more comfortable using the following: When it comes to computing the cost of storing records in offices, studies by national research institutes and professional organizations all come up with very similar figures. For example, the average filing cabinet, standing on an office floor, costs about $1,300 a year.

My own calculations arrive at the same total, although the line items vary. One national association study breaks down the yearly cost as follows:

	Yearly Cost
Equipment (amortized over 15 years)	$ 26
Supplies	130
Floor space	65
Supervisory	208
Direct filing personnel	871
Total	$1,300

I have some problems with the assignment of these figures, however. First, I don't know a chief accountant who would let you depreciate a file cabinet over fifteen years. Most scream at five years and would prefer three years.

Second, I usually consider supervisory costs to be no more than 10 percent of personnel costs. Third, I doubt that there are many metropolitan offices whose square footage, including taxes, cleaning, heating, air-conditioning, lighting, and security, can be purchased for $7 a square foot. New construction in the Midwest is currently going for about $32 a square foot, unimproved, and taxes not included. Prices are even higher in some major cities.

The interesting point is, though, that while I disagree on the break-down, my figures do yield the same bottom line:

	Yearly Cost
Space ($10 per square foot, 9 sq. ft.)	$ 90
Supplies (folders, tabs, labels, guides, color-coded identifiers)	130
Equipment ($400 per cabinet, low-bid-depreciated over 5 years)	80
Supervisory (10% of labor cost, including front office "burden")	90
Filing personnel (90 hours per year per cabinet, about 1 3/4 hours per week)	900
Distribution (delivery of items sent to/from the files in the cabinet)	10
Total	$1,300

I think you will find this figure conservative enough to fit almost any economic market today. But if your information indicates it should be much higher or lower, by all means go with your data. You might also want to use both your and my figures to emphasize your research and dedication to accuracy.

Also, on the subject of equipment costs, national surveys conducted by office systems research centers advise us that one full-time person is required for every twelve file cabinets. Personally, I find this too low. Remember, only 15 percent of documents in a file cabinet are ever looked at again. And 98 percent of that 15 percent are looked at in the first year. After that, studies show that less than 2 percent of the files in any cabinet will ever again be referenced. After the second year, the figure drops so dramatically, it is equivalent to what the Food and Drug Administration calls a trace element.

Therefore, use the ratio of one full-time equivalent person (FTE) for every twenty-five file cabinets. Remember, you will be telling management that these are average figures. You may be describing highly active files, such as personnel files for a company with 25,000 employees, or your personnel staff may have set other guidelines, as has the U.S. Army. You will have to settle on either the national averages or on your own, however, because you will be projecting an annual increase. In so doing, you will gear the annual increase in volume to the number of new personnel required to manage the new records.

Since the early 1960s, when computer people began telling us that the computer would make paper records obsolete, paper records have increased by 3,000 percent. Some of this is due to computer output, and a good deal of the responsibility also must be awarded to copy machines.

But a change in management style is at least as responsible and ensures that volume will continue to increase, no matter how closely we monitor copy machines nor how hard we try to control computer reports. Many staff members receive copies of memos, reports, letters, reading files owing to status, not because they need to know. One company I worked for had a staff of three people devoted entirely to keeping the interoffice mailing lists up-to-date, yet they were falling behind; it's an impossible job. Remember years ago when we had no copy machines? We had to stick carbons between sheets of paper to make copies, and if we made an error, we had to erase all the copies as well as the original. Way back then a boss would tell an underling what, and only what, the boss felt like passing on. Now, with correction typewriters, PCs, and copy machines, everyone on the staff can hear the good news and the bad, almost instantly. The need for instant communication isn't diminishing, either.

Changes in style of management have introduced quality circles, "flat" management organizations, ad hoc project teams. Has this affected the volume of records? Yes. Volume is increasing annually at an average of 15 percent. It would take more than reorganization to reduce the volume of records accumulating. Here's a partial list of what would be needed to reduce the records volume:

1. Total analysis and restructuring of each process within a company
2. Releasing employees from the need to CYA*
3. Reduction in the number of lawsuits and million-dollar settlements

Do you see any of the above happening in most companies? Neither do I.

Hard times, such as a depression or recession, which results in a shortage of funds, probably do more to restrict the flow of paperwork than does

---

*Rough translation: Be sure your rear flank is covered.

Exhibit 3-6. ABC equipment costs, current plus next five years.

Year	Linear Feet	17% + Increase	Number of Additional 6 - D Cabinets, Holding 18 feet (@ $600 Each ÷ 5)	Annual New Cost	Cumulative Total
CY	3,837	-0-	-0-	-0-	
CY+1	4,489	652	36	$4,320	$ 4,320
CY+2	5,252	763	42	5,040	9,360
CY+3	6,145	893	49	5,880	15,240
CY+4	7,190	1,045	58	6,960	22,200
CY+5	8,412	1,222	68	8,160	30,360

good advice. If instant communication is the flint that sharpens the competitive edge, you will be continually looking for more effective ways to file and retrieve records, to amalgamate information, and to dispose of records no longer needed. Here are a couple of assumptions to speed you on your way:

1. Check that filing equipment currently in use is fully depreciated. The current cost should be zero. After all, you wouldn't want to be chasing the status of every file cabinet in the company; that way madness lies.
2. When any new equipment is purchased (as your increase in volume indicates will be necessary), it will be, most likely, of the most efficient, durable, aesthetically pleasing variety.

Six-drawer lateral cabinets holding about 18 linear feet of records are the most efficient. You, as records manager, will select brands that meet your criteria for style, durability, and color to fit with the decor. Such cabinets cost about $600 each. Depreciated over a five-year period, this amounts to $120 a year for each new cabinet.

If you know for a fact that your company pays $500 for such cabinets and depreciates over a three-year period, by all means use the company's figures instead. But do not hesitate to use my figures and my methods of calculation to save time and be consistent. You may be called upon to survey more than one company within your organization, and then you will have a standard with which to work.

Always, always include a page in your report that explains your average figures. Thus your readers can raise or lower the figures as they are privy to exact numbers. I have never had a manager object to this method, or at any rate, not so long as I described exactly how my figures were derived.

Now you must plot out your equipment costs over the next five years. Remember, in the ABC Company example, the cost for the current year's equipment is zero and the volume of record growth is increasing 17 percent a year. In the CEO, Human Resources, and Engineering departments, there was a total linear footage of 3,837. The annual 17 percent increase will bring that total to an astounding number requiring an additionally astonishing number of cabinets. The ABC calculations will look as shown in Exhibit 3-6. As you can see, in the fifth year, ABC will be paying over $30,000 for new equipment purchased during the previous five years. Use the following checklist as a summary of the steps involved.

Equipment Cost Checklist

☐ The current linear feet × 17 percent = the increase for the current year + 1 (CY + 1).

☐ The increase is divided by 18 feet, which is approximately the amount of records that will fit into a six-drawer lateral cabinet. This figure represents the number of new cabinets required to hold the increase.

☐ The number of new cabinets is multiplied by $600, the average cost of a deluxe new cabinet.

☐ This total is divided by 5 to arrive at the annual costs, depreciated, for the new equipment.

☐ The previous year's investment is added to the total cost so you know what the actual costs will be at the end of the next five years.

In the example, the total cost amounts to a little more than $30,000. Naturally, if you were projecting more than five years, the cabinets bought in CY + 1 would be fully depreciated and fall off your schedule. "But," you ask, "won't some of the directors send old records in the old cabinets to storage?" Yes, they might. And yes, there might be a Santa Claus. At ABC, the directors had no plans to remove any records from their offices, much less dispose of any. So you will also need an official retention schedule, monitored with an iron will, to effect any changes resulting in dollar savings.

One of my early clients was spending in excess of $100,000 a year on filing cabinets. By recommending (and receiving approval for) a freeze on new purchases and by enforcing the retention schedule I proposed, the company saved $500,000 over a five-year period—not bad for the evaluation and program implementation, whose total cost was $32,000. The entire cost was recovered in four months!

Cost of Personnel

Personnel will probably be the biggest item in your cost breakdown. It is also the most difficult to get a handle on and the most difficult to prove—that is, to make your readers understand and believe what you are saying. And while I'm telling the bad news, I should mention that at least 50 percent of the companies I have worked for have had no official position of file clerk. This was interpreted to mean that doing without file clerks "keeps the managers and supervisors busy and doesn't cost us a thing, and look at the money we are saving. Just one big happy family, everybody doing their thing."

Let me tell you what this leads to. In a very large mining company, all the mining engineers did their own filing as part of cost-cutting measures. As a result, the only set of blueprints for a particular area or piece of equipment was often in the hands, desk, truck, or on the dining room table of one engineer. If that engineer was at another site—a very common occurrence—blasting, all the attendant activities regarding the blueprint had to be put on hold until the engineer returned. Delays ensued and costs rose. As times grew tougher and competition stronger, many staff members, engineers included, were laid off. Often the blueprints disappeared altogether. I am not suggesting for one moment that this practice caused the demise of the company, but it certainly didn't help.

For every record created, there are filing and retrieval costs. You need to determine these costs as closely as possible, for these three reasons:

1. Most offices have 70 percent more records on hand than necessary. When you set up a retention schedule, many currently filed (or piled) documents can be discarded at once. The time saved can be as much as 50 percent of a staff worker's time. If this means the company can operate with fewer people, or avoid hiring additional staff, or not engage temporary staff, or free up professionals to work full-time at their profession, these are dollars saved.

2. The fewer records placed in the file, the faster stored records can be filed and retrieved. My time studies have shown that this can result in a 35 to 50 percent reduction in filing and retrieval time.

3. Before you attempt to find out "why nobody around here knows how to file," and to set up standard filing systems with written procedures, you must eliminate all nonessential records. Then you will be ready to set up the best system to deal with the remainder.

Going back to the American Bagel Company, you see that the filing and retrieval costs are broken down into three personnel categories: senior management, middle management, and clerical support. ABC's human resources director provided the mid-range salaries for these three categories:

Senior management	$60,000
Middle management	$30,000
Clerical support	$22,000

In studying the ABC grid, you'll see that the detail that screams out is the senior manager, who spends 50 percent of her time filing. In addition, three of the middle management group spend almost 20 percent of their time filing. Yet I doubt very much if this is in their job descriptions. These numbers indicate more than just staffing problems. They seem to be symptoms of filing system problems as well. Either of these areas might well prove to be a good pilot program for an automated filing index, a file tracking system, or an electronic imaging system. Or, hey, why not all of these?

You are saying to yourself, "I'm just a beginner. Who am I to tell top management to stop filing? Or even how to file?" Your very first recommendations—the records inventory, retention schedule, and disposal program—will drastically reduce if not eliminate management's need to file. And besides, it *is* your job to tell all staff members how to file.

Filing, in and of itself, is not usually the problem. The filing usually comes at the end of a process. It's with the retrieval of filed records, whether on paper, optical disk, microfilm, or other, that frustration sets in. When that happens, time and money (as in sales, customers, lawsuits) are lost.

So, with every spare moment you have, start talking to your vendors. Look at what they have to offer, but *don't buy anything*. It's not too early to start looking. Somewhere, you'll come up with a system that connects your problem with a possible solution. Put the details of the problem together with your notes on the vendor's products in a tickle file. Include a copy of your evaluation as well as any flowcharts you may have made during interviews.

When you point out in your report that a senior official is spending 50 percent of her time filing, you will get the question, "What should we do about it?" You can smile, with confidence, and respond, "I am exploring several systems that may be of help. But I really need to be able to cost-justify one or more before I give you my recommendation."

As for calculating personnel costs, there are two methods you can use, based on the annual percentage increase in records volume:

• You can assume that the same people will continue to file, buy more cabinets, and add more space to accommodate more records. Thus they will increase the percentage of their time spent filing and decrease the percentage of time doing what they were hired to do.

• You can assume that any increase in records will be handled by newly hired personnel.

History shows us that in most companies, the increase in records volume is handled by current personnel until they scream for mercy. Then new staff is hired. Since you have no way of knowing when this breaking point will be reached, I suggest you merely take your known annual percentage increase across the board and assume that new personnel will fall roughly into the same categories as current personnel. In the ABC example, the current cost of filing is $108,979 a year. Management will want to know how the 17 percent increase will affect this cost. Compute the 17 percent increase and add it to each of the next five years. Using the numbers gathered, this is how the table of personnel costs would look:

	Increase	*Total*
Current Year (CY)	—	$108,979
CY + 1	18,526	127,505
CY + 2	21,676	149,181
CY + 3	25,361	174,542
CY + 4	29,672	204,214
CY + 5	34,716	238,930

Make a note to mention in your report that the personnel costs for filing and retrieval will double in the fourth year *if nothing is done to control records.*

The First Power Graph

Now you are ready to pull all your numbers together and prepare the first really telling picture of current costs for handling records. Not only that, your graph will depict the projected costs for handling records in each of the next five years. If management makes the decision to do nothing about your recommendations, then at least it will know what these costs will be—and be willing to swallow a *doubled* overhead on a non-revenue-producing activity.

Exhibit 3-7. ABC records management costs, current and projected.

	CY	CY+1	CY+2	CY+3	CY+4	CY+5
Space:	67,100	78,507	91,853	107,468	125,738	147,113
Equipment:	– 0 –	4,320	9,360	15,240	22,200	30,360
Staff:	108,979	127,505	149,181	174,542	204,214	238,930

Exhibit 3-7 shows the current and projected costs for the ABC example. The bottom line is that costs will go up 235 percent at the end of five years.

Now that basic costs are determined, as in the ABC example, what other issues should you address?

The Other Issues

Security of Vital Records

Next to determining the cost of handling records, the most immediate priority of any company has to be the security of its vital records and its private and confidential records.

Many employees will swear to you they have a good security program in place. But there's a great deal of mythology in most companies. That is, many employees believe a thing is true, but in fact it is not.

In one company, more than two dozen staff members assured me that all vital records were routinely backed up in the basement of a branch office about fifty miles from headquarters. In my innocence I thought this was ideal.

Nearing the completion of the inventory process, I signed out a van from the company motor pool, dressed in grubs for the day, and tooled off to the nearby town, planning to work in the basement.

In fact, the "backup vault" was one (count it, one) file cabinet. It was less than that, actually. It was one envelope in one drawer of one cabinet. Nothing had been added to the envelope in over a year. There was, therefore, no backup of the vital records of a company highly regulated by federal and state agencies.

So when you asked the question in your company, "Are any of the records you work with vital?"—and of course you define *vital* so everyone knows what you are talking about—you probably got more yeses than no's. People like to believe that "their" records—and, in fact, "their" work—is important, nay, essential to the organization. So it may be. Your job is to find out if the data are essential, and if so, if they are adequately protected in the event of a disaster.

From your own survey, you will have obtained good data to prepare a telling graph on the subject of vital records and their security. Based on the ABC evaluation (see Exhibit 3-8), we find that *everyone*—100 percent of the employees—had (or thought they had) vital records. Yet only 24 percent of those interviewed thought these vital records were properly secured and backed up off-site.

This means that in the event of a disaster, 76 percent of the company's vital records would be lost.

In your report, you will not only hit this hard but include in your recommendations the development of a disaster recovery plan. The plan will identify all vital records, describe the backup procedure, and detail how and when the records are to be delivered to the recovery worksite. In going through this process, you will have completed one third of the company disaster recovery plan.

In addition to vital records, there is also the security of day-to-day working records. Remember the harassed human resources director with his boxes of records piled all over the office? In government agencies, and in some private agencies regulated by governmental agencies, the privacy issue is a volatile one. Records that are considered private or confidential must be unavailable to persons unknown. Keeping such records around the office instead of in a secured room, or at least in locked files, leaves them vulnerable to access by visitors from the outside, by the staff's internal part-time staff, by cleaning crews and service crews, and by the occasional staff worker who comes in to work evenings, weekends, or holidays.

In a case where job openings were microfilmed at 4:30 in the afternoon, duplicated, and dispatched to the 750 Job Service locations around the state by 8 A.M. the next day, the microfilming was being run at a service bureau. It

Exhibit 3-8. ABC estimate of vital records security.

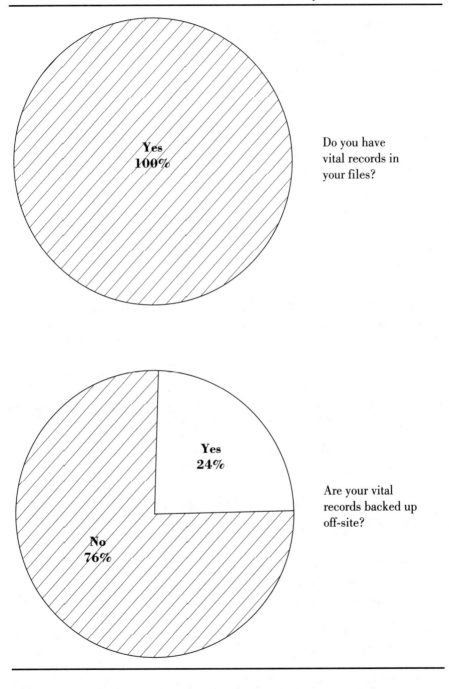

Do you have
vital records in
your files?

Are your vital
records backed up
off-site?

came to my attention that the details of certain openings were sold by micro-film night-crew operators to a select clientele. The bottom line was that the service bureau lost the state account (about 50 percent of its business), several people lost their jobs, and the state brought the whole operation in-house.

So privacy and confidentiality are security issues, as are corporate trade secrets such as formulas, patents, legal records, accounts receivable, bank deposits, strategy-planning-session minutes, and reports. Each company has a different set of records that need protection. During your survey you will have come across instances where this need is desperate to the point of dangerous. These are records you simply must secure. Security must have the highest priority.

Assorted Additional Issues

Take a serious look at other issues that your interviewees raised (albeit with your help). My usual practice is to abstract from each person's comments each and every point of the conversation. Remember to reproduce positive comments as well as those that seem to build a case for your program.

After all, no manager is going to believe that nobody had anything good to say about the company's handling of records. If you have found truly nothing good to be said, and if no one makes an attempt to say anything positive, then there is nothing you can do; you can't manufacture data. But rest assured, management will be skeptical if the picture is all black.

Let's tally the remarks made by employees in the ABC example. Keep the original survey sheets handy to ensure you are being as unbiased as possible. In the "Comments" section, we find these needs expressed:

- An optical disk system
- Filing space
- Security for records
- Forms program
- Storage space for old records
- A file tracking system
- A records retention program
- Filing staff and cabinets
- Vital records protection program

When you survey the records for the entire company, you will find these same needs expressed repeatedly. The lack of a records management program affects the entire company, not just one or two departments. But even in the small ABC sample you can see that four of the remarks are directly concerned with filing. Two deal with security for confidential and vital records, and two relate to retention schedules.

Here, then, is the heart of your program. The filing problem seems to be one of overcrowding rather than the need for new systems. In summarizing these remarks so that management can see the dangers, list the needs as perceived by the staff as follows:

1. Inventory and retention and disposal systems that identify and protect vital and confidential records.
2. An image-reduction system to reduce the volume of records that must be kept for long periods of time and/or that have very high access by multiple employees.
3. An off-site storage site in a low-cost facility to secure vital record backups and that can be hooked up to the inventory and retention and disposal systems.
4. A file tracking system so that the company will not let certain files "fall through the cracks," resulting in the company's failure to meet federal regulations.
5. A forms management system that will eliminate duplicate forms and/or the collection of redundant information, plus improve the appearance and understandability of its forms.

Naturally, in conducting your evaluation, you will have a lot more data to work with; as an example, these figures are simplified. Nevertheless, your totals might work into a pie chart like the one shown in Exhibit 3-9, or something even more elaborate.

Very often an employee will make a statement that crystallizes an issue. These comments should be reported verbatim. I usually include a page with just quotes from staff members, trying not to be repetitive but to create a mood. (Remember that old sales motto: "First you make 'em sick, and then you make 'em well!)

Actually, it's necessary for management to understand that all is not peaches and cream. They should know that the staff has been thinking about specific situations for some time, and that employees have some very definite ideas on the subject which should be heard. The frustrations should come through in the comments.

These are some that stand out in my mind (direct quotes):

Exhibit 3-9. Evaluation totals shown as pie chart.

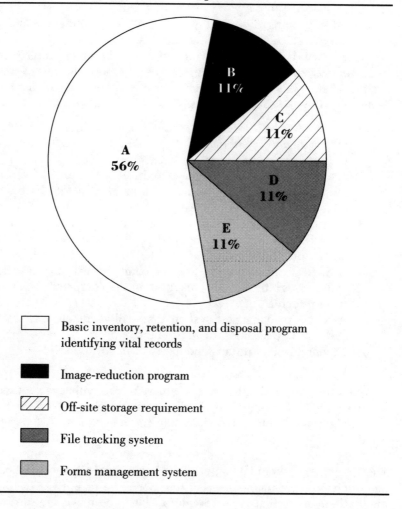

Basic inventory, retention, and disposal program
identifying vital records

Image-reduction program

Off-site storage requirement

File tracking system

Forms management system

"Going into our storeroom is a trip to hell."

"We are losing thousands of dollars a day because we can't find
files. The Feds are fining us daily, but soon they'll be closing us
down."

"Our forms are so awful they are embarrassing!"

"The mistakes we make in records management we pay for in the Legal Department!"

"We kept that memo thirty-two years too long and it cost us hundreds of thousands of dollars."

"When we wash the fire engines, the records stored in the garage get wet."

"I keep all my records in my office because if I ever sent them to Central Files, I would never see them again."

"There's two of us in this office, plus all the boxes of files, and if either of us needs to open the file cabinet, the other one has to get up from her desk and leave the office. But we only leave to do this five or six times a day."

Honest, guys. Those are from major American organizations. With your pie chart and the quotations, the priorities will fall into place almost automatically.

Chapter 4

Your Recommendations for Change

The various elements of your evaluation will lead you directly to the recommendations you need to make. Always keep in mind the dollar savings to your company that will result from implementing the inventory, retention, and disposal program. Dollar savings has to be priority one.

With a top-flight records management program in place, the costs of handling records will rise no more than 5 percent annually. And this seems to be the case whether additional programs, products, or staff are added. It may not hold true if your company acquires other large companies. But even then, with a retention schedule in place and annual disposals enforced, you'll stay pretty close to the 5 percent average.

"How can this be?" you ask. "If the size of our company doubles, won't the cost of handling records double?" With controls in place, that shouldn't happen. But those controls must include:

- An official retention schedule with a disposal date in place for each record series, by custodian.
- The rule that no new records series is created without a retention entry into the schedule.
- A low-cost off-site storage for little-used records.
- A vital records program in place that includes routine backup of essential records.
- An image reduction system in operation so that records series of large volume can be reduced to microfilm or optical disk to conserve space and reduce retrieval time.
- A forms management program in place to reduce waste and redundancy, and to speed up processing.

Exhibit 4-1. Projected net savings under a records management program.

	Costs w/o Rec. Mgt. Program	12% Reduction	CY Net	5% Increase	Annual Savings
CY	$176,079	$21,129	$154,950		
CY+1	210,372			$162,698	$ 47,634
CY+2	250,394			170,833	79,561
CY+3	297,250			179,375	117,875
CY+4	352,152			188,344	163,808
CY+5	416,403			197,761	218,642
	Total 5-year net savings				$627,520

- Procedures in writing for each employee using one or more of the preceding programs. Procedures are also used for training new staff.

How do you get management to say yes to such a grand program? Look at the numbers you have just come up with for the ABC example and you'll see that the overall annual increase in records will be 17 percent. Your program will reduce that increase by 12 percent. (We'll concede a 5 percent increase, though experience shows us it is very often less than 3 percent.) Exhibit 4-1 shows the annual savings possible to ABC under a records management program. Go back and review the power graph (Exhibit 3-7) carefully to be sure you understand this.

Do you see where the savings have come from? We're talking about $627,000 saved in a five-year period! You may have rescued the company from having to build a new wing, lease additional floor space, or rent offices in another part of town. And in five years, the costs for handling records have increased only about $20,000.

A full-scale records management program designed to achieve that 12 percent savings will cost ABC, including the records manager's salary, approximately $100,000. As you can see from Exhibit 4-1, the entire program is paid for in the second year. This leaves a net savings of close to half a million dollars over a five-year period. How can management not respond to those numbers?

You are now at the most critical part of the evaluation process. The recommendations you propose will be the foundation of your own records management program. So they must have some possibility of accomplishment, whether by you alone, with the help of staff, or with a consultant team. But your recommendations must be realistic. Management must be able to see that dollars spent for the program result in tangible benefits—that is, real dollar savings.

Lets review your options. What, after all, is there to recommend? We'll analyze the comments received from the ABC staff and the data compiled on volume, space, and personnel costs.

The consensus of opinion at ABC is that they need more space to put all the records. But is that the problem—or the symptom?

If the records manager could get rid of 70 percent of the records on hand in prime office space, would there be room for the other 30 percent? If the answer to that is yes, the next question is, "How does the records manager know which records can be disposed of and which can be transferred to low-cost storage?"

Fortunately, there's an easy answer. A detailed records inventory in conjunction with a company-wide retention and disposition schedule will take care of the problem once and for all time. The inventory will also prescribe the frequency for backing up vital records, the media that should be used for the backup records, and the time frame for transferring records from offices to storage centers. Also, the inventory will detail which records series should be disposed of or kept forever. So with this one recommendation, 67 percent of the ABC comments, suggestions, and frustrations have been taken care of.

You still must consider the security of private, confidential, and vital records. Granted, the groundwork is laid for the backup of vital records. But the inventory doesn't do anything about image reduction or for the forms area, which also needs attention. It should be made clear to management that the greatest and most immediate benefits will be reaped by implementing a records inventory and retention schedule and the initial annual disposal. The good news is that you now know what your *current costs* are, so you will be able to calculate accurately the *savings accruing* from this one recommendation.

Now, having said that and recognizing that the inventory, retention, and disposal program is the logical way to proceed, you should know that not all good records management programs have had the luxury of beginning logically.

Not that many years ago, a governor of Minnesota heard from an old friend of his, the sheriff of a small town near the state's northern border. His message was to this effect:

"Governor, I have been filling out a Firearms Use Monthly Report for you folks in the Capitol for nearly twenty years. Now you know, Governor, we only got one gun up here and it hasn't been fired but once in twenty years. And that was at an old dog—and I missed. Can you do something about these dang forms?"

That one letter started the records management program for the state of Minnesota. The governor asked me, "How many forms have we got, anyway?" Taking a wild guess (don't ever do this, I surely wouldn't now, knowing what I know), I said, "About 30,000!"

"But," I put in quickly, "if we took an inventory, we could eliminate at least a third!"

"If you can get rid of 10,000 forms, you've got a deal," said the governor.

Did I say, "Well, that's nice, Governor, but we really need to take a records inventory first?" Nope. We took the forms inventory first. It took three months and three people. We collected about 34,500 forms, which the press made a good deal of since we had only 32,000 employees (including faculty and all employees in the entire state university system)! But the bottom line was that we eliminated more than 11,000 forms, most of which were dropped during the inventory process itself. The balance were eliminated when our computer printout showed us the redundancies. Annual savings in printing costs were $120,000. The governor was as good as his word. I had my records management division, staff, and budget.

But here *you* are, about to embark on a logical and well-organized records management program. So organize your recommendations.

Recommendation 1. A Single Records Inventory, Retention, and Disposal Program

If your organization has never taken a records inventory, has never identified its vital records, has no disaster recovery program, and is buying filing cabinets at an alarming rate, you can make an excellent case for beginning your program the way it should begin, with a records inventory. The space, equipment, and personnel savings will pay for the program thirty times over.

Your next question may very well be, "OK, what if management does agree with me? How do I proceed? How to I determine the cost?"

That is a very good question, for two reasons: First, it is logical for management to be concerned about the cost. But second, *you* are getting into the habit of equating records management with dollar figures. Think of yourself as a key player contributing substantially to the bottom line.

Let's pretend you work for the Terrific Lotion Company (TLC), with 1,000 employees. In conducting your records management evaluation, you have interviewed about 30 percent of the people who have records in your company. But you have measured *all* of the records. Let's say you measured the total linear feet at 26,000. This is a fairly typical amount for a company with about 1,000 employees.

On average, it takes about a minute to inventory a linear foot of records. Often you will have a huge storeroom with, say, claim files. These will require but one inventory sheet. Other times you will be inventorying a file cabinet with a hundred different records series. But about a minute per linear foot is a good average for purposes of providing estimates.

In addition to completing the inventory sheet, you must consider data entry time because, of course, you are not going to keep this inventory manually.

In estimating your 26,000 linear feet, you will have approximately 4,000 individual records series. There will be among these duplicate records series. For example, perhaps twenty employees will have purchase orders. Another forty may have personnel files. There may be fifteen budget files and ten files of freight bills. Depending upon your company's business, there may be 100 expense account files and 200 sales reports. Nevertheless, for purposes of your inventory, each must be listed separately.

When you assign retention periods to each of these entries, you will make one copy the copy of record—that is, the company's official record—and assign to it the full retention period. Then you will shorten the retention period of all the other copies of that record.

For example, Procurement, or Purchasing, will hold the copy of record for all purchase orders. The retention period may be six years, based on your state's statute of limitations. Everyone else who has kept a copy of the goods ordered for departments may throw such copies away as soon as the goods have been received and accepted. Do you realize what you have done here? You have wiped out about twenty drawers of files in that one item alone! That's equivalent to five four-drawer cabinets, with combined costs of $6,500 a year!

With every records series having its own entry in the inventory, you can begin to estimate the cost of assigning the retention period to each entry. For someone who has done a lot of retention work, it takes an average of one minute to do two records series. Four thousand series would take about thirty-five hours. But because you are new at the business and will have to do some research, you should double this figure. (In Chapter 6 you will find a great many retention guidelines, and these might further impel you to do your own research. This is the right and proper way to proceed.) Research time is difficult to estimate. I know that just looking up a word in the dictionary takes me twenty minutes because I cannot resist reading the rest of the definitions on the page. But when faced with 4,000 retentions to do, your curiosity may be curbed somewhat, and your speed will increase rapidly.

A good software package to run your inventory will cost about $1,000. There are packages for $400 and there are packages for $5,000. Somewhere in between will be sufficient unless you are planning to hook on a file tracking system as well as control of an off-site records center. The addition of these other items brings you to the high end of these figures. For example:

Estimating the cost:	Look at what you have available to compute the cost and the savings of a records inventory, retention, and disposal program.
Given:	Since each of you is working under a different compensation structure, for the sake of our exercise, imagine your wage is $12 an hour, including fringe, and your helper's is $9 an hour, including fringe.
Total elapsed time:	About 29 weeks.

If you have more help, the time frame can be cut somewhat, specifically the time spent taking the inventory. But as this is a learning process for you, be leary of accepting help that will not be part of your staff eventually. You will be spending as much time reviewing the helper's work as if you had done it yourself.

The inventory, retention, and disposal program is the keystone of your recommendations. The necessary tools to do the job appear in Chapters 6 and 7 of this book.

Let's compute the savings for our example, the Terrific Lotion Company (TLC). You can then make some assumptions regarding your company's inventory and use these figures as benchmarks when you have actual figures from your evaluation. See Exhibit 4-2 for the time and cost recommendations for TLC.

1. Of the 26,000 linear feet of records currently on hand, 18,000 are in offices and 8,000 are in storage in the TLC basement.
2. Office space rents for $25 a square foot, including taxes and utilities and cleaning.

Exhibit 4-2. Time and cost estimates for recommendation 1.*

Activity	Labor Required	Hourly wage Including Fringe Benefits	Number of Hours	Cost	Elapsed Time (weeks)
Inventory of 26,000 linear feet	Records manager	$12	320**	$ 3,840	8
	Helper	9	320**	2,880	8
Retention assigned to approximately 4,000 file series	Records manager	12	80**	960	2
Data entry 4,000 file series	Data entry	9	60	540	1.5
Corrections and approvals Preparation Manager's meetings Corrections Management and legal approvals	Records manager	12	80	960	7
Disposal, first annual	Records manager	12	80	960	2
D-Day	Helper	9	18	162	0.5
	All records holders		2	N/A	N/A
Totals				$10,302	21

*Based on 26,000 linear feet of records, 4,000 record series.
**I have added an extra 33 percent to accommodate those new to taking a records inventory and assigning retention.

Exhibit 4-3. Chart showing savings at TLC.

Location	Cost/Square Foot	Percentage Disposed	Linear Feet	Occupying Square Feet	Annual Savings
Office	$25.00	33*	6,000	3,600	$ 90,000
Storage	4.50	40	3,200	1,000	4,500
Office	25.00	40	7,200	4,320	10,8000
Added to storage from office	4.50	—	7,200	3,085	−13,883
				Total	$188,617
Cost of records inventory, retention, and disposal					13,902
Net savings					$174,715

*Approximately one-third is the national average.

3. Storage space rents for $4.50 a square foot, unimproved.
4. 30 percent of the office records will be eligible for disposal.
5. 40 percent of stored records will be eligible for disposal.
6. 40 percent of the office records will be placed in storage.

The result is shown in Exhibit 4-3.

You will have to decide if the records removed from offices should go to the basement storeroom or if they might be better off in a commercial records center costing about $.25 or $.30 a cubic foot per month.

Labor	$10,302
Inventory retention software	1,000
Manager's time to review	1,200
Attorney time to review	800
Disposal day souvenirs	500
Printing and notices	100
Total	$13,902

As a records manager, these are the kinds of decisions you will be making. Knowing your current cost is basic to the decision process. On average, it should take a manager about two hours to review and correct his list, plus an hour at the manager's meeting when the lists are distributed. The attorney will take from one day to two weeks, depending upon how familiar she is with the company, its history, and the appropriate legal citations. The total cost estimate for Recommendation 1, therefore, is $13,902.

A word of caution: If you do use a commercial records center, be sure *your* retention schedules are observed. Unless you go the center annually and personally supervise the destruction of records eligible for disposal, you will find yourself in the same position as thousands of other companies—paying to store obsolete records. And worse, you'll be paying to store records that could put your company in legal jeopardy.

Even though your storage costs have increased, you can claim a space savings of almost $175,000 a year. If your office costs only $12 a square foot a year, as opposed to $25 per square foot, your net savings are still almost $90,000 a year. And the savings over a five-year period are almost too embarrassing to mention.

Eventually, as you go about implementing your program, document your savings, preferably with photographs of space that has been recycled and statistics or studies on reduced filing and retrieval times.

Recommendation 2. A Two-Phase Records Management Program

You might well consider breaking your recommendations into two phases. Management can see that the top priorities are being met before others are begun. Also, you don't ask for dollars for the entire program, just a piece at a time. At the same time, you have an opportunity to learn as you get one project under your belt at a time.

For a moment, let's go back to the ABC example and prepare the recommendations. With ABC, you can comfortably break the recommendations into two phases:

Phase I:

• Records inventory
• Retention schedule
• Disposal system, initial and annual
• Vital records protection

Phase II:

- Off-site storage
- Image reduction
- Forms inventory

Phase I should have the highest priority, with the second phase beginning when Phase I is completed.

But there is always the off chance that you will face a management team that says, "Listen, why not contract for the whole program right now? It will save our time, eliminating our need to meet again to approve what we already know we need. And it will save our records manager's time, the time it would take to convince us of something we are predisposed to undertake."

Your chances are about three in ten that this will happen, so you will want to have your initial presentation as complete as possible. Even if there isn't immediate and unanimous approval of the entire program, your description of Phase II could have one or more of these effects:

1. Someone may see in your recommendations a real priority and urge you to get on with it at once. An example might be the disaster recovery plan. Remember, also, that the governor and his friend the sheriff started the Minnesota Records Management Division via a forms inventory.

2. Management will have an opportunity to digest the scope of the program. Everyone must understand that even though the inventory is completed, the program is just getting started. The inventory is only step 1.

3. You will aid the budget process in that you are asking for funding to be included in the next annual budget, and have indicated what you will need in the budget after that.

4. You will have an opportunity to point out that although you have computed the cost of the inventory using every anticipated expenditure, only the $1,000 for software and the D-Day incidentals are currently non-budgeted items. Things will be different in Phase II.

So let's look at the recommendations for Phase II.

Off-Site Storage

You have probably come to the conclusion that your basement storage area really is not adequate. It needs better or more shelving, better or more cleaning, and removal of extraneous materials such as paint or electrical appliances that are plugged in. It needs secured or controlled access.

At TLC, with 1,000 employees, 8,000 linear feet of records could be stored in the basement. You would be safe in estimating that about 3,200 linear feet will be disposed. This is probably very low, but it is a good starting point. In addition, you may estimate that about 7,200 linear feet will be transferred to basement storage from the offices at the time of the initial disposal. That means you will be storing about 12,000 linear feet of records, allowing for records transferred in from branch offices, temporary storage of files from departed employees, and miscellaneous items that you didn't expect, such as original artwork, obsolete training tapes, maps, flags, and banners—all of which somehow are part of the general housecleaning in the offices. Indeed, you will scratch your head in wonder, "Where did they keep all this stuff?"

Given the security necessary, you may wish to plan for space for a part-time clerk to manage the 12,000 linear feet of records. This may be especially true if you are given a few record series that are only a year or two old; there could be significant retrieval from these files. Consider carefully if the room currently in use can be successfully expanded and secured. Is the light sufficient? Is it fire resistant? Also consider that even if all these criteria are met, a storage area in the same building cannot be used to house vital records. Vital records simply must be kept outside the main building, preferably a few blocks away. A ten- or twelve-minute drive is certainly feasible. With adequate planning, a low-cost records storage facility outside the building could also be used for backup computer tapes as well as the vital papers, microfilmed records, floppy disks, optical disks, and other backup and/or reduction media.

Suppose you have found adequate space in an old but solid warehouse a half-mile away. The cost is $2.75 a square foot. Here's a real plus: The ceilings will safely allow shelving twelve shelves high instead of the seven in your basement.

This means you can stack 12 linear feet of records in 1 square foot of floor space instead of 7. Your cost goes from sixty-four cents per linear foot to twenty-three cents per linear foot. This is not the whole story, of course, because you have such considerations as aisles, desk space, and washrooms. But by and large you can count on storing double the records at half the current cost.

Two additional ways to keep the storage costs down are (1) recycling the shelving currently in use in the file rooms, basement storeroom, and file cabinets emptied as a result of the disposal; and (2) persuading the landlord to install a security system and a smoke and fire detection system if one is not already installed.

In your proposal, recommend that you will control the retrieval and replacement of records stored there. That way your assistant will have daily retrievals as an assignment duty. Department managers can forget this headache forever and clerical support staff will kiss your feet.

Exhibit 4-4 is a computation of the costs of this grand scheme.

The benefits of off-site storage are as follows:

1. There is $15,000 in savings over a five-year period.
2. The basement storage space is freed up for storing desks, PCs, or quantity lots of supplies purchased at discount.
3. The vital records program can be activated.
4. There is control over stored records, ensuring confidentiality and enforced disposal on a routine annual basis.
5. An issue causing frustration to staff is eliminated.
6. The records are in a secured location with full alarm systems.
7. The records necessary for disaster recovery are easily available for transfer to the recovery site.

You may even wish to include a floor plan with your report, suggesting how the shelving and control desk might make full use of the space you are requesting. The plan can be detailed or as simple as the diagram shown in Exhibit 4-5. This is a time when one or more of your vendors can be of enormous use, also. If you are up-front with them, explaining how this is just a proposal and that you may be as much as a year away from making a decision, and also that you are considering used shelving, many vendors will be willing to draw up a floor plan for you. You should, of course, expect them to recommend their own shelving.

On a tangential note, even though movable shelving is transportable, think carefully about installing it in leased space. Movable shelving is defined as rows of shelves mounted on tracks. The shelves move together to form a solid block. When a particular file or box is needed, the clerk turns a manual crank or pushes a button and the row to be accessed separates to allow user access to the files. Approximately one third more records can be accommodated in the same space occupied by open shelving. I have seen remarkable space savings with movable shelving, justifying its additional expense, and at least one vendor will guarantee to pull it out and reinstall it elsewhere if that becomes necessary. But you will have to cost-justify this kind of purchase carefully if it is to go into space your company does not own.

Exhibit 4-4. Current basement storage costs at TLC Headquarters Building.

TLC Headquarters Building

Space	Cost/Square Foot	Annual Cost
2,000 square feet (8,000 linear feet jammed in shelves, floors, aisles)	4.50 per square foot	$ 9,000

Personnel	Time Spent on Retrieval	Annual Cost
Clerical time	1 hour/week × 20 departments $9 hr × 20 hr. = $180 × 52 weeks	$ 9,360
Managerial time	1 hour/month × 20 depts. $12 × 20 hr. = $240 × 12 months	2,880
Total annual cost		$21,240
Five-year cost		$106,200

Current Problems

- No security of stored records, no installed fire or smoke detectors
- No room for one more box
- No confidentiality of private records
- No backup for vital records
- Staff visits the area only under duress

Proposed Off-Site Warehouse Storage

Space	Cost per Square Foot	Annual Cost
2,750 square feet (10,000 linear feet stacked 12 high)	$2.75	$ 7,562.50
Shelving		
Recycled materials first year		0.00

Exhibit 4-4. (*continued*)

Space	Cost/Square Foot	Annual Cost
Additional used materials		
Construction for security; fire/ smoke protection, tape storage		6,000.00
Personnel		
Clerical support	1 half-time at $9/hr.	9,360.00
	Mileage, 1 mile/day	
	@ $.30 per mile	78.00
Total cost		$23,000.50
	First year	$23,000.50
	Second year	17,000.50
	Third year	17,000.50
	Fourth year	17,000.50
	Fifth year	17,000.50
Five-year cost		$91,002.50
Average annual cost		$18,200.50

Image Reduction

Image reduction calls for a study of a whole area, not just the file series you have identified through the evaluation as prime candidate for image reduction. This is when you polish your flowcharting skills.

Going back to our ABC example, recall that the CEO's secretary was especially interested in image reduction. He may have told you that he would love to free up the file room he is now using to store long-term-retention documents. He indicated he would like to see the originals stored off-site, and that he would be happy to work with the reproductions. If the originals were ever needed for legal activities, they could be retrieved from the storage area. Certainly, the CEO's secretary not only has a good grasp of his requirements but a pilot project in his area would bring excellent exposure to department and division heads. But who else could benefit from the image-reduction system? Ask yourself:

Exhibit 4-5. Overhead view of suggested shelving layout.

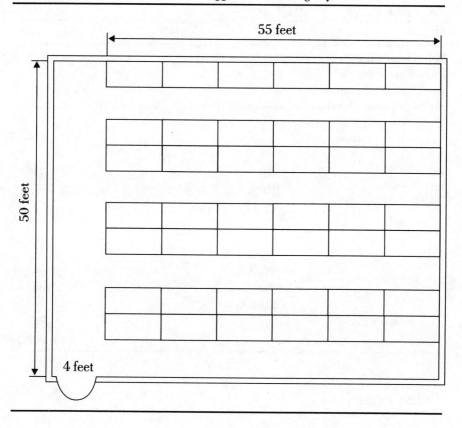

☐ Is there a need for more than one station, during both the conversion process and the operating process?

☐ Should the conversion process be part of a centralized service?

☐ Which departments have a need to share the same documents?

☐ Is that need sequential or simultaneous?

☐ What is the nature of the documents to be converted—size, color, paper weight, single or two-sided, volume, peaks and valleys (of production), turnaround time requirements (how soon the department needs the reproduction after the documents have been sent for imaging)?

☐ Who should be involved in the study?

☐ Should you turn to vendors for advice?

☐ Should you have a consultant do the study?

Imaging equipment ranges from $30,000 to $250,000 and more for complete systems. But the major costs are not the study or the equipment. Indexing the documents to be imaged is critical to the operation. The software for a reliable optical disk system can cost upwards of $7,000. Also, scanning the documents and then entering the index data can amount to as much as $1 per page, depending upon the complexity of the index.

These numbers are not meant to scare you away from the task. But you should realize that the initial study is just the tip of the iceberg. If you set the estimated cost for an in-house study at $3,000, and the cost for a consultant to do the study at $5,000, you'll be in the ballpark.

Note: Most vendors of imaging equipment will do the study at no cost. You will have to know a great deal about electronic imaging and micrographics to avoid going along with what may be a biased recommendation. On the other hand, if you are already predisposed to a particular vendor and you have confidence in the company and its service, this is not the worst way to go.

The worst thing to do is to do nothing. Electronics imaging is here to stay and will provide many solutions to image capture, reduction, and transfer problems.

However, there are some specific records series that adapt more readily to one technology than to another. For example:

• Files to which documents are added over long periods of time are ideal for optical disk. This is because, if the index is designed effectively, optical disk software will pull all relevant documents to the screen at one time, in either ascending or descending chronological order. The viewer can then select which documents he wishes to view, read, or print. Erasable optical disk is also available.

Examples of these kinds of records are personnel files, litigation files, claim files, and accounts payable and receivable. But note: Those companies that have a large investment in micrographics systems and equipment should consider a microfiche jacket system. This is a labor-intensive system that requires a jacket loader and duplicator (or large expenditures if a service bureau is used).

• Records that are of permanent nature, which cannot and must not be altered, are good candidates for CD-ROM because the encoded image is burned into the disk and is permanent. Again, the indexing is critical because each disk may hold 6,000 to 10,000 images and capacity seems to increase every month).

Examples of CD-ROM applications are: corporation and merger documents; pension plan files; construction contracts; patents, formulas, designs; advertisements; and historical records.

At the moment, most optical disk and CD-ROM systems will scan documents up to 17 inches long, so larger engineering drawings are better placed on 35mm microfilm, which can then be jacketed or left on roll film.

Micrographics

Micrographics is the overall term for all types or styles of records placed on microfilm. The compaction of records is amazing: a 100-foot roll of microfilm holds from 2,400 to 4,800 images (or sheets of paper); one 5 1/4-inch CD-ROM can hold up to 10,000 (soon up to 20,000) images; and one 5 1/4-inch optical disk can hold from 10,000 to 20,000 images.

There are also differences in equipment. A full-scale micrographic laboratory can run from $100,000 to $250,000. CD-ROM entry-level systems start at about $17,000, with additional costs for burning the image. Optical-disk systems start at about $35,000 for a stand-alone system. But as with CD-ROM and micrographics, these cost figures grow dramatically with the addition of workstations, sophisticated software, juke boxes (holders for the disks), and so on.

These are very big numbers, so extreme caution is advised before decisions are made. One micrographics system, which is el cheapo and highly underutilized, is computer-output-to-microfilm, or COM. Data on mainframe tapes or disks can be transferred to microfilm. A 4-by-6-inch sheet of film, called a fiche (pronounced *feesh*), will hold 307 computer pages, plus 1 page of indexing. Service bureau costs for COM range from $.10 a fiche to $1.50, depending upon local competition. Currently, we have computer-output-to-laser disk (COLD), which is the same idea, with images encoded on the optical disk instead of on film.

Applications for COM and COLD include: general ledgers, customer lists and histories, sales figures—year-to-date, year-end financial reports, accounts receivable, and accounts payable.

Many technological changes will undoubtedly take place in the industry because of the resistance the product is meeting in the marketplace. So the systems of today may bear only slight resemblance to the systems of tomorrow. This should not in any way deter your study of image reduction. Microfilm was in use in 1870, but it didn't really come into its own until the 1940s, 1950s, and 1960s, when microfilm readers were finally improved to the point where the medium was a feasible substitute for the original. I discuss image reduction in greater detail in Chapter 11.

Forms Management

In your proposal to management, you will want to make the forms management recommendation last. This is because (1) you will have become much more familiar with the company's documents when you have completed the inventory and retention process; and (2) you will need the cooperation of almost every living soul in the organization. It's better that they have seen you for some time as a cheerful and confident records manager.

Assuming that you have an estimated 4,000 records series, about 80 percent of these will contain at least one form. Some records series, such as purchase orders and invoices, will be made up primarily of forms—the company's forms, plus those of vendors and customers or clients. For the sake of explanation, estimate that you have 1,000 forms. This includes those that are "bootlegged" by individuals at the copy machines as well as those that are officially printed and warehoused. It is vital to capture the bootlegged, informal forms because:

- Even if department staffers proclaim that "they are for our own use only," often these forms find their way out to the public.
- Even informal forms cost money to design, copy, process, distribute, store, and retrieve.
- Informal forms tend to lose consistency and the most recent version differs from previous versions. There may be very good reasons for the changes, but are staff workers using multiple versions of the same form?
- Forms, official and informal, reflect an image of your company, not only to the public but to your employees.

What constitutes a form? Usually I consider a form to be a document that requires completion, by either the staff or someone outside the company. For example, a form letter to a client containing blanks that have been completed by the sender and/or that the client must complete, is a form. On the other hand, a form letter that is a preprinted notice advising clients of a price change is *not* a form. If this distinction seems too rigid as you become familiar with your company, you certainly may modify the definition to suit your particular circumstances.

When estimating your time to perform a forms management study and make recommendations, allow at least six months. The project is not going to have a high priority among staff members; in fact, it may be perceived as a threat. But then, what isn't perceived that way these days?

Here are some of the tasks involved in conducting a forms inventory:

• Collecting two copies of each form generated by the company. These copies should be blank, not filled in. One copy goes into your reference file at once, and the other will be used for analysis. Do not use photocopies of forms. And your copy should contain all the multiple copies, just as printed. If the form is numbered, have the manager void two numbers for you.

• Developing or purchasing a software program to assist you with the analysis. Some of the fields you will need are:

Originating Dept.:	Name
Description:	Size, color, number of copies, construction, paper weight, distribution (who gets which copy)
Purpose:	For example, requisitions for supplies, requests for vacation time, repair orders, overtime records, overtime approvals
Retention:	Retention period for each copy; when your forms program is in operation, you may wish to include the retention period at the bottom of new forms, along with distribution instructions
Duplication of Data:	Which other forms collect most or all of the same data

• Analyzing the results of the study.

• Meeting with each concerned user to see if you can, in fact, eliminate or combine the items in question. Then make recommendations for eliminating and/or combining forms.

• Starting the process to improve the content, appearance, and ease with which each form is completed.

• Initiating a numbering system for the remaining forms and for new forms, and making sure that obsolete forms are removed from offices and supply rooms when revisions are issued.

• Storing copies of all forms for reference when new forms are proposed; keeping your PC database up-to-date for search purposes.

• Working with staff and vendors to set standards for design, quantity, storage, and minimum stock levels for all forms.

That's not all of it, but it's enough so that when you are budgeting your time for the study, you will be almost 100 percent occupied for six months, plus about one half that time for your assistant. In addition, data-entry time and the cost of a software package must be included. Total costs, then, would look like this (figures projected from the TLC example, with 1,000 employees):

Item/Task	Responsibility	Cost
Forms collection and analysis	Records manager (full-time, 6 months)	$12,480*
	Assistant (half-time, 6 months)	9,360**
Data entry	Operator, 2 weeks	720***
Software	Vendor	500
Estimated cost for Forms Management System		$23,060

Problems and Overview

Check your figures. It is so important, I must say it repeatedly: Check all your figures, not once, not twice, but over and over.

You're probably inclined to say, "I'm dealing with so many estimates anyway, what if there is a slight error in calculation?"

Well, the fact is that in almost any management meeting there will be someone whose job it is to check figures. She has no time for anyone who can't keep figures straight. To this person such mistakes are evidence of not just carelessness but of something sinister, bordering on sly manipulation of numbers or even downright lies. And even if she can't find anything wrong with your numbers, you may be asked, casually, "Just how did you come up with these numbers?" The mere fact that you have gone over them so many times will give you the confidence to reply smoothly.

If, in spite of all your efforts, a mistake should creep in, say stoutly, "I will correct these sheets at once and have new copies in your hands by 3 P.M. today." And, of course, you will. *Do not,* in your meeting, blame your staff, the computer, or the copy machine. Take responsibility.

At least two other disturbing things may occur during the course of your evaluation and analyses:

1. You will come across employees who are total zeros in their jobs. They don't know and don't care to know how to do a better job.

*$12/hour.
**$9/hour.
***$9/hour.

2. You will come across some really neat people who are getting the job done, barely, by coping with some awful workflow procedures.

What should you do about this? The first is a no-win situation. If you are good buddies with the personnel director (no lower), you may confide your observations. Chances are he knows all about it and has the situation under control or observation.

The second situation is an entirely different story. If the really awful procedures impact, or will impact in the future, on your records management program, you should document each case. Use your flowchart skills together with a narrative to describe the situation. When you are analyzing the data, you may come up with solutions for some of these problems.

If you can document substantial savings (in time, equipment, labor, or dollars), by all means include these recommendations in your report; your flowchart will be a powerful convincer.

My flowchart template has stood me in good stead, both as Minnesota Director of Records Management and as a consultant. I never go out of my office without it. Over the years, I have used the workflow technique of my evaluations to help later install some of the following:

- An optical disk system for the large number of IRA applications stored by a bank's home office
- A central file room—and I do mean central—for the legal department of a large holding company
- An optical disk system for the personnel records of a nuclear power plant
- A new filing system for a regional medical center
- Streamlined processing systems for city and county licensing units

Not one of these was an easy sell. Each one had to be cost-justified, even those where no momentary investment was required. The time saved had to be proved beyond a shadow of a doubt. Intangibles like improved accuracy, employee job satisfaction, or enrichment weren't enough.

If your program is not affected by the poor procedures, hold on to your documentation. Sooner or later poor systems have a way of impacting records management. Then haul out your data and make your recommendations at that time.

Chapter 5

The Report and Your Presentation

We all know the powerful effects a great advertising campaign can have. Think of your report and presentation as your ad campaign.

You have great data. You probably know more about your company than anyone else except the founders, the CEO, and the CEO's secretary. Your recommendations are worthy of respect and serious consideration.

Now it is up to you to package them in an attention-getting format and present them in a sharp, concise, and confident manner. You are "selling" in the best sense of the word. After all, what is the use of all your good work, careful analysis, and thought if nobody buys?

When you prepare your report, keep in mind that (1) only a select group will hear your presentation as well as read your report; and (2) the rest of the staff will only read it. So the report has to be understandable and convincing to those who will not have the benefit of your charm and persuasive skills.

Elements of the Evaluation Report

The records management report should have at least these elements:

Cover

Put a crisp, clear cover on your report. The report is important, and it should look it. Spell the company name correctly, including all abbreviations, as the company prefers to see it. If your company has a logo, you may certainly use it here. Put the name of your department or division as the source of the report in a prominent place. (I have never used my own name on the cover, although using names may be a policy in your company.) Also, check out your company's policy for claiming copyright.

Letter of Transmittal

State who approved the study, who conducted it, who took part, and where, when, why, and how. Give special thanks to your contacts and those who were interviewed. Sign the letter.* The transmittal letter is not listed in the table of contents; it is simply the first page after the cover.

Table of Contents

All significant headings, graphs, tables, and additional material must be listed.

Introduction

Provide a short description of why the study was conducted, qualifications of the study team (don't be shy), number of those who took part, and significant aspects of the scope of the study—for example, all members of the personnel department, all department heads, and the entire headquarters building staff, plus a short description of the method employed to perform the study.

Findings

Describe the volume of records, security of records, filing systems, equipment in use or in disuse, forms, storage, and computer systems. This is a description of what you found to be "the true facts" of the study. If you have actual space or personnel costs, be sure to mention them. But do not point a finger at anyone for not having received the exact figures in time for your report.

The findings for each area should detail the results of your study for that area: records inventory, security, vital records, filing equipment, disposal of records. Do not assume that your readers will know what a records inventory or a file series is, or even what a vital record is. In the gentlest of terms, explain.

---

*As a beginner, you may ask your boss if she wishes to sign the letter of transmittal. If the answer is yes, take it to mean your report is a humdinger!

You will want to make liberal use of the comments you received during the interviews so that this section is believable and creates a sense of urgency. Make use of the pie chart to illustrate your points. Include any specific data you may have been asked to study, such as image reduction, filing systems, or use of storage space.

Sometimes, when the picture you have to describe is particularly bleak, you might slip in a cartoon depicting the universal need for records management so that no one will begin to feel "picked on."

This section is the guts of the report. It's where you set the stage for your recommendations, and by citing the severity of the problems, you justify the cost of solutions. But don't let me scare you.

Recommendations

Based upon the findings, these are your solutions. Put these recommendations in the same sequence as the findings. Also, do not recommend a cure for something that has not previously been diagnosed as an illness. Build your case in the findings, not in the recommendations.

Let's talk morally and philosophically for a moment. Suppose you are certain in your own mind what the recommendations should be but are unfamiliar with some of the areas. You can't perform the tasks yourself. The question is, should you recommend only what you know you can accomplish, or should you recommend those other areas as well—those tasks that you feel you are not at the moment competent to tackle?

This is not an easy question to answer. After all, you were hired (or perhaps had the job thrust upon you) because you were perceived to be an expert, possibly *the* expert. How will it look if, at the first meeting, you have to admit you're in over your head? I have seen top management people who admire candor, adjust to it comfortably, and say, "Go for it; get the help you need." But let me tell you, such folks are mighty few and far between.

Therefore, divide your recommendations into phases. Phase I would be those items you are confident you can accomplish within a reasonable time. Phase II should be those items you will be somewhat skilled in by the time those skills are required for implementation. And Phase III might be those items that call for outside help. Presumably these last are the most complicated and logically fall at the end of the program, when you will have become much more experienced. (If you are absolutely brand-new to records management and have no idea how to perform even the most basic tasks, take heart. This book will get you through Phase I as we have described it.)

Cost and Time Estimates

Explain what each recommendation will cost and how much time is involved in implementation. In some recommendations there is a conversion period as well, so the costs of converting must be considered. This would be true, for example, if you were recommending a new filing system to replace the one currently in use.

Also, differentiate between the costs related to outside help and the costs of using company staff. If you recall, in the case of the forms program, the total cost was estimated at $23,060, but only $1,220 related to nonbudgeted expense. You might want to discuss internal staff time in terms of hours, instead of dollars. But never lose track of the fact that, in the end, hours cost dollars.

Also, be sure to include the cost of any new equipment, software, space, staff, or overhead expenses that might be incurred as a result of implementation. Keep nothing back. Tell the complete story.

Benefits

This is another of those "most important parts." But truly, this is where you live or die. Hard dollars are saved, costs are avoided, and intangible benefits described. (Guess which ones will be considered the most important?)

Your report should indicate you know how to accomplish what you are recommending and how much time it will take you to do it. Some of the benefits might depend upon a department's timetable—for example, a move to a new building: "Let's get rid of those old records before we move!"

Action Plan

The next page of your report should be an action plan. It should detail which activities will come first and which come sequentially or simultaneously. Try to be as specific as you can, given the limited knowledge you have on the conversion process and the limited control you will have over equipment delivery and construction schedules. As you will note, however, the areas where you personally are in charge can be fairly accurate.

Try to make use of what is known as a Gantt chart,* a simple presentation of a timeline. A Gantt chart offers a look at a project as a whole, without going into the details that simply bore your audience and/or scare them away from taking further action. Without including the timelines that make

---

*A Gantt chart can be found on page 242 of the evaluation sample in Appendix A.

up the Gantt chart, the following are the activities that usually are included, with some of the tasks involved:

Inventory of Records, Retention, and Disposal:

- ☐ Volume/inventory process
- ☐ Retention process
- ☐ Data entry/software program
- ☐ Manager's meeting
- ☐ Correction process
- ☐ Data entry corrections

- ☐ Legal approval process
- ☐ Written procedures
- ☐ Disposal procedures
- ☐ Disposal day
- ☐ Updating the system

Storage Program:

- ☐ Location/selection
- ☐ Shelving research and selection
- ☐ Requests for proposal/bid process
- ☐ Conversion procedures
- ☐ Software/data entry

- ☐ Maintenance procedures
- ☐ Installation of equipment
- ☐ Conversion
- ☐ Security system
- ☐ Open house/orientation meeting

Vital Records Program:

- ☐ Listing of vital records
- ☐ Recommendations for backup—frequency and media

- ☐ Written procedures
- ☐ Documentation for disaster recovery plan

Filing Systems:

- ☐ Studies
- ☐ Recommendations
- ☐ Approval/orientation process
- ☐ Purchase of supplies

- ☐ Conversion procedures
- ☐ Conversion
- ☐ Written procedures

Imaging Feasibility Studies:

- ☐ Scope of study
- ☐ Flowcharting
- ☐ Verification
- ☐ Analysis/design
- ☐ Research equipment/software
- ☐ Requests for proposal
- ☐ Selection/procurement process

- ☐ Installation
- ☐ Orientation
- ☐ Staffing: job description, recruiting, training
- ☐ Written procedures
- ☐ Data conversion

Forms Management:

☐ Scope   ☐ Analysis
☐ Software/equipment selection   ☐ Approval process: staff meetings
☐ Forms collection   ☐ Forms design orientation
☐ Data entry   ☐ Written procedures for mainten-
                                               ance

Obviously these are not the sum total of recommendations you will be making, nor is the list of tasks all-inclusive. But the list will give you an idea of the depth required for an action plan. Try very hard to compress the plan to one sheet; it seems to be more digestible to do so.

Lastly, include the estimated start date and the estimated completion date. When computing the time it will take to accomplish the tasks, you have a number of estimates to use from your recommendations and findings sections. Allow a lot more time for meetings than is really necessary, unless you work for a company whose policy on meetings is that they are for the most part useless and enormously costly. Count yourself lucky if this describes your management philosophy.

Summary of Recommendations

The summary should be as barebones as you can make it. You may want to withhold this sheet when making your oral presentation and then distribute it at the end. That gets a little play-acty for me, but you know your audience, so use your judgment here. Many people in your audience will immediately turn to the summary and study it, so you will not have their attention while building your case. Also, after looking at the summary, many managers never read the entire report.

Sometimes I cope with this situation by saying, "There is a summary of findings, recommendations, and costs at the front of my report. On your honor, please do not peek at it until we are ready for questions." Even so, about 10 percent will insist on peeking.

Team Qualifications

This section lists the people who are going to work on Phase I of your recommendations, plus possibly those who will work on Phase II, if you have made your selection. Where possible, list the qualifications you think will signify each person's ability to perform the tasks assigned. As the in-house records manager, try to select people who know the company and its records well, and who understand the politics of the company. Pick a staff that management will regard with respect. Get the very best people you can—remember, if they look good, you'll look good. The glory in being a records manager is usually reserved for the manager who has the best staff.

The Addendum

The addendum will include the abstract of the interviews, the grid, and any other materials you might find useful. Don't overdo this, however. Managers have a short fuse when it comes to reading; the bare necessities take twenty-five hours a day as it is. So be sure that what you include speaks to the point and backs your position 100 percent.

The originals of your interviews should be kept in your own file for a year after the report has been released; then dispose of them. (Be sure to add this record to your own file series inventory and establish the one-year retention period.)

Preparing the Report

If a picture is worth a thousand words, an example is surely worth as much. Review the sample evaluation in Appendix A. When you begin to write your report, you will have the benefit of my thinking as you put your individual stamp on your own report.

Once the report is nearly finished, prepare the final draft on your PC. Also make final versions of the graphs, charts, and tables. Here are the final steps I take:

1. Assemble the report in sequence—the letter of transmittal first, followed by the table of contents.
2. Number all the pages, beginning with the introduction.
3. Proofread every line and check all figures. (Preferably, get someone else to proofread your work.) Make any corrections necessary.
4. Print the full report.

If you know how many copies you will need at the presentation meeting, make them now, plus two extra copies. One of the extra copies is your permanent file copy; the other should be the original, or master copy, you will use for making corrections (God forbid!) and for running off additional copies.

When the graphs for the data are completed, they can be converted to overhead transparencies for your presentation. You'll be able to refer to the image on the wall and your listeners can be following by looking at the same data before them—offering positive reinforcement of your ideas. Also, you can respond to questions articulately and promptly—no chances for questions to lurk among your audience.

For overheads, use the following:

- Volume graphs and maps
- All charts and graphs
- Lists of findings
- Summaries of recommendations
- All benefits sheets
- Action plans
- A cartoon or particularly nifty quote
- Plus one other page you simply can't live without

Try to keep your overheads to about ten in number. And each overhead should have no more than eight or nine words. Graphs are the exception, but keep them as simple as you can.

The Meeting

Schedule a management meeting to hear your report. Explain to your boss that so much work has gone into the project, and the ramifications are so great, that a meeting is essential. Promise to be done in about forty-five minutes (sounds better than one hour) and that you will be crisp and concise.

At least one major U.S. company pays serious attention to such meetings. The decision makers must be present and a project is voted up or down right there at the time. I can't tell you what a blessing this is.

So try your hardest to get the decision makers at your meeting. See that your supporters are included in the list, but do not be dismayed if the opposition is there in force, too. Remember the company's mission statement: You're there to help accomplish its goals. The worst that can happen is that the opposition will be a minority; the best is that you will persuade them to your cause. Set your meeting for morning, midweek if possible. Don't pick a Monday or Friday, nor the day before a holiday or the day after.

Avoid surprises, if at all possible. Nobody wants to appear to management as though he didn't know what was going on in his area. Talk up your plan and try to get a consensus before the meeting. Go over the data with your interviewee. If an individual denies your numbers, be certain you are right before you go public. You can be sure your objector will do just that—object loud and clear, possibly in advance of your presentation.

You will have to weigh the benefits of a compromise; that is, you may have to give the objector the benefit of the doubt versus the end product you are trying to reach. Every company has one or two people who object to everything as a matter of practice; nothing you can do or say will please them. These people can hurt you very much, sometimes fatally. Usually management knows these people, too. And for reasons that I have never completely figured out, the front office seems to condone their destructive behavior. So:

• *Rehearse the night before.* Speak out loud to your mirror, to your family, or to your dog. I used to hate the rehearsal, especially to my staff. But it made me a better person, and I had better presentations.

Wear something fairly conservative, but definitely on the stylish side. Don't be dowdy. If you know you look nice, you'll be able to forget your appearance and concentrate on what you're saying.

• *Get to the meeting room a half hour early.* Set up your overhead projector. Get your overheads in order. I usually use one copy of the report to make notes in the margin. Then I insert my overheads into the report and they come up at the appropriate times. When all is in readiness, relax.

• *As people come into the meeting, adopt a friendly, confident attitude.* Introduce yourself to those whom you don't know. Take your place at the head of the table, or midway down one side of the table, or at the head of the room at a lectern—whichever suits the configuration of the room. If you are to be at a lectern, and somebody is going to introduce you, try to mingle with folks until the meeting is called to order. The idea is to cross any bridges that may exist between you and the audience. This is not an adversarial meeting, and you want to show as clearly as you can that you are a member of the team.

• *When the meeting starts, introduce yourself (unless someone else has done so).* Describe, very briefly, the evaluation process.

• *Show your first overhead.* This should be the cover. Ask your audience to follow using their own copies, and to note their questions in the margins. Tell them you will take all the time necessary to deal with each one at the end of your remarks. Acknowledge positive comments with a smile and a nod, but save the questions for the end.

• *Proceed through the report, using your overheads to keep you on track.* I shut off the projector between overheads for two reasons: so that the audience can concentrate on what I am saying and so that I can make good eye contact.

• *At the end of your formal presentation, ask for questions and comments.* Let your "friendlies" speak up. If there are questions you cannot answer, *don't guess.* Instead say, "I'll have to check on that. May I call you with the answer?" And, of course, follow through.

• When the questions seem to have run out, *ask for the sale.* I often look at my watch and say, "I can start the inventory at 1 P.M. today. Is that OK?"

Most of the time this is followed by laughter. Government agencies, in particular, usually cannot move that fast. But in at least two cases (one of which was a municipality), the answer was "yes, 1 P.M. is fine."

On one occasion I made my evaluation report presentation to a decision-making committee of a Fortune 500 company at 10 A.M. I recommended replacing the central file with microfilm. We finished with questions at 11 A.M. The committee asked me to return at 1 P.M. (at my suggestion). When I returned, the central file was *gone,* modules had been set up in its place, and computer analysts were at work on a new program. Now that's what I call affirmative action!

You may have to wait a bit longer. But if you have asked for, or suggested, a start date (and the compelling reasons for that date), you may ask politely when a decision will be forthcoming. Then thank everyone for their attention and put your overheads and reports together with confidence.

Stay as long as anyone has a question or wants to talk—or even ask your opinion. The longer people stay after a meeting, the more successful the meeting is likely to be.

All your hard work leading up to this meeting is over. You have performed one of the most exacting records management tasks you'll ever do: the records management evaluation. Frankly, if you have followed all the steps suggested in this book thus far, there is very little you cannot accomplish as a records manager.

On to the next step. *Bonne chance!*

Part Two

What to Do When Management Says Yes!

Well, how did it go? Were you dazzling? How I wish I could have been there to see and hear your presentation! But now we must deal with the aftermath: what to do when management says yes!

The mechanics of the evaluation are about the same for every company. The guidelines I've given are easy to follow, as you have just seen. But the implementation of your recommendations will differ greatly from company to company.

No two companies are going to need or want the exact same index to their files, for example. And while there are similarities, it is up to you to use your ingenuity to design a system that gives your company the competitive edge by retrieving vital information. This is why your analysis of information needs is critical. Even companies in the same line of business have different needs based upon location, organizational structure, internal politics, and outside competition. You are, of course, duty-bound to do your very best. This may include having to tell management that you will need help in certain areas, either in-house staff or outside expertise.

That's not only not bad news, it's a very positive position for you to take. It's always more productive to work with someone with whom you can talk over ideas and options. The implementation of your recommendations will only benefit from the input. Besides, when it's over, you can't give a triumphant high-five to yourself, can you?

Another difficult task that, rightfully, will cause you worry is advising management if the wrong people seem to be in certain jobs. I am speaking here only of jobs that *impact your proposed systems*. Don't try telling the boss that his brother-in-law lacks vice-presidential capabilities. Chances are he knows it, but whether he does or not, it's none of your business. What *is* your business is if the data-entry operator can't key data correctly or never is available when you need those services. Stick to only what concerns your implementation and don't try to be a personnel expert.

Having said that, there are exceptions, of course. There may be at least one situation when you may wish to step slightly out of your territory. Suppose while you were conducting the evaluation, you came across one or two employees who would be tremendous assets to your records management operation. They could be of either permanent or temporary assistance during the inventory, for example. If management, in the process of approving your recommendations, asks if you will need any help, it's nice to have a few names ready.

Compared to the rest of the items on your list, these issues are relatively easy to solve. Either you'll get additional help or you won't, and either miscast personnel will be given other tasks or you'll have to learn to work with them. Once you have stated your position clearly and positively to management, live with their decision and don't *ever* complain about it.

In the unlikely but possible event that management has said no to your recommendations, what should you do?

If the word is given during your presentation, while you are bundling up your overheads and reports, it can be momentarily disturbing. But it's very important to keep your cool and follow these steps.

1. Start by saying to your boss:"I understand your decision. I will put the inventory aside for now and proceed with [the task which caused the original assignment]."
2. Thank everyone for his or her cooperation and return to your office.
3. Review the meeting and report to see if there is anything you left out or too much you left in. Are your figures correct? If you come across something significant, you may wish to address it in a memo to your boss. If not, file the report, along with your interview sheets and flowcharts. And flag the file to be included in your work when the next budgeting process rolls around.

If the no comes to you after the meeting, you've had a little time to reflect and prepare yourself. Then follow the three steps above.

As I said before, it's unlikely you will get anything but yes. So let's concentrate on what to do when you get that go-ahead from management. It's mind-boggling, isn't it? Don't panic. The following chapters take you step by step through implementation. Depending upon what was approved, you can turn to the specific chapter and follow the instructions. Good luck!

Chapter 6

The Records Inventory and Retention Schedule

The initial tangible results of a records management program may be seen companywide at the first disposal of records. So it is with a certain sense of urgency that you must gear up and start the inventory process.

Let's begin with some definitions for the basic tools of your trade, which will become as much a part of your kit as your flowchart template, pencil, and eraser.

copy of record The official copy of a particular record, though not necessarily the original. For example, the original purchase order may go to the vendor. The purchasing department will hold the second sheet, or copy, and the ordering department keeps the third. In some companies, the receiving department also has a copy. Thus, Purchasing has the copy of record, which is the one that will receive the long retention period. All other copies may be disposed of when administrative needs are fulfilled.

custodian The name or title of the person who has physical possession of the record series or file.

disposal date The date on which the record series has fulfilled legal, administrative, and historical needs and may be destroyed.

file The file folder relating to single copies (for example, Union contract, 1996; Couter Pond correspondence, 1995; Smoke-free ordinance, 1997).

file index A listing of all file folders within a company or agency, including detailed information about each file, where it is located, and who has physical possession. Files may be on paper, disk, film, or some other medium.

file series   *See* record series.

index   A listing of the items that make up a retention schedule, a paper filing system, or an electronic imaging system, such as a computerized or a micrographics system. A good index includes the location of each item listed.

off-site storage   Low-cost separate facility that is secured and has 24-hour access. Used for storing vital records, backup, and long-term or permanent storage records with low retrieval needs.

records   All forms of communication or information relating to a company or agency, regardless of medium.

record series   All records that relate to a single topic (personnel files, litigation, claims) or that are uniform documents relating to the same process (invoices, purchase orders, applications).

records inventory   A listing of all record series, giving detailed information about each entry, including the retention period and the citation upon which the retention period is based.

records retention schedule   A list of the length of time each record series must be kept.

retention period   The period of time a record series must be kept before it can be destroyed.

vital records   Those records essential to ensure that a company or agency will be back in business within X hours or days following a disaster or business interruption. Examples of vital records are accounts receivable; payroll; vendors or suppliers lists; general ledger; deducation register; current contracts; customer lists; personnel home addresses and telephone numbers; the disaster recovery plan; corporation or merger documents; outstanding stocks, bonds, and accounts payable; and patents, formulas, designs, and recipes.

Let us assume that management has approved Phase I of your recommendations and has given you the go-ahead to develop the records inventory, retention, and disposal program. This assignment will include:

- Taking an inventory of existing records
- Drawing up a retention and disposal schedule
- Backing up all vital records
- Finding off-site records storage

If you take it one step at a time, it's not as overwhelming a task as you might think.

In this chapter, we look at how to take the inventory and develop the retention schedule.

The Importance of the Inventory

The cornerstone of any records management program is the records inventory. You need to know what you have in order to manage it, and not only do you need to know *what*, you need to know *who, when, where, how much*, and in many cases, *why.*

The detailed records inventory tells you not only the title of the record, but all of the following:

- [ ] Who holds the copy of record
- [ ] How much of the series is produced annually
- [ ] How much is on hand at the moment
- [ ] Whether it is a vital record
- [ ] If there is a need for confidentiality
- [ ] If the record is of historical value
- [ ] How long the record should be kept

The "copy of record" concept is one of the most important cost-cutting tools available to a records manager.

When duplicate copies of a record are distributed, one copy is specified as the copy of record. Its custodian is listed in the inventory, and she is instructed to retain or store that copy for the full retention period. This might be from one year to forever.

All other staff members who receive copies of that same record need keep their copies only as long as they are useful. In many cases, such copies may not even reach the file cabinet. Since the average number of copies of a record is eight, this means that seven copies can be disposed of, not filed. Can't you just see the tremendous savings this generates?

"But how," you ask, "will a custodian know whether she has the copy of record or a duplicate?" This is where your automated system comes in. You will have generated and distributed the official inventory, retention, and disposal listing to each custodian. It's a simple matter to look up the record title to determine who has the copy of record. And, more important, it gives the other seven users the authority to dispose of their copies as soon as their usefulness is at an end.

The second and third items above are helpful in the event you wish to target this series for image reduction or off-site storage. In other words, the inventory is a critical planning tool. You cannot consider that you have a records management program until your records inventory is completed.

Exhibit 6-1 will give you some idea of the amount of data necessary to achieve a detailed, consistent inventory. As always, these examples are intended to give you an indication of what can be done. You may want to modify the form to suit your own needs, or you might use the form as a guide to develop your own.

Keeping the Inventory Manageable

The main pitfall in taking a records inventory—one that has baffled records managers and consultants for many years—is: What is the scope of records inventory, and how does one keep it from becoming an index of records? We know that a record series is a collection of records about the same topic. For example, it could be personnel files, legal files, accounts receivable, or accounts payable. It could also be a collection of identical records of the same size, format, and content, such as would be the case with invoices or purchase orders. But sometimes this definition blurs.

Here are two typical files:

The Lake of the Woods Project, 1968. Completed.

Mayor's Notes on Tax Subsidies for Tobacco Growers.

The first is clearly a project file. But as for the second, we have a choice: We can consider it part of the working files or administrative files and deal with it as such in our retention schedule, or we can inventory each and every folder individually.

Before we make a decision, let us think for a moment about the two basic types of records inventory: detailed and generic. We define a *detailed* records inventory as one that fully describes the series. That is, it lists the following:

- Title
- Description
- Location
- Original or duplicate
- Volume
- Frequency of issue
- Responsible authority (for approving disposal)
- Dates of the series (from/to)
- Whether vital or nonvital
- Custodian
- Retention
- Governing authority (legal or industrywide requirement)

Exhibit 6-1. Records inventory data collection form.

RECORDS INVENTORY DATA COLLECTION FORM

Facility   Division   Department   Image

Custodian position   Custodian name

Record series title

Record series description

Media   COR   If NO, who maintains copy of record?

_____

Date range on-site   Volume (ln. ft.)

Thru

Date range off-site   Volume (cu. ft.)

Thru

Storage Location:

Frequency   Privacy/secured   Vital/backup

Filing sequence (alpha/numeric/chronological/subject)

Retention:
Years   Instructions   Office   Storage   Off-site

                                                                      Dispose
Governing authority

The *generic* schedule includes only the following:

- Title
- Retention
- Governing authority

A generic schedule takes broad blocks of records, such as accounting records, and assigns to them an overall schedule—for example, six years. I bring the generic inventory process to your attention not because I have any faith in it but because many others do. Records managers who have not held many other jobs, or who perhaps do not know the personnel of the company well, see a generic records schedule as a tremendous shortcut. It's not—and it is totally useless.

If your company has followed a generic schedule, rest assured that beyond the first effort, nothing has been accomplished. The generic schedule is not self-perpetuating. It requires untold amounts of decision making on the part of every manager whenever a disposal day is set. And there is absolutely no control over the disposed items. Disposal is as much a matter of choice as if no retention schedule existed.

So, if management has agreed to having an inventory and to assigning retention periods to all record series, then by all means put something in place that will not have to be redone in a few years. Install a system that will deal with the unique needs of individual staff members. It must, as well, be controllable.

Since you will produce a detailed records inventory, go back to the dilemma of the general versus the specific. Because you are new in your job, possibly new to the company, consider the day-to-day files relating to projects or assignments *in progress* as administrative files (though you may use individual titles in the description area of your form). Working files often become completed projects and as such will have a much longer retention period. Also, every manager has dozens of working file folders that are for her own use and never see the light of day. Don't get caught up in trying to detail these and thereby cluttering your inventory with data that will either be discarded at the end of the month or be added to a larger project file. Individual managers will love you for this decision.

You don't want to confuse your records inventory with a filing index. The two are not the same. Remember:

Inventory = File series
Index = File folder

Ultimately, the retention period will be the link between the records inventory and any file index you eventually prepare. In Chapter 9, I will explain how this works, but for the moment think of the retention schedule as the umbilical cord between the records inventory and the file index. This may seem confusing now, but it will become clear as you get into the inventory.

Action Plan for Taking a Records Inventory

A good beginning to the inventory process is an action plan for yourself. You will enumerate each of the tasks that must be accomplished. That way the program won't be so overwhelming and you can proceed in an orderly manner. Here is a sample action plan; modify it as you wish.

☐ Prepare your own inventory sheet form:
Modify sample (see Exhibit 6-1). Add elements as necessary for your system.

☐ Select software (or use the RIDS Manual at the end of this book)

☐ Select and train helpers. Based on the evaluation, you will need:

Space to Inventory	Inventory Takers
10,000 linear feet of records	4
5,000–10,000 linear feet	3
2,000–5,000 linear feet	2
Less than 2,000 linear feet	1

Note: Later in this chapter I equate the amount of help you will need with the records series, rather than linear feet. Use whichever measurement is most comfortable.

☐ Prepare news item or office memo regarding the inventory. Include beginning date, staff names. When sent to department heads, include boss's signature.

☐ Establish the schedule and make assignments to helpers.

☐ Send out notices of the schedule.

☐ Complete an inventory sheet for each record series or duplicates.

☐ Enter data on computer system.

☐ Run listings by custodians.

☐ Schedule managers' meeting.

☐ Hold meeting and distribute custodian lists.

☐ Allow for custodians' review period.

☐ Negotiate changes.

☐ Make corrections.
☐ Enter corrections on computer system.
☐ Generate two alphabetical lists for legal department or company attorney.
☐ Schedule disposal day.
☐ Run lists of records eligible for disposal, by custodians.
☐ Send out news of D-Day (disposal day).
☐ Arrange for pickup, recycling, or incineration of records.
☐ Arrange for mementos of the event, such as photographs.
☐ Collect disposal lists.
☐ Enter data into computer.
☐ Generate lists of records disposed, then reset computer system for next year.
☐ Send backup list of disposed records to off-site storage.
☐ Send out news of disposal: amount of records disposed with photos, number of file cabinets emptied, dollars received for recycled paper, special mention to particular units.
☐ Prepare written procedures manual.
☐ Maintain system with new entries.

Do not be dismayed. It is easier than it looks. Actually, it's not that much different from the evaluation process, and you lived through that, didn't you?

Staffing Requirements

For the first few inventories you undertake, it may seem difficult to estimate the resources necessary to accomplish the tasks you have set out. Keeping in mind Murphy's law, it always seems better to allow more time for the job rather than to use more people. If you err and come in early, you'll gain more points on your personal balance sheet.

There are, however, some rules of thumb to assist in planning your schedule:

Number of Record Series	Number of Staff Required
50–1,000	1
1,000–2,500	2
2,500 +	3

But how do you know how many record series you are dealing with? As stated, no two companies are the same. But as an example, suppose a company employs 750 people. This is what you are likely to find:

Department	Number of Record Series
Front office, CEO, president	20
Administration/administrative services	300
Sales, marketing	300
Accounting/finance	450
Personnel	250
Manufacturing/operations	250
Purchasing	200
Claims	100
Credit	50
Treasurer	100
Legal	100
Planning, research & development	400
Testing	200
Public relations/advertising	200
Safety	150
Taxation	200

In addition, governmental units will have:

City council	100
Public works	300
Police/law enforcement	200
Fire department	100
Mayor's office (*see* Administration)	
Permits/licensing	250
Inspections	250
Plus assorted boards and commissions	200

You can see that it doesn't take very long to add up to more than 4,000 record series. You may be surprised to learn that departments with long banks of file cabinets may not be the ones that have hundreds of file series. For example, claim files and personnel files take up a large amount of space, but each may be only one record series.

Remember, in each company, these record series will have unique titles. By all means use the titles specific to your situation. If someone calls the daily financial report the "green sheets," identify them as green sheets and in the descriptive field call them "Financial Reports—Daily."

It is difficult to take a records inventory by yourself. First, you need a second pair of eyes to check your work. But also, because we all bring different skills to a job, some people will be better at the interview process while others will shine in getting the powerful records management message across.

Also, you will need to follow up on staff members who may have been missed in the evaluation. This can be done by others while you are working on the retention portion of the inventory.

In making your staff assignments, try to have the records of an entire department covered by the same person. I recommended the same routine during the evaluation and the same reasons apply:

1. The helper-interviewer has the opportunity to become familiar with the department's special lingo and its personnel.
2. Even if that knowledge is limited to knowing which department member has the information you need, your helper will have developed into a valuable asset.

Go over the interview sheet with your staff so that everyone is familiar with each item and the responses called for. Rehearse their opening remarks. It is important to create an impression of professionalism and trust. You don't want them to be put off while the people your helpers are about to interview try to figure out if they are qualified and if they are wasting time.

The Inventory Interviews

Follow the same procedures for scheduling the inventory interviews as you did for making your evaluation meetings. Give people notice that you will be with them in the morning or afternoon, but probably you won't be able to be much more specific than that.

Take twenty or thirty blank inventory sheets to each interview. There may be times when you'll have to make additional copies on the spot. But except for storage areas, twenty sheets should suffice in most cases.

Again, explain to each interviewee who you are, what you are doing, and sit comfortably so that you can write quickly and accurately. Keep smiling even though the person you are interviewing shows signs of testiness or even downright antagonism. Keep remembering that you are here to make his job easier. So keep cool. Be friendly, interested, but certainly keep the project moving. You have too much ground to cover to discuss extraneous subjects. On the other hand, your interviewee may be able to give you insight into the importance of specific records, especially those which might have misleading titles.

I am thinking particularly of records called "General Ledger," which aren't *the* general ledger. Some are not even a close relative. Also, you will find records called by a common term, such as "Pink Sheet" or "Blue Book"; these may, in fact, be *the* general ledger. It happens, time and again.

The interview is the best time to learn about such singularities, and so your notes are essential for assigning retention. Place such information as "backs up the general ledger trial balance at the daily cut-off" in the "Record Series Description" column of your sheet, if at all possible, with additional data on the back of the form. With the full-search capability of many software programs, you can then search such key words as *general ledger, daily cut-off,* and *backup.* These will be important to you in the future.

We generally reserve the balance of the "Governing Authority" section for instructions to the custodians, such as "review before disposing" or "dispose when no longer active."

Likewise, the interview is the best time to pick up information on computer output. Such remarks as "I get this report every day and never look at it" or "I don't know why I get this report" or "I only use the last page of this 700-page report" will be interesting to the computer systems management staff. They are as interested as you in conserving time and resources, so passing on these remarks can save them money, too. (One major company that had issued tons of computer output daily suddenly decided to cut down to zero. No reports went out for a week. Only those who called up to complain "Where is my report?" were put back on the mailing list. The savings amounted to thousands of dollars a week!)

If you find after an hour or so that you are only halfway through the total series, or that your interviewee's interest is less than enthusiastic, you might suggest a ten-minute break and then come back to finish up.

Let's face it: Records inventory is not the most riveting subject in the world, and a busy employee watching her phone light up with calls or the clock for the next meeting is just as anxious to finish as you are. Try hard to keep your interviewee's interest up and maintain momentum.

One question you should be prepared to answer is, "I thought you people did this just a few weeks ago. Why are you doing it again?"

The question occurs because most of the people you interviewed for the evaluation do not know the difference between an evaluation and an inventory. You should have an answer ready. For example:

"Oh, yes. That was the records management evaluation we did a few weeks ago. We needed to determine our current costs of records handling and the ways in which we can improve the process and cut the cost. The records inventory we are taking now is just one of the ways that were recommended. But it is the *most* important so we are starting with an inventory of every single record in the company. Now, let's look at what you have. Shall we start with that cabinet?"

Having spent considerable time with the inventory sheet, I should point out that there are alternative methods for completing the form. Instead of hand-writing each sheet, you could use dictating equipment or a laptop computer. If you have reliable staff available to transcribe dictation, you may certainly use a hand-held dictating device for taking the inventory. However, remember that you will not be able to assign retention schedules until the transcription is completed and printed out. This is not particularly a hardship, as I have several times assigned retention periods to printouts. The laptop is clearly an advantage because it eliminates rekeying of data.

I personally love my laptop. It is also the speediest method. The person doing the retention schedule will, of course, work from the printout or the screen, completing the process. If you are fortunate enough to be able to use such equipment and technology, by all means do so.

As mentioned before, sometimes a record series may escape your notice. It's a good idea to leave a few blank inventory sheets with your interviewee. These can be completed when a new series is added to the master file, or when an old series is suddenly noticed.

During the approval process there are at least two other opportunities to add items to the inventory list, so it isn't the end of the world if one is overlooked in the initial process. I get about 95 percent of the record series in the first go-round. As a consultant, I am on a very tight schedule, as you can imagine. But I pick up most of the missing 5 percent in the correction process. You will be amazed and pleased at how dedicated many staff members are in making the inventory correct and complete.

I think the reason for this is that you have said to them: "Look, these are your records, and it's time you managed them. We are going to set some guidelines with the retention schedule. If you don't agree with those guidelines, we can talk about it and perhaps change. But once agreement is reached, it will be up to you to follow up by filing, storing, retrieving, and disposing of these records on schedule."

When you have finished going through all the record series belonging to the interviewee (custodian), stand up, offer your hand, and thank her for her time and interest. You may leave your card with your telephone number, as well as the blank forms mentioned earlier. If you haven't already done so, explain the correction and approval process briefly. The employee will then be on the lookout for the notice of the manager's meeting and the need to go over the printout for corrections and additions.

Written Procedures

Whichever method you use to take the inventory, it will be a wasted effort if you do not finish off the process with a written procedures manual. A written procedures manual is a must because:

1. Ongoing maintenance of the system remains consistent.
2. The manual becomes a training tool for new employees, both in the records management unit and elsewhere.
3. When or if your company merges or acquires another organization, the same procedures can be adopted by the new employees.
4. When modifications or changes to the system become necessary, the manual is updated and all concerned receive copies, so that everyone works with the same basic information.

Retention Schedules

Meanwhile, back at the retention desk, big things are happening. A records manager, even a world-class records manager, cannot be everywhere at the same time. You cannot purge every staff member's files on an annual basis. Nor would the company's staff, for the most part, welcome your doing so. The retention schedule takes care of this problem:

- It absolves custodians of having to make decisions on how long to keep each record.
- It directs custodians to dispose of specific records according to schedule with impunity.

In other words, it tells the custodian when to dispose of which records and eliminates all guesswork on their part.

Let's face it. Very few staff members are going to throw away records that are not specifically named by record title and custodian's name. Do not kid yourself on this subject. Even if you get through a first disposal day with a generic schedule and are tempted to say, "I told you so," resist the temptation. Your program will fall apart when new people are hired, when you leave, or when management changes. This may be sooner or later, but it will happen.

Certain people, possibly 10 percent of employees, will continue to observe the generic schedule and do their annual disposals. The other 90 percent who have records which should be disposed of won't. When faced with litigation, an organization's files that *should* have been disposed of will be subpoenaed. The company is now in the position of having to testify against itself. With a generic list in hand, it's very hard to convince custodians that they must match their records to the list and dispose of appropriate records. If a record title is listed as "Daily Accounting Transactions" and the worker knows the series as "4 O'Clock Greenies," do you think he will throw these records away? No way. I wouldn't, either.

Even if the titles are identical, a worker may decide, "I might need this. And since everyone else is throwing their copies away, I had better keep mine. Just in case." Your retention program has just collapsed. You don't know that copy exists. You don't even know that compliance has broken down.

There is only one right way: Assign a specific retention schedule to every entry—originals, duplicates, office copies, and storage copies of the same records on the same or different media. Of course, the retention period for copies is different from the retention period for the original (or copy of record).

The Components of Retention

Retention schedules are derived from four basic needs:

1. Legal
2. Administrative and fiscal
3. Disaster protection and vital records
4. Archival

Unfortunately, these are not separate, discrete needs. One file series may meet or contain all four needs—payroll registers and financial statements come to mind.

1. *Legal needs.* The most easily determined, these records retention requirements have been issued by a government agency and are printed in black and white for all to see. Examples of resources are: codes of federal regulations, state statutes, state rules and regulations (administrative codes),

and county or municipal ordinances. The appropriate legal references can usually be found in major libraries in your community.

2. *Administrative and fiscal needs.* Set by the organization itself, these records may be held slightly longer, but *never shorter* than legal requirements. An example is accounts receivable.

Normally, a company will write off an uncollectible debt three years after all reasonable methods of collection have failed. The total elapsed time, therefore, is usually about six years. During this period, if the deadbeat client tries to buy something else from the company, the records will indicate that he is a bad risk.

However, in the case of one of our customers, a drug and alcohol rehabilitation center, the decision was made to keep such documentation for seven years after the debt had been written off, bringing the total elapsed time for such records to about ten years. It seems that rehabilitated clients often feel it important many years later to reimburse the organization that effected their recovery. Such bills are very often paid in full.

Administrative needs also apply to correspondence from and to senior officials. While most correspondence is obsolete within one or two years, suggestions, plans, and ideas put forth by executives may be valuable to their successor for some longer period. However, there is a very specific danger here.

In one company, the notes a vice-president made on a laboratory test more than thirty years previously stood up in court and caused the company to lose a lawsuit involving product failure—in spite of the fact that the product had been out of warranty for more than twenty years.

When the company's records were subpoenaed, the vice-president's memo was caught up in what at first had been just a "fishing expedition" by the prosecuting attorney. The bottom line is that the memo should have been discarded years ago—especially since it apparently had never gone further than the VP's filing cabinet.

Administrative need is a rationale for retention that you want to use judiciously. It is not your purpose to remove records before the staff is completely finished with them. But at the same time, obsolete records must not be allowed to linger and do harm, either.

3. *Disaster protection and vital needs.* You will select out of the mass of records those that are absolutely essential to the organization and that will be necessary to the recovery process in the event of a disaster. Examples are accounts receivable; payroll; incorporation, merger, or acquisition files; board minutes; outstanding claims and credits; customer or client lists; supplier lists; inventories; insurance policies; contracts.

As you can see, these items must be kept for various lengths of time. Some of them are vital for only a short period or until superseded. And every organization will have a slightly different set of vital records. Depending upon many facts, the percentage of total inventory that is considered vital will vary from 5 to 20 percent.

The important thing to remember about vital records is that if you designate a record series as vital, you must be prepared to back up those records—that is, duplicate them on the same or other medium routinely and store either the original or the duplicate off-site. The backup, of course, must be updated whenever the original is updated. This is central to protecting vital records and forms the basis for your disaster recovery plan.

4. *Archival needs.* Historical records show the place the organization has in the community and the world at large. These are documents that record the founding, growth, and landmark events in the life of the company. Such documents may be used again and again for training manuals, anniversary observances, written histories of the company or its founders, annual reports, public relations stories, and advertising.

Determining the Retention Periods

Let us assume at this point that you and your helpers have completed taking the inventory and you are faced with about 600 completed inventory sheets. How should you select the appropriate retention period for each item? Here is a checklist outlining the thought process, which goes like this:

☐ What is the record?
☐ What it is used for?
☐ Is this the original or a copy (the copy of record or a duplicate)?
☐ What is the time span of the series—from and to?
☐ Where are these records located?
☐ How often is it produced, and how much is on hand?
☐ What do you know about the legal or administrative requirements for this series?
☐ Is there any reason to suspect the government, any agency, might be interested in this record? If so, who?
☐ How about the courts? Has there been a recent decision that might affect how long this record is kept?
☐ Do you know anything about this record that might make you want to lengthen the legal requirement?

The answers to these questions will have you well on your way to making rational decisions. If there is a legal citation, certainly you will go with that unless there is some overriding knowledge, such as in the case of the drug and alcohol rehabilitation center mentioned earlier. If the custodian thinks you are recommending too short a period, you can count on it that she will let you know.

One personnel manager once told me he needed to keep terminated personnel files eighty-eight years after termination because he might have to give a recommendation on a former employee. Visions of ninety-five-year-old ladies applying for bus driver positions floated through my mind. I reminded him that unless he was in the habit of hiring five-year-olds, most of those terminated employees were dead and gone. He could not see the humor and certainly did not agree. I set the retention on terminated employee files at four years after termination.

When the law or a rule specifies the retention period, a company is wise not extend the retention period beyond the prescribed limit. Otherwise a company may find itself testifying against itself.

For example, a personnel placement company lost a six-digit amount of money on a lawsuit brought against it because the company had maintained personnel records on ex-employees—twenty-five years after termination. An ex-employee claimed she had received a bad reference in an application for a job fourteen years after she had left the company.

Personnel records are indeed tricky. As in most basic questions there is often the other side to consider. I am reminded of a midwestern utility company whose holdings include a nuclear power plant. The plant is going through the decommissioning process. Several years of personnel records relating to terminated employees who never worked in the plant but who had visited it could have been legally disposed of.

The company, however, made the decision to retain these records so that twenty or thirty years from now, should new information surface that might impact current employees and their health, all possible data will have been retained. In my opinion, the current and future employees of this company are very lucky indeed.

If the custodian has indicated that the record series is vital, you have an additional set of questions to answer:

- [ ] Is it truly vital, or is it like beauty—only in the eye of the beholder?
- [ ] If it is vital, what is the medium used? Paper, tape, disk?
- [ ] What is the volume and how frequently is it produced?
- [ ] For how long is the record vital? A day? An hour? A year? Is it vital only until the next report is issued, or until the next year-end report is issued?
- [ ] Should it be backed up by simply photocopying the record as it stands or would it be more efficient to reproduce it on microfilm or electronic imaging?

☐ Does this record contribute to the history of the company and/or is it totally irreplaceable at any cost? Or is it perhaps too costly to recreate so that if it were destroyed, it would never be reconstructed?

In the last case, such records might be blueprints of original stores or manufacturing sites, photographs, newsletters, awards, benchmark studies, proclamations, or congratulatory correspondence with famous signatures.

All of these questions about retention are not equal. By far the vital records criteria and the legal requirements are the most important. If you don't have enough data on your sheet to make a decision, you must seek out additional information.

☐ Is the title unclear?
☐ Was the description omitted?
☐ Is any other necessary data missing?

Use your telephone or go in person to the custodian to get your questions answered before making a judgment. Remember, you are taking your organization out on a long limb when you set a retention schedule. Although the schedule is dynamic and certainly can be changed, nevertheless you could do a whole lot of damage by setting incorrect retention periods. This is *why* you get the big bucks.

Before you panic, let me assure you that a good deal of help is out there. *Legal Requirements for Business Records*, by Donald S. Skupsky,* is everybody's retention bible. This reference contains the results of a search through the code of federal regulations and state statutes. The result is an organization of retention periods in the same sequence as the original code and laws. Read the instructions carefully before you attempt to use the two-volume books.

Once you use Skupsky's book, the original codes should hold no fear for you.

- If your company ships across state lines, you will want to make heavy use of the Commerce Code.
- You will also need the Labor Code for many records.
- Financial records will be referred to in the Banking and Securities Codes.

*Skupsky publishes his own books out of Denver and updates them annually. You may subscribe to his services.

- Separate codes are issued by the Department of Agriculture, Health and Education, IRS, and Food and Drug Administration.

Once you begin to use the codes themselves for your work, you may find that you prefer them. Any reference material other than the codes will be accompanied by a disclaimer to the effect that the author has put this data together to the best of his ability but is in no way responsible if, in relying on it, your company loses in court. If you have any doubt about the retention given in a citation, go directly to your company's legal counsel. In my years of retention research I have found conflicts in legal retention periods. Usually these are between state and federal codes. The simplest solution is to take the longer period. This is particularly true if your company is doing business in more than one state, or more than one country. Laws differ.

The Government Printing Office has several volumes available that condense retention guidelines for most business and office records. These do not have the force and effect of law, but they have been well thought out and well organized. Keep a volume of *Federal Government Retention for Federal Records* on your desk. It is available from the Government Printing Office, Washington, D.C.

Most state, county, and municipal agencies have put very little in the way of retention requirements into their bill and ordinance drafting process. More is the pity. But each state does have a statute of limitations. This means that if legal action is not brought within that period, the case cannot be brought to trial. Note that many states have differing statutes of limitations for civil and criminal cases.

Many states use six years as their statute of limitations, but several are much longer. Find out the actual period in your state and in each state in which your company does business. Then you can make the decision either to invoke the longest period that applies or separate records by state and use the appropriate period for each. I have used both methods successfully.

A word of caution here. Lately, the courts have been rather lenient in opening cases that have exceeded the statute of limitations. This is particularly true when personal injury or product failure is a factor. And of course some types of cases have no statute of limitations, such as murder.

The retention on workers compensation cases at the federal level is five years after a claim has been closed, but many states have allowed such cases to be reopened many years later, even after a previous settlement has been reached. So keep these records permanently, especially the form called First Report of Injury. Microfilm or optical disk imaging is recommended if the files are as large as I think they are.

Your computer system should also calculate the disposal dates for each record series (based on the dates of the records themselves and the retention period you've set). From this calculation, you will produce lists, by custodian, of those records eligible for disposal.

You have now taken the guesswork and decision making out of the disposal process. You can also key in the disposal date and update your records for each disposal that takes place. This is a programming decision.

Every year after disposal has taken place, print a list of records destroyed. This list itself becomes a vital record, and it is entitled to all your backup procedures.

When a records series is ongoing—that is, new editions are issued periodically—you will want your system to remind you when the old editions are eligible for disposal. Some computerized systems do this automatically, but if you have a system that doesn't, here's what you do:

Lets say the retention period for terminated personnel files is four years after the termination date. On your screen, that entry might look something like this:

> 1990 Terminated Personnel Files
> Retention: 4 y TER   Disposal date: 1995

In 1995, the 1990 files will be disposed of, and your 1995 disposal list will confirm that these records have been destroyed.

You may go into your system and change the title "years from 1990" to "years from 1991," and the new disposal date will change to 1996. When your list of records eligible for disposal in 1996 is run, the 1991 terminated personnel files will appear.

The retention schedule procedures sample in Appendix B mentions the possibility of overriding the system in the event that a manager must hold on to records for an extended period—e.g., due to pending litigation or, as in a case we had in Minnesota, an investigation.*

You can tell your system that such records are "on hold." Remember, it's the records you don't know about that will get you in trouble.

Collect any industry guidelines that have been approved by boards or committees recognized by your company: trade associations, national professional groups, or national publications of long-standing merit. The im-

---

*We held up disposal of purchase orders for several years while the attorney general's office investigated a suspected case of collusion in the purchase of a certain product.

portant criteria are that the guidelines relate to your company's products or services and that such recommendations have been arrived at after due deliberation by knowledgeable members.

If all else fails, and you cannot find citations that fit the record series in question, you may have to set some standards on your own. This process is called "administrative decision." It is arrived at by questioning the involved custodians and using good common sense.

For example, consider a record series called "Correspondence." As far as I have been able to determine, there is no applicable legal citation for correspondence. But after speaking to hundreds of managers and supervisors, it seems clear that if you haven't looked at or needed a piece of correspondence for the past four years, you're not likely to need it again. And even if you did need it, judging from the thousands of correspondence files I have seen, you might not be able to find it. So I have set the retention schedule for correspondence at four years, with the comment to "review before disposing."

How many times have you needed something the day after the paper recyclers have hauled it away? I don't know how active Murphy's law is in your company, but it does happen. So what do you do?

There is life after disposal. In the long run, it is better to get rid of old correspondence; however, the same is not quite true for the correspondence of officers of a company. I have set the retention schedule for officers' correspondence at ten years. First, most top officers don't keep a lot of correspondence; they pass it on to managers for action. Second, if correspondence is kept, it may be refiled as part of a planning or project file, which will be culled upon the project's completion.

Completed project files are usually kept for ten years—longer if they have historical significance. Many secretaries to CEOs keep what they call a chronological file. A copy of each incoming and outgoing missive is filed and cross-indexed. (The sharper secretaries keep their indexes on a PC; this allows them to find anything, anytime. Your off-site storage center or basement file room will need a system very much like this, so you will do well to study it. Isn't it nice you became friends when you were looking for the company's mission statement?) Nevertheless, be judicious in assigning disposal times to Administrative Decision files.

Other references you may find useful—if you are careful to remember they are not legally binding—include:

- Publications of the Dartnell Institute of Business Research, Chicago, which occasionally issues retention guidelines

- National Association of Bank Auditors and Controllers
- *Federal Government Retention for Federal Records*, a booklet available
  from the Government Printing Office, Washington, D.C.

Remember that the custodians of these records, and the custodians' supervisors, top management, and legal counsel will all be looking at your retention schedule. Yours is not the final word; rather, it is the first step toward setting up an official retention schedule. If you are too far off base, people in the chain will be only too happy to point out your error. Throw yourself on their mercy and explain that you will make the requested changes. Be sure to thank them for their interest in helping with this important work.

Assigning the Retention Periods

There are two ways to approach this phase of the retention work: (1) You may assign the retention periods to the completed inventory sheets as each department is completed; or (2) you may wish to arrange the company's entire inventory sheets in alphabetical order by record title and do the whole project A through Z.

I think the second approach works better, but you will have to use your own judgment. If your company offices extend over seven or eight locations, the second option may not be feasible.

Time will be one of the governing factors in choosing which method you use, but not the only one. There is significant advantage in starting the retention assignments while the inventory is in progress. If you have questions, for example, they can be answered most easily while the data are fresh in everyone's mind.

The advantage of alpha sorting is that when you have selected the copy of record—for example, purchase orders—it is a simple matter to assign the shortened period to duplicates. It *seems* to make the work go faster, although I'm not entirely sure of this. But I do think it makes for consistent work and less correction later on. The other advantage to the alpha system is that you can achieve some standardization. If one purchase order series is titled "Purchase Orders" and the other "Orders for Purchase" and still another "Purchasing," you can select the most appropriate title and call them all the same. If in doubt, look at the inventory sheet to see what the form is called and use that. Caution here: Do not venture too far from what employees call the record. It must be recognizable to them.

In my opinion, there is room for compromise between the two methods:

1. Do the completed department. When you have assigned a retention time to each inventory sheet, arrange the sheets in alphabetical order by record title. Do this at the end of each day.

2. The next morning, go through the completed sheets and try to pick out any discrepancies in retention times. This will refresh your memory for the day's work ahead.

3. Arrange the next department's records in alphabetical order by record title. Using your completed work as reference, you can now go through that department and do research only for those records that are unique to the department. You will be surprised at how much duplication there is and how much time this saves you.

When the inventory has been completed and all retention times are assigned, the records for the same title will come together. I have seen many instances where different record series have the same name. I cannot urge you strongly enough to be sure to understand just what it is you are dealing with. Read the description field carefully; if there is any doubt in your mind, call the custodians for clarification. If there are many such instances, set these aside and go over all such questions at the end of the inventory.

You will want to have your reference material lined up before you. From the sorting you will have an idea of just what material you will need: OSHA regulations, Securities Exchange, product liability, interstate commerce, etc. Get it all ready.

Set up note paper so that you can record any citation you use. You will note that many citations run to fifteen or more characters; lately we have been using the entire citation. Remember that the goal is to allow each custodian to manage his or her records. By providing the entire citation, custodians will feel comfortable in following your retention schedule and be more willing to dispose on schedule.

Head your note paper as follows:

Citation   *Topic*   *Retention*

This becomes your own reference as well, so that when you see a record for the second time, you can refer to the previously set retention period.

When you've finished your notes, you will want to enter the data into your PC so that you can produce the official retention schedules for distribution to all custodians.

In Appendix B is a retention and disposal procedures manual with examples of the inventory sheet, code sheets, and maintenance procedures.

Records Retention Myths

You will remember that I mentioned that myths exist in most companies regarding their records storage and protection. Here are some regarding retention:

Myth 1. *The federal government expects you to keep records forever.* Not so. In most cases the specified retention period is relatively short—two to five years. Many specified periods are one year.

Myth 2. *The federal government tells you exactly how long to keep all records.* Not so. Many laws, rules, and regulations have no retention period for the paperwork they have created. Many others simply state "shall maintain . . ." What does that mean? The bill drafters and the regulation promulgaters act as if they will be around forever to check up on you. Attempt to ascertain what "shall maintain . . ." means exactly. If in doubt, mark such items as permanent, at least until you can determine otherwise.

Myth 3. *State and federal retention periods are usually the same. When in doubt, use the federal retention period.* Not so. Very often state and federal retention periods differ widely. Taxation records come to mind: Adopting the federal period across the board might be ill-advised if your state has a ten-year statute of limitations. Adopt the longer period, whether it is state or federal.

If your company has experienced no dispute in federal returns, going back four years not counting the year in which you file the tax return, you may be safe in disposing of these returns when they are five years old. But in the past year, two corporate tax officials asked for a seven-year retention on tax returns and supporting documentation because similar cases have been allowed in court. Many companies prefer to keep tax returns permanently in support of financial statements in the event of mergers, stock issues, and acquisitions. You will have to do your own research on this and, together with your company's tax and legal counsels, arrive at a company-wide standard.

Myth 4. *If there is no legally specified retention period, it is OK to dispose of records as soon as you have finished using them.* Not so. Many records are vital to the company's operation and should be kept in a rotation mode: grandfather edition, father edition, son edition.

An example is: accounts receivable register, June 1, 1995 (grandfather); accounts receivable register, June 15, 1995 (father); accounts receivable register, July 1, 1995 (son).

In other words, when the July 1, 1995, register is produced, the June 1, 1995, register may be destroyed. This ensures that a backup register is always on hand. (Because accounts receivable are vital records, a copy of each issue is placed off-site. And the off-site situation is the same for disposal: When the "son" is placed off-site, the "grandfather" is destroyed.

Also, many records are of historical value to the company, such as awards, photographs, maps, plans, special anniversaries, celebrations, community events, and programs in which the company played a part. Personnel handbooks, advertising layouts, original artwork, exhibits, blueprints, and studies are other records that have significance long after their immediate usefulness has ceased.

Finally, the official copy of record may be of importance to research, cost-accounting, budgeting, planning, forecasting, modeling, and other departments after its immediate use is completed. If there are multiple copies of these records, obviously only the copy of record need be kept.

Myth 5. *Companies that are involved with medical and disability claims can follow the published rules and dispose of closed records when the statute of limitations has passed.* Not so. Though the Code of Federal Regulations specifies that workers compensation claims can be disposed of after five years following the time the case is closed, many courts are allowing very old cases to be reopened. If a case has been adjudicated, the company is on safest ground by microfilming or imaging the complete file.

You should also provide documentation that the copy is "full and true," using the dates and signatures of the appropriate manager and the camera or scanner operator. It is very costly to attempt to reconstruct a case. While the court may have the bulk of records, the portion that tells the company's side may not be complete, or even may be missing after several years. We are hearing of cases today where survivors and beneficiaries have opened cases many years later.

Myth 6. *Once a retention schedule is set, the individual retention times never have to be touched again.* Not so. Oh, would that it *were* so! Unfortunately, state and federal legislatures change the law. In many cases, a retention period is added where none existed before, and so the new period may not agree with your prior decision. Also, new products and services continue to come before regulatory bodies and these bodies promulgate rules and regulations affecting retention periods.

Your own company changes as well. Items that were of no particular concern a few years ago may be of major importance today. Price quotes, vendor listings, job applications and résumés come to mind. A retention schedule is dynamic. It may change with the speed of a glacier, but it does change. Be sure that yours can be updated and that such maintenance is a simple task.

Management Input

The purposes of the managers' meeting are threefold:

1. To keep everyone apprised of the project's status
2. To inform the key players about how the inventory, retention, and disposal system works
3. To enlist the help of management in correcting, adding, or deleting records on the inventory

The value of this meeting is that the managers will now understand what records management is all about, particularly as you insist that their department be in charge of the records in that unit. (You will be surprised to learn what a relief this is to the managers who thought that you were planning to take over this duty from them. They will be happy to learn that you are just the tour director.)

The agenda for the meeting is usually something like this:

- Introduction by your supervisor
- Summary of the purpose of the records inventory
- Brief preview of how the records inventory, retention, and disposal program will work
- How the inventory was prepared and the timetable for completion
- Details of the inventory sheet
- Distribution of custodian listing and appropriate code sheets
- Instructions for making corrections
- Due dates for corrections
- Concluding remarks by your supervisor

I usually project a picture of the inventory form on the wall and go over each element so that the managers understand the data making up the inventory.

Make it very clear in the course of the meeting that when a suit is filed against the company, prosecutors may subpoena *all* records in existence. It will not matter if any records have passed their legal retention period. If they are on hand, they will be swept up in boxes and carried off for study by the other side. If anything incriminating is found among these records, out of context though it may be, that information will be used against the company.

This gets to the main point of your program. It is crucial that you have a detailed and enforceable disposal schedule. It is a waste of time and money to put a retention and disposal system in place if the disposal is ignored by the records custodian. Top management must realize this and give the disposal program wholehearted support, not only because of the money to be saved but because of the heavy legal liability.

As in everything else, there are always a few managers who are "too busy" or too something else to complete the assignment on schedule. It's nothing personal. These people don't perform on schedule in their day-to-day work either. And their bosses know who they are.

On the other hand, a surprise may be in store for you. Back in their offices, some people will remember other record series that should have been included. Some will simply write down the title and expect you to complete the rest of the data, but many will go right across the sheet, filling in the correct data for each series added—including the appropriate codes. This has never ceased to amaze me, and I always make a point of calling these people to thank them. It's a way to acknowledge a true professional.

There are two ways to set the deadline for returning the corrected sheets to you. One works better than the other, but neither is perfect. You can set a due date and ask that all completed sheets be returned by that time. Or you can state that you will pick the sheets up in person on that date. Generally, I phrase it this way.

> "In order to save you the trouble of finding me, just put the completed sheets on the corner of your desk by 3:30 p.m. on Friday (allow about ten working days for completion) and I will pick them up. If you have questions, I will have my calendar with me and we can set a time to meet to go over the list."

Making the Changes

When you go over the returned retention schedules, mark each change or addition with your initials so the data-entry operator will know you meant the change to stand.

If you can't live with a manager's changes, schedule a meeting with the person to iron out the difference. You may not have understood the nature of the record series; or the manager may have good reasons for keeping the record longer than the law states. For example, if it's a matter of a year's extension, and the reasoning sounds appropriate, agree to the change. But if the manager wants to extend retention for several years and the legal basis for your shorter time is clear, hold fast. You may want to pass the buck to the company's attorney for a ruling.

Don't let yourself get stampeded when a powerful manager yells at you something to the effect, "Then I'll take it home with me and keep it in my basement!" This kind of response should be reported to management at once, since a lot of harm can be done when a manager thinks like that. Stand fast.

If you have done the necessary research, you may be willing to add a year or two's life to legal documents to satisfy administrative requirements. This is true in the case of laboratory tests of products that have never made it to the marketplace. It is also true for salary garnishments, disciplinary records, and terminated personnel records; you might set a retention period of three or four years after completion of the last transaction, clearly labeled as an administrative decision. (To keep them longer is to open your company to the possibility of heavy losses in the event of litigation.)

Once you have reached consensus with the custodians, submit the corrected retention schedules to each manager for signature of approval. When the managers have signed off, present two copies of the alphabetical records listings to the company's attorneys. Include a code sheet if you have abbreviated in any way. Very possibly, the attorneys will select only those items that may be exceptions to the retention times you have proposed. Since most attorneys do not find this fascinating work, try to present well-organized materials. Go the extra mile.

Also, because you are making it so clear-cut, do not be afraid to set a date for final corrections so that you can keep on your schedule. Three weeks is ample time for legal consideration, given the fact that the attorneys probably are very familiar with the material and the legal citations you have used to back up your decisions.

If you explain that the first annual disposal date is scheduled for such and such a date—possibly six weeks from the time you are submitting the material to Legal—you will no doubt receive full cooperation. It doesn't hurt to mention that the CEO has approved the disposal date.

Chapter 7

Disposal of Old Records and Protection of Essential Ones

Disposal of obsolete records and the protection of vital records are not mutually exclusive. As vital records outlive their usefulness, the retention schedule kicks in. The old are destroyed and the new editions or versions take their place. An example of this is an accounts receivable listing. Can there be a more essential record in any company? Yet it is only of value until it is superseded.

Of course, not all obsolete records were vital and not all vital records become obsolete, as you will discover during your first disposal exercise.

Housecleaning Records

Disposal is not only easier but goes a lot faster than you'd think. The main bottleneck may occur in storage areas where records have no custodian: There may be boxes of records with no labels; the contents may have spilled out; or some boxes or files may contain the records of departed managers.

One person must go through these records while another checks the retention schedule. Then the records that appear eligible for disposal can be separated out, clearly marked, and moved to a staging area. The most appropriate manager can sign off, approving the destruction.

A list *must* be made of these and all other records destroyed. This means that even the storeroom records must be on your retention schedule. If you have completed your inventory of storerooms before disposal day, you will thus eliminate this bottleneck.

D-Day Procedures

Now, having said all that, a good deal of other planning must take place before the first "D-Day" is a success. You don't want to turn everyone off on your program. After all, this is the payoff you have promised.

To begin, generate a list of records eligible for disposal for each custodian. Make sure that, if the custodian cannot dispose of the records at this time, there is a mechanism (your software should do this) in place to catch up with the eligible records next year. Also, ascertain that the custodians have an acceptable reason for not disposing of certain records and that you can track these during the coming year.

Give ample notification of D-Day so that those who wish to dress casually may do so, and so that those who will not be available on that day may dispose of their records a few days *early*. (*Never* settle for a few days later. When you have finished with D-Day, you want to be done.)

Arrange for sufficient trash barrels or pallet-ainers* to be placed in strategic locations. Some companies use runners to take the disposed records to the dumpster. Alert the trash-removal people as to the proper time for pickup and for cash payment if the paper records are sold for recycling.

Keep track of all records disposed of. *This is essential.* If your computer software doesn't provide this feature, you will have to do it manually. This information completes your records retention schedule and proves that disposal can be accomplished in a routine manner during normal office procedures. This is done most easily by having the custodians make appropriate notations on their disposal lists, which you provided.

You will have to ensure that private or confidential records are shredded before being disposed of.

Reward each participant for his or her efforts. You might want to think about T-shirts, mugs, posters, banners, appropriately inscribed prizes or certificates, even a little plant for the desk. The significance of this last item will not be lost on those who are environmentally conscious.

The Results

You'll want to document to the one-half inch the amount of floor space, shelf space, and cabinet space that has been freed up. You'll record the tons of paper recycled, take before-and-after photographs of the pack rat's office,

---

*Large boxes of chicken wire fastened to a pallet.

and collect any other great-sounding statistics or evidence that will serve to illustrate the success of your program.

"Isn't this a little bit self-serving?" you ask. You bet. But if you don't do it, who will? And if not now, when? After all, this is mainly company-serving. The company has spent a lot of money and time to get this program under way. Management should be informed that the efforts and cost were worth it, as you promised they would be.

Remember a few things about those records now that you have followed through to their actual disposal:

- Over 90 percent of a record's life is spent in the file cabinet or storeroom.
- 85 percent of all records are never looked at once they are filed.
- Of the remaining 15 percent, 98 percent of remaining activity takes place in the first year after filing.

Small wonder that you could say with assurance, "30 percent of this stuff can be dumped!"

Holding On to Important Records

Two types of records are stored off-site—that is, out of the company complex: (1) vital records, and (2) long-term or permanently stored records for which there is little need for recall.

Vital Records

If any of your company's buildings, or the floors on which your company is located, were destroyed or became unusable, which records would management need to get back into business? How fast could you get your hands on those records? And to whom would you send them? Who would need them to document the expenses of the disaster, the work in progress, for recovery purposes?

These questions are, of course, part of a company's disaster recovery plan. But you would be surprised to find that many such plans do not contain a specific section detailing which records are vital to recovery nor the logistics of getting them to the recovery site.

As mentioned in Chapter 6, vital record series include the following:

- [ ] Accounts receivable
- [ ] Customer lists and files
- [ ] Payroll records
- [ ] Personnel files
- [ ] Pension files
- [ ] Credits and claims
- [ ] Corporate documents
- [ ] Litigation in process
- [ ] Current sales details
- [ ] Inventories
- [ ] Formulas, patents, trade secrets
- [ ] Engineering drawings, tests of new or current products
- [ ] Bills of materials on current products
- [ ] Vendors or suppliers listings
- [ ] Listing of employees' home telephone numbers, special skills

Some, but not all, of these records are computer files. Computer tapes are often backed up off-site. But there are a couple of important items to consider here too:

1. Even backed-up computer tapes are not kept for very long periods— from as little as a son-father-grandfather rotation to as long as six months or a year. By their very nature, computerized data are meant to be updated. That very often means only the very latest version is available.

2. Very often paper records support computer tapes, not only the data-entry sheets but the original computer program documentation and/or the system description.

In the past businesspeople considered computer files to be fairly secure because, in order to read them, there is a need for appropriate hardware. We know now that this gave a false sense of security. Computer systems need to be secured as do paper files. Since the management information systems (MIS) department in most companies is heavily involved in trying to make the company's systems impregnable, it is important for you to work with the computer staff so that all records will be secured and protected under company-wide standards.

In addition to protecting records from natural or man-made catastrophes, there is the security of private and confidential records. It is of no value to call a record series private or confidential if it is kept in a high-traffic area with access by anybody who happens to pass by.

Unfortunately, security is not achieved cheaply or with small effort. On the records inventory sheet, regarding vital records, you recorded the frequency of issue and the volume. From this information, you can suggest appropriate backup media.

For example, an annual report of thirty pages can easily be photocopied, with the copy sent off-site to storage and the original in the office as the working copy.

Things get a little more complicated when we talk about daily, weekly, and monthly reports, however.

- [ ] For how long is the information vital?
- [ ] Do you have to back up every day, or once a week?
- [ ] Should the backup be a duplicate floppy disk or a paper copy? Is the volume sufficient for microfilm? Optical disk?
- [ ] Who is responsible for making the copy and sending the copy to storage?

And here's a truly key question:

- [ ] If the volume is sufficient for microfilm or optical disk, shouldn't the record be produced on optical disk in the first place? That way, only the disk would have to be duplicated at intervals. Or can the system's backup tape become the security copy?

It is up to you to weigh these backup alternatives, provide the necessary cost estimates, and recommend the most effective method for each record series.

And that's only half of it. Every vital record that is to be backed up must have its own set of backup procedures. Every person involved must know what his duties are and when they are to be performed. *Do not even think of proposing a backup procedure without detailed written procedures.*

As you know, to arrive at procedures acceptable to those who will be doing the work will require meetings, recommendations, and revisions before final approval of a procedures manual is given. This takes time. The good news is that the material fits directly into the disaster recovery plan, and when completed, you personally, will have contributed about one-third of the material in the plan.

It has come to our attention that companies having completed and tested a disaster recovery plan become eligible for enormous savings on insurance premiums. Check with your company's risk manager. If your company does not have this office, meet with the person who handles insurance. You will be amazed at the savings possible.

Long-Term or Permanent Storage

Certain records belong in off-site, low-cost storage. Usually it is possible to combine vital records and long-term storage needs, and records managers should keep this in mind when shopping for a site.

Examples of long-term or permanent storage records include:

- Old payroll registers
- Terminated (more than two years old) personnel files
- Old policy or procedures manuals
- Old (more than three years old) general ledgers
- Year-to-date financial reports
- Completed capital-improvement contracts
- Old engineering drawings, plans, blueprints, (if company still owns the property or is still responsible for it)
- Old studies, surveys that have ten-plus years' retention, or data have been fully utilized
- Workers compensation claims involving a fatality or permanent disability
- Expired insurance policies

You get the picture. These are records that have fulfilled their administrative usefulness and are now being kept for legal reasons. Because of the legal connection, these files are not dead and certainly may be recalled from time to time.

Before you start shopping for a site, find out just how fast your users (those who send records to you and retrieve them) need to receive the files back when they ask for them. If the answer is, "I need it with the speed of light," get a fax machine and start thinking about a networked electronic imaging system.

If the answer is, "within two hours (or four hours, or next day)," your options are a courier, several-times daily delivery by helper, once-a-day delivery, or "pick it up at the counter in ten minutes."

More factors to consider in selecting an off-site location are described in Chapter 8.

And if retrieval of certain records becomes frequent—say, more than once or twice a year—think about returning them to their custodian. This may be on a temporary basis, such as for a research project, or long term, such as for litigation.

Software packages are available to help you track your records, including off-site records. More about that in Chapter 8.

Private and Confidential Records

Most companies have certain record series that are considered *private.* (Usually this means they may be seen only by the subject of the file and the key worker—a salary garnishment, for example.) Or the records may be considered *confidential,* meaning they may be seen by several key workers and usually the subject, but not always; medical files would be an example.

Other records requiring security come to mind:

- Customer lists
- Sales commission detailed reports
- Patent drawings, applications
- Employee stock option plan details by employee
- Contracts currently in effect
- Litigation in process

Some of these are, of course, vital records and will be backed up and kept off-site. But the working copies that remain in the office also need security.

In dealing with security, weigh the pros and cons of locked and fire-resistant cabinets versus a secured storage room. Fire-resistant cabinets retail from $3,000 to $6,000. If you need several dozen, a manned and secured storage room might be cheaper, especially if that room serves other purposes as well.

There should be a certain amount of secrecy about the secured room. For example, it need not be common knowledge as to what is in that room. I would even subscribe to some sort of mild subterfuge, such as that the room is "just a place for semiactive records, more than one year old but too new to be sent off-site." Then, of course, exactly such records may be stored in the room as well.

If you do establish an in-house records storage room, be sure that all records housed in it are a part of your retention schedule, and that the schedule is followed.

Written Procedures

Whether you are dealing with vital records, long-term or permanent storage records, security-risk records, or semiactive records, *you must have written procedures.*

Do not expect records custodians to go along with your plans unless they have something from you *detailing* what must be done every step of the way. Believe me, they won't. And one day top management will be looking for records you are supposed to have and you don't have them. You want to talk stress? That's stress!

The custodian just looks innocent (possibly smirking as well), saying, "Well, nobody told me!"

The boss is furious, "Nothing is where it is supposed to be around here. . . ." You don't want to hear the rest.

So, whichever plan you adopt, let the custodians know what each is to do with each record series—in writing. (More on these procedures can be found in Chapter 8.)

Chapter 8

The Off-Site
Records Center

Now that you have determined just what belongs in an off-site records center, you can start to plan seriously. Your records inventory picked up the volume of such record series, so you have a fair idea of how much will be transferred to an off-site records center. You also determined the frequency—how often the records are generated. Together, these numbers will help you to plan your ideal records center.

Most records managers determine early in their careers that a low-cost storage area in an off-site location saves thousands of dollars each year. "Off-site" might be an unused building near the company complex, some rented space outside the company complex, rooms in a branch office outside the company complex, or space rented from a commercial records storage company. *Off-site* means, literally, "not in the company complex."

Ideally, the storage area should have a high ceiling so that boxes can be stored ten to twelve shelves high but not closer than eighteen inches from lights and pipes. The lighting should be bright enough to allow the staff to read labels. You don't need a lot of windows. You must be able to secure the facility, to install smoke and fire detectors, fire-fighting equipment, motion sensors, and all the other trappings that go with making a place secure in these times.

Your evaluation and inventory figures will provide good estimates of the amount of space you will need for an off-site records center. Unfortunately, there are no rules of thumb for how many record boxes fit into how many square feet.

Configuration of the space plays a key role: Pillars, restrooms, elevators, triangular corners, stairwells, heating, air-conditioning, and ventilating equipment—even doorways—affect the square footage available for erecting shelves. The ceiling height, overhead pipes, and lighting affect how high you can stack.

Two examples come to mind, but follow them cautiously: I once fit 26,000 boxes into 16,000 square feet of an old warehouse-type building loaded with 3-feet-in-diameter pillars. And I also saw 400,000 boxes stored on four floors of an old manufacturing plant with about 100,000 square feet on each floor.

General Physical Considerations

In addition to physical security, there are important points to keep in mind when establishing a records center and/or using commercial storage facilities:

• Aisles in the records center should be at least three and one-half feet wide, or wide enough to accommodate a skid or a four-wheel dolly. You will need a ladder, library style, for the upper shelves, or a forklift if the budget permits.

• Allow room for a staging area large enough to accommodate at least two long tables. Here you can stack incoming records until you are able to index them properly, enter the data on the computer, repack the records if the boxes are broken, and, perhaps most important, see that the contents are free from vermin and other basement soil. It is also vital to confirm that the box holds what the label or indexes say it holds.

• Standardize your storage boxes, using the records center box that is about 12 by 15 inches. These boxes hold about 1.25 cubic feet of records and weigh about thirty pounds when fully packed. Bankers boxes, which are twice as long and hold twice as much, can weigh up to seventy pounds when fully packed. Depending upon who is going to be doing the lifting, you may find it preferable to use the smaller box.

• While most of your long-term-storage records may be kept in boxes, many departments make an extremely good case for storing their semiactive files on open shelves. Generally this is because they must retrieve files one at a time, or because additional files may be created regarding the same client, account number, or project and they want them stored next to each other. Lastly, the boxes may be heavy and they don't want a lot of boxes coming back from storage, just the pertinent files.

• Microfilm vaults should be kept at between 30 and 40 percent humidity, and between 65° and 75° Fahrenheit. Original silver film should be kept in nonmetal containers; also, make sure the film has been tested so that the chemical residue (after processing) is under .05. The methylene blue test will give you this information and can be done by an independent microfilm testing laboratory. Tests should be made within forty-eight hours of processing.

• Computer tapes stored in the vault should be hung on racks, with labels clearly visible as you walk down the aisle.

• If you are building your records center from scratch, plan on additional space or secured space for computer tapes, floppy disks, optical disks, microfilm, exhibits, original advertising boards, and archival material.

• If you are remodeling, review the floor plans for records center staff offices, shelving, high-security vault, staging, and review areas. Some records centers have "break rooms," lavatories, conference rooms, and other amenities. What you can have will depend upon the available space in the building.

Record Keeping and Procedural Considerations

Don't get bogged down with more than one records control system. If you are careful in the beginning, the records in offices, central files, and storage areas will keep the same index number in the off-site center as they had before shipment to the center. Then, as the record series moves from one location to another, all you need do is change the location code. The entire box has been assigned with very little difficulty.

Many records managers change the custodian name to their own when a box comes into the records center. I tend to think this is a mistake, because the custodian and her manager still will have to approve disposal when those records become eligible. You don't want to lose track of the players in your system.

Never forget that even though you are the master of all you survey in the records center, the records belong to the company, not you.

Your records center computer system can generate the label for each box going off-site, possibly even give you a bar-coded label, and assign the next open spot. And if you use bar coding, you will find it particularly time-saving in the checkout process. The volume of anticipated retrieval will determine if bar coding is a worthwhile investment for you.

You might elect to use file folder labels that fit over the existing edge of old files in order to accommodate your new numbering system. But whatever system you use, give a lot of consideration to the design of the box labels. You want the space big enough so that you can write location numbers large enough to be read from the floor up to twelve boxes high.

Also, if you are using bar coding, you will want to leave space so that the computer-generated bar code label can be applied and scanned or pre-printed on the label. The labels must be pressure-sensitive so that they can be peeled off and applied, but make sure the label vendor knows the temperature and humidity conditions of your storage area. You don't want the label's sticky substance to dry up and cause it to fall off. Nobody knows trouble like a records manager whose labels have fallen off!

Record keeping will be a very large item during the conversion process, and diminish to perhaps an hour a day as the system is up and running. The conversion process may require temporary assistance, but the ongoing tasks will be part of your helper's job description.

Written Procedures

Never install a records center without providing detailed written procedures for managing and controlling the operation. When dealing with complex procedures, each person involved in then able to read the big picture and at the same time target his specific responsibilities in order to bring about successful completion of the project. And after the procedures are completed, if you flowchart each step, you will find that the correct procedures are exact and totally comprehensible. The flowchart is sort of self-checking, like adding a column of figures from the top down, and then from the bottom up.

Procedures are written in a format similar to that of a play (see Exhibit 8-1). Are there other ways to write procedures? Yes. Are they as effective? No. Don't even consider them.

Control and Security Issues

Security of a records center includes fire and smoke detection, fire-fighting equipment, and motion-detection sensors to announce intruders to the police.

There is some dispute regarding sprinkler systems versus halon gas as a means of fighting a fire. You will have to meet with your fire chief to make this decision as there is a good case to be made for each. The main problem with sprinklers is that if they go off accidentally, they can do a great deal of damage. If the building you select is already equipped with sprinklers, then changeover to halon is an expensive proposition. A lot will depend upon the construction of the building, its location and surrounding industries, or lack of them.

Exhibit 8-1. Procedures for accessing records into the records center.

Who	Step	Action
Records custodian	1	Complete Records Transfer Form (TLC 851-rev. 9/9/97). Check to see that boxed records are in the same order as listed on TLC 851.
	2	Notify Maintenance to pick up boxes.
Maintenance driver	3	Count boxes to verify the number stated on TLC 851. Transfer to records center.
Records center manager	4	Verify number of boxes received matches TLC 851 number. Sign third copy and give to driver.
Maintenance driver	5	Return third copy to records custodian.
	6	Using the TLC 851, verify that the boxes contain the records described. Notify records custodian of any discrepancies.
Records center clerk	7	Enter Transfer Form data on computer system. Assign center's storage location (some systems will do this automatically).
	8	Print newly entered data, including the center's storage location for each box. Attach the printout to the second copy of the TLC 851. Return printout and TLC to records custodian.
	9	Print box labels (or bar code labels) and attach to appropriate boxes.
	10	Shelve boxes in assigned locations.
	11	File first copy of TLC 851 in temporary file for thirty days, then dispose.
	End	

Controlled access, however, is not even in question. No one should be allowed into the area without signing in. I prefer to have access to the stacks limited to the records center staff, for both pulling and refiling. You may, however, set up comfortable areas for users to work while they look through several boxes or files on-site, rather than having the records sent back to their offices.

Files and boxes should be requested and delivered only to authorized persons. These persons will have submitted authorized signatures to be kept on file, and records center staff must scrupulously observe such requirements.

Cost Considerations

What should it cost to store records off-site? That depends upon the following:

1. Do you have a records center at present, or is one going to be set up from scratch?
2. What system are you using now?
3. Are you using a commercial off-site storage facility?
4. What system does the commercial center use?
5. If you are setting up a new records center, where are the records that will go into it now stored?

The software and hardware costs of a records storage system are infinitesimal compared to attendant space costs. You may already have a computer that can be used for the control system; if not, you're probably talking about not less than $2,500 for the hardware.

Software will on average run about $500, although you certainly can go as high as $2,500.

Assuming you have selected a site for your records center, and have satisfactory hardware and software for its management, the following are other costs you must estimate:

1. File folders and boxes
2. Box labels
3. Shelving
4. Labor

As I mentioned in regard to the evaluation process, you will be able to reuse all shelving freed up either by records disposal or by transfer to the off-site records center. Open shelves, file cabinets, movable shelving, power files—all these can also be used satisfactorily in a records center. Do not worry if the overall effect is Early Scrapheap. Looks aren't everything.

For those records that cannot be accommodated on recycled shelving, there are vendors who specialize in used shelving, and often the classified sections of newspapers will contain their ads. If you find it essential to buy new shelving, there are multiple vendors to assist you.

What you want from each vendor is a floor plan detailing how their shelving works with your recycled units to make the most of available space. You will then be able to compare inches to total cost (including installation, freight, and taxes). Don't do the measuring and draw a plan yourself; there's too much you don't know about bracing, end stations, construction, and other matters. Let the vendor supply this information.

As to labor costs, you can divide them into the "before" and "after": before is the conversion and after is the ongoing maintenance.

"Before" costs include:

• *Construction and/or cleaning of the new site.* You will need to estimate number of hours required, number of people necessary to get done according to your timetable, equipment, and supplies.

• *Transportation costs.* Will you use in-house vehicles or the services of a commercial hauler? The number of hours and trips required depends upon the capacity of the vehicles, loading and unloading facilities, distances from pickup at offices to the trucks, and from the truck to the staging area in the records center. If you use a commercial hauler, he will be able to give you estimates.

• *Review of the boxes and assignment of locations.* Your staff must check that boxes and files are in good enough condition to sit on shelves and clean enough to be accepted. If not, the contents must be reboxed or inserted into new folders. (In the process, you'll remove strange things that seem to creep into files: coffee pots, empty three-ring binders, unused adding machine tapes, trashy novels.) At the same time, the boxes and files can be keyed into the computer system, the location assigned, and the bar code label generated, if this is part of your system. This is when staff also determine that the file or box does contain what its label says it contains. New labels are then applied to the boxes and files, and the work is verified.

• *Shelving.* You will want sufficient staff to shelve the boxes so that the work in the staging area can be completed without the clutter of boxes or files waiting for shelvers. At the same time, it is a good idea for another verifier to check the shelves to see that all items are placed properly.

When your remodeling is complete, here are the basic items you must take into consideration under the heading of "ongoing costs": rent/taxes, heat/air conditioning/power, labor, transportation (vehicle, mileage, insurance, license), supplies, supervision, security system, cleaning (interior, possibly exterior), snow removal, miscellaneous repairs, insurance, legal advice, and maintenance. Many of these costs can be obtained from vendors.

A Dress Rehearsal

Before undertaking so mammoth a job as setting up a records center, you will want to be certain that each person involved in the transfer of files will know what to do. Walk through these procedures with the staff in a rehearsal. Get the kinks out. There will be kinks.

For example, one night, during the rehearsal for a hospital file room conversion, thirty-seven volunteers were on hand. The files folders had been reprinted and shipped by the vendor. As we started to transfer the file contents from the old folders to new folders bearing the terminal digit labels, we found that the vendor had packed the files in the boxes out of sequence. We have to repack 60,000 folders before the work could begin. It took eighteen people four evenings to accomplish the task. The vendor paid for the labor, but four days were lost from the conversion timetable. However, that was minor compared to the mess we'd have had if we had not had the rehearsal.

Life is too short to go down in flames over a simple mistake that can be corrected easily, in the early stages. From this point on, the job gets easy.

Part Three

Other Issues in Records Management

You've tackled the basics. Now it's time for "designer" systems—with *you* as the designer! Each company is unique in its filing needs. Certainly you will work toward standard filing practices, practices that dovetail into your records inventory. But be prepared to hear this:

"Nobody knows how to file anything anymore!"

Chapter 9

Effective Filing Systems for Today

"Nobody knows how to file anything anymore!"

I could set that remark to music, I have heard it so many times. It is almost impossible these days to conduct an evaluation or take an inventory and not hear 50 percent of the staff complain about filing: their filing, which is never done; the crazy filing system used; the lack of a system; and especially, "When so-and-so is not here, none of us can find anything."

What does all that mean? *No filing procedures!*

We could spend the rest of the day discussing what's wrong with filing in offices today. But the problems can be summed up in one sentence: We have too much information flowing in through multiple media to be accommodated efficiently with old filing structures.

Types of Filing Systems

What are the problems with old filing systems?

• *Alphabetical.* Everyone knows the alphabet, right? With America's population at the two hundred million mark and growing, we have duplicate names—literally hundreds of thousands of duplicates, including middle names. In some cities where much of the population has descended from immigrants of a particular foreign country, you will find this especially true. In addition, many ethnic groups place the surname first and given name second. Some families have several last names, yet members are all of one family. These cultural variations have caused particular consternation in the ranks of health-care workers trying to coordinate family medical records.

• *Subject filing*. Another form of alphabetical filing, subject filing, is an even worse disaster. Why doesn't subject filing work? One reason: On any given topic, my idea of the subject is different from yours. For example, a file on the topic "Southeast Florida Water Treatment Study" could be filed under:

Florida
Environmental studies
Ecological studies
Southeast Florida
Water treatment studies (and the year)

or by the name of the author, team, department, or agency issuing the study.

Unless you know my thinking, or I have provided an extremely detailed, cross-referenced index, you are unlikely to find that study in my files. Even *I* probably won't be able to find it in six months! I may have been so tired of the whole thing, I put it under Miscellaneous!

And let me add that taking brand-new folders and sticking colorful letters on them won't help one bit. In fact, it makes matters worse because now you have a big investment in a dreadful system that's even harder to change to something useful.

• *Geographical*. How many file clerks today know enough geography to set up and maintain a national or international geographical system? If the geographical system depends upon sales territories, these change so frequently that tracking is almost impossible.

• *Chronological*. At least a chronological file is not difficult to comprehend. But not very many record series lend themselves to filing chronologically. A tickler file is a good example of filing by date.

As you can see from above, except for systems relating to names filed alphabetically, all other methods require an index. That's the bad news. The good news is that with an index, anyone who needs to use a file, is able to find it. And an index that is kept up-to-date, computerized, and available in central locations is the most useful of all.

A *numerical system* is ideal for today's business. In fact, it's made to order for computerized file management. These are some of its characteristics:

• The files are accessed via an index.
• The system can be used with individual files as well as boxes of files.

- It is applicable for files in offices, file rooms, off-site records, commercial storage, even files that have been destroyed.
- The system works regardless of medium: paper, magnetic disk, microfilm, optical disk, or a mixture of the above.

Planning Your New Filing System

Look carefully at your evaluation notes on the company's filing situations and styles before making any recommendations for change. You will need to take several items into consideration:

☐ What kind of computer capability is available and to whom?
☐ What kind of shelving is available and will it work with your proposal, or is new shelving required?
☐ How much space would be saved with a central file, or with satellite filing stations?
☐ Where should a central file be located?
☐ Who is going to do the filing, who the retrieving?
☐ Can you use the same file folders with new numbers, or do you need to buy new ones?
☐ Do you need controlled access?
☐ How does your system fit in with the company's disaster recovery program? Are vital records protected? How will they be identified?

Remember, your aim is to achieve some sort of standardization that will be simple enough for everyone to learn and accept. It must have enough flexibility so that it can be used in diverse programs within the company, each of which may have different informational needs.

Study those needs. Looking at your organizational chart, for starters, discover:

☐ Which departments require information from one another?
☐ Which share the same information?
☐ How are these departments physically located in relation to each other?
☐ Do their locations facilitate or hamper the flow of information?
☐ What is the sequence in which the information is developed?
☐ Do staff members require the information because it is news or for historical purposes? Is it reference data?
☐ How do people ask for, or look up, the information—by title, date, subject, name, or all of the above?

Suppose, for example, you are dealing with just one secretary, and she has just one large set of files, with only her boss as a user of those files. You may wish to create a system of filing that will be unique for her purposes only. But beware.

Be alert when the secretary says things like, "And I always file under who sent the letter." To her, "who" means person. Or, "I always file under the main subject of the letter." So you set up an alphabetical system, thinking, "Wow! That was easy. I'm done." Then that secretary leaves and the new secretary can't find a thing. That's because the new secretary thinks that "who sent the letter" means "company" or that the main topic of a letter is different from the one the previous secretary had selected.

Now suppose you are trying to standardize the filing in the entire company. When you have a lot of users of a system, you must sit down with each of them to determine each one's needs and timing. Then you digest the data and transform it into a system that can be consistently documented and maintained.

Never lose sight of the fact that a record is a record is a record. The medium upon which the record has been created may have only the skimpiest relation to the system under which the data is to be stored and retrieved. Therefore, you will want to develop a filing system that accommodates any medium now in use and any that will be used in the future.

In addition, you want to identify location. You need to locate the records regardless of where they have been stored, filed, boxed, filmed, imaged, even disposed of. Remember, *the purpose of filing is to retrieve*—even though 85 percent of the stuff will never be retrieved.

You may have a file created on computer printout stored in a manager's office, while the computer-output-to-microfilm (COM) copy of the same record is stored in the records center off-site. When you look at your index, it should tell you and your users the locations so that the user can make the decision: "Do I want to view the record on film, or get the record from the manager?"

Disposal of Old Files

So far so good. The index elements are fairly clear, especially after your interviews. The next item you want to consider is tying in the disposals of your file folders to the disposal system for record series.

This consideration impacts heavily on the selection of filing system. For example, say we have a record series called "Purchase Orders." If purchase orders are filed numerically, the numbered P.O.'s can be separated by year: P.O.'s for 1994, 1995, and so on. If your retention period is five years, the

1994 P.O.'s may be disposed of in 1999 (or 2000, depending upon your company's fiscal year). So if your P.O.'s are filed alphabetically by supplier or by product or service, you will have to cull your file annually to pull out the old files.

Therefore, when you assign a retention period to "Purchase Orders," you have automatically set a retention period for each file folder in that series. You can look up purchase orders in the records inventory, and you find the five-year retention and the disposal date.

As a result, following the scenario above, in the year 2000, you will notify the custodian responsible for purchase orders that all 1995 purchase orders may be destroyed. So when selecting a filing system for purchase orders, chronological may be the way to go. The user either will have a computer printout listing vendors by P.O. number or will file alphabetically by vendor name within a given year. Companies making thousands of purchases a year will use the first method.

You will gather from the above discussion that I am in favor of breaking up files that continue on for several years, such as administrative files or working files. It's best to break these up by year. That way the custodian will not have to go through a huge file to find and review material eligible for disposal. Remember that if the custodian is not ready to dispose of a record, he can override the system. All it takes is a note to the systems manager and the clock is reset.

Indexing the Filing System

As noted before, every filing system except an alphabetical one requires an index. Think of the files you keep in your PC. You have to index them to retrieve them. Your file cabinet is no different.

How many times have you gone to a file cabinet to find something and said to yourself, "Now where did I put that?" Didn't you ever wish you could go to your computer, tap in a few key words, and watch your screen show you not only the file you were looking for but all files in the company that carried related information?

With the help of a computer you can do just that. (I know you're way ahead of me on this one.) All you need is a good index. And designing the index is the guts of your filing system. For example, I was consultant for a company with twenty-one employees that wanted a company-wide filing system. Many files in the offices were extremely confidential. Management did not want me to even see the file folder titles. However, it was agreed that a central index to files could be created on the computer, protected by password, and have one trusted employee to manage the system.

Every employee was given a number from 1 to 22. The employee number was followed by a dash. Each employee then filled out a file identification sheet for each file. The employees numbered each file and its corresponding identification sheet in sequence: 1-1, 1-2, 1-3, and so on.

The system monitor entered all the file identification sheets in the computer. (I supplied the software.) From then on, when an employee opened a new file, she used the next available number, completed a file identification sheet, and sent it to the systems monitor.

The data were entered. At anytime the boss could review a printout of the index to see who was working on what. Some other neat features were added to allow transfer of files among staff and use of the index to research previous work on a subject. All in all, it was a very simple system. Things get more complicated when several hundred employees have files.

One word of caution: Whether you are designing a filing system for one person or a thousand, whether you are using one filing style or several, *every* file folder should be included. One major American company has just issued an edict: There are no personal files. If the document is in this building, it is a company file. Period.

Because of my own experience, I favor numerical filing systems. But I shy away from systems in which the numbers mean something—the previous example was one argument I lost. Numerical systems are impersonnel. They are adaptable to computerization. They are flexible. Files can be transferred to other users and tracked more easily. For these reasons, when designing a filing system, you had better have a compelling reason to go with either alphabetical or subject files. Keep in mind that the biggest files in the country—Social Security, Medicare, and the military—are numerical.

A final word: If you include on your computer form a description regarding a certain file, and other users wish to add their input of key words and phrases, this can be done. When searching such words, selected files will appear on the hit list and users will have a broader field to search. Not only will users find the file they are looking for, they will find other files on the same or similar topics, which they may or may not know existed.

Can mistakes occur in a numbering system? Yes. Can staff members sometimes fail to describe a record fully or even accurately? Of course. But compared to all the other systems available, you will find the numerical system most effective, the least expensive in the long run, and the easiest to document and maintain.

Terminal Digit Filing Systems

A variation of numerical filing, terminal digit filing is one of the few things that's the reverse of the oft-used phrase, "Easy to say, hard to do." Actually, terminal digit is difficult to explain and simple to use. Its chief characteristics are:

- It may be used successfully when the total number of files is greater than 5,000 or when the addition of new files is so heavy that personnel are constantly having to readjust whole shelves of files.
- File search time is drastically reduced because the search space can be limited to ten files.
- Security is increased because the filing number does not appear to be an account number, a Social Security number, or a project number.
- File maintenance is practically nonexistent—that is, the necessity to move files to accommodate those removed or those added is eliminated.

In terminal digit filing you use the last pair of digits (or sometimes, the last three) of the file number as the primary filing identifier. The second pair of digits reading from right to left, is the secondary identifier, and the third pair from the right is the tertiary identifier. Usually, no more than three pairs are necessary unless you are working with a very large file series, perhaps 5 million files. For example, in the Social Security number 244-81-9001, the file would first be filed and retrieved under 01. If there are two files with the last pair of numbers 01, 9001 would be after 8901 and before 9101.

If you decide to use terminal digit filing, block off your files evenly so that an equal number of files will fall into each section. For example, the sections might be labeled:

00–09	50–59
10–19	60–69
20–29	70–79
30–39	80–89
40–49	90–99

or

00–19
20–39
40–59
60–79
80–99

As you can see, this is the strongest argument against sorting and filing by last name, since so many names begin with C, G, P, and S. In the Upper

Midwest, where we have a large population of Scandinavian ancestry, we have a preponderance of Carlson, Johnson, Swanson, Nelson, and their variant spellings. Personnel in Minnesota are constantly running out of filing space in the C, J, P, and S sections.

The Changeover

The items you must consider, once you have decided on your new filing system, are:

1. Can you do it yourself, or do you need outside help?
2. What is a realistic time frame for the project, beginning with the overall design through orientation of staff?

Exhibit 9-1. Records inventory form.

Please Complete All Numbered Items

ID#: _____
1. Facility: _____   2. Department: _____   Image: _____
3. Custodian: _____

Record Series or File Folder

4. Title: _____

5. Description: _____

6. Medium(F4): ___   7. Copy of Record: Y or N
8. Date range: on-site: ___/___/___ thru ___/___/___
9. Volume: _____   Box #: _____
10. Storage Location(F4): _____
11. Frequency: _____   12. Privacy: Y or N   13. Vital: Y or N
14. Backup: Y or N

Retention

Years: _____   Instructions: _____   Office: _____   Storage: _____
Off-site _____   Governing authority: _____

Reprinted courtesy of Lee Barnard.

To aid you in arriving at a decision, Exhibits 9-1 and 9-2 are data collection forms used to compile information on filing needs. Modify as you see fit. Don't worry if some phrases seem unfamiliar; go with what you know.

Use either of these forms to help you arrive at a filing style. When your system is designed and approved, you will need to design an input form for collecting the description of each file so that data can be transferred to the computer. Most recently, I have been using the records inventory form to study files as well as to take the inventory. Perhaps I am not as pure as I once was, but the results have been clearer, both to me and my clients. However, if you have a mind to go into deeper analysis of the files, Exhibit 9-3 is an example of an excellent form used by Patti Zimmerman, CRM, president of Info Tech. A sheet must be completed for each file folder in the company.

Generally, custodians can complete their file identification sheets for their own files. But depending on the numbers of users, you may want to give them some help. Note also that the forms can be used for feasibility studies on electronic imaging.

Exhibit 9-2. Abbreviations and acronyms used in retention.

A.D., Adm. Dec., various   Administrative decision.

ACT   Active. These records may be kept in your office while active, and then sent to storage or disposed of.

ATC   After the last transaction is complete.

AUD   After *tax* audit. This means that the record may be disposed of *before* the full retention period if the tax audit has taken place.

SUP   When superseded. The record must be kept until its data have been superseded. In computer systems, four generations—current plus three—are required.

OBS   Obsolete, no longer useful.

REVIEW   Files contain some records eligible for disposal and some that are not. Please review and separate these files by disposing of the older ones. Check the retention period to see the cutoff date.

TER   After termination of employment/contract/lease/etc.

PER   Permanent retention.

Exhibit 9-3. File management study form.

DATA COLLECTION

FILE ORGANIZATION

Record series: _____

File media: **Paper**   _____

                    Microfilm   _____

                    Microfiche   _____

                    Other   _____

Indexing scheme: **Alpha**   _____   by   _____

                    Numeric   _____   by   _____

                    Chrono   _____   by   _____

                    Other   _____   by   _____

File contents (document descriptions): _____

_____

_____

_____

_____

Contents of core file: _____

_____

_____

Folder index fields: _____

_____

_____

Unique field: _____

FILE ACCESS

Number of users filing: _____

Number of users retrieving: _____

Departments accessing: _____

_____

_____

Average number of retrievals per user/hour/day: _____

Time of high filing activity: _____

Time of low filing activity: _____

Courtesy Patti Zimmerman.

Exhibit 9-3. (*continued*)

Time of high retrievals: _____
Time of low retrievals: _____

FILING LABOR

Daily retrieving hours by clerical: _____
  supervisory: _____

Daily filing hours by clerical: _____
  supervisory: _____

Daily refiling hours by clerical: _____
  supervisory: _____

ACCESS REQUIREMENTS

Is simultaneous multiple retrieval required? _____

If yes, are there multiple retrieval sites? _____

Need specific document _____ % of time
Know document needed when retrieving _____ % of time
Need entire file _____ % of time
Is 100% availability required? _____

Read only: _____ %
Read and copy: _____ %
Make copy for distribution: _____ %
Generate new document from retrieval: _____ %
Number of copies per hour/day: _____

File backup needed? _____

FILE VALUE

Number of files lost per day/week/month: _____
Number of files misfiled per day/week/month: _____
Number of files out-of-file per day/week/month: _____

Time to locate: lost file _____ misfile _____ out-of-file _____

Cost to recreate a file: _____

Legal velue of file: _____
_____
_____

Proprietary value: _____
_____
_____

(*continues*)

Exhibit 9-3. (*continued*)

Consequences of lost/misfile/out-of-file: _____

_____

_____

FILE VOLUME

Number of folders:

        Active: _____

        Inactive: _____

Number of cabinets: _____   type: _____

                     _____   type: _____

                     _____   type: _____

Space usage: _____ linear feet of records

              _____ square feet of records

Estimated annual growth rate (% and if): _____

NOTES: _____

_____

_____

_____

_____

DOCUMENT INFORMATION

Record series: _____

File indexing scheme: _____

Document index fields: _____

_____

_____

Unique field: _____

Document flow (attach flowchart):

_____

_____

_____

Exhibit 9-3. (*continued*)

Average number of documents per folder: _____

Average number of pages per document: _____

Number of characters indexed per document: _____

DOCUMENT ENTRY

Number of new folders created per day/week/month: _____

Number of new documents created per day/week/month: _____

Number of new pages created per day/week/month: _____

Number of pages added to existing documents per: _____

Number of files purges per: _____

Average growth: _____ % per day/week/month

DOCUMENT CHARACTERISTICS

Size of document pages
legal/letter/single-sided/double-sided/color/multi-pages/etc.: _____

_____

_____

DOCUMENT NOTES: _____

_____

_____

Chapter 10

Forms Management

During your evaluation, what was the response when you asked, "Are you satisfied with the appearance and usability of the company's forms?"

Was everybody happy?

The answers to certain questions will help you determine if there is a forms management problem in your company:

- Do people complain about not having up-to-date versions of their forms?
- Are some of the staff always running short of forms?
- Are there several versions of the same form in use?
- Does anyone think there are too many forms? Not enough forms?
- Does everyone just "make up their own" forms?
- Are the forms professionally produced or are they done by just anyone as the need arises?
- Do the forms have the company logo, contact name and/or telephone numbers, address, and zip code?
- Are the forms printed in easy-to-read type?
- Are there instructions, somewhere easy to find, on how to complete the form? Or as to who gets each copy?
- If the form is produced with multiple copies, do all the copies get used?

It is likely you'll need to take a forms inventory. Don't back away from this. First, it's easy to do. Second, it will save the company tons of money. The most costly activity an employee can perform is to "run off a few forms" on the office copy machine; your in-plant print shop or an outside vendor can do it cheaper (unless we're talking about an experimental form, where it is not known if the form will be used at all). Indeed, having done many studies on the subject, I have found that commercial and in-house printers win every time in terms of unit cost. Plus their output looks so much more professional.

Someone in the company must read the printer's proof, checking spelling, dates, times, addresses, and so on, to determine that everything is exactly right before printing. But it is just this attention to detail that makes professionally done forms superior to those churned out on an office copier.

Exhibit 10-1 is a copy of the worst form I've ever encountered in twenty-eight years of active records management. A government agency instigated the form, and each of the thousands of copies printed were done on the office copier at about $.06 each! On the other hand, look at Exhibit 10-2.

Analyzing the Forms

In examining the current forms, consider first:

☐ The purpose of the form. Is it:

    ___ To requisition purchases?
    ___ To request leave or sick leave?
    ___ To record deposits?
    ___ To file claims?
    ___ To order files?

☐ The physical characteristics of each form:

    ___ Its size
    ___ Single sheet or multiple copies
    ___ Paper stock and color

☐ Its appearance:

    ___ Company identification
    ___ Adequate spacing for completion of data
    ___ Zoning of data for understandability (blocks of related data outlined or boxed in)

☐ Its comprehensibility:

    ___ Form title present?
    ___ Clear instructions

Exhibit 10-1. Example of a poor form.

Exhibit 10-2. TLC forms inventory survey sheet.

G. George
Records Management Unit
Room 234
Ext. 5678

Form ID#: _____   Date: _____

Division: _____   Custodian: _____

Department: _____   Ext: _____

Form#: _____ Revision: _____

Title: _____

Two-word description: _____ _____

                                   [verb]   [noun]

Users: _____

Retention: original _____ copies _____ governing authority: _____

Characteristics

Size: _____ Number of copies: ____ Colors: _____

Paper stock: _____ Minimum stock level: _____

Last vendor: _____ Cost per 1,000: _____

Lead time: _____

Analysis

Comprehensibility (1–10):
Arrangement/appearance (1–10):
Spacing allowed for completion (1–10):
Instructions for completion (1–10):
Company identifiers (1–10):

___ Explanations, e.g., of codes or abbreviations?
___ Blanks clearly labeled, visible to typewritten completion?
___ Form number included in an appropriate location?

Add such items to your analyses as necessary for your company. But largely you should be able to go over each form quickly and complete a forms inventory sheet.

What you learn from your forms will help you determine if there are:

- Duplicate forms
- Forms that collect the same data for various purposes (redundant forms)
- Obsolete forms
- Nonstandard forms
- Vital forms

Use a computer to assist you in this task, since you will eventually want to add the following information to your forms records:

- Form number
- Minimum stock level
- Previous vendor
- Number ordered, cost per unit
- Lead time necessary from date order is placed until receipt of new order
- Revision dates
- Departments that use the form and must be notified in case changes are requested

Estimating the cost of taking the forms inventory will involve determining the amount of cooperation you will receive from the rest of the staff. But let's say there is sufficient help so you can collect the forms without difficulty. The analysis of each form will take about twenty minutes. Because you have other duties and responsibilities, and may not be working on the forms inventory full-time, you should allow about six months to complete this task and to make your recommendations.

Develop your computer program (or ask MIS to do it for you) so that the fields appear on your screen in the same order as on your form.

Now you have a choice: You can gather all the forms examples and enter them directly onto the computer, or you can complete a survey sheet for each form and then enter the data from it. Personally, I prefer the first method.

When the data are entered, you are ready to analyze the company's forms. You may ask, for example, how many different forms are used to requisition supplies? How many different forms are used to request vacation or leave time? How many have poor (or no) company identifiers (name, telephone number, or address)?

How many forms are redundant or totally obsolete? Can some be combined? Which ones can be improved? There are several form design books on the market; there are also some excellent seminars, which are probably even more useful. You will quickly see your own aesthetic appreciation and design technique improve.

Once created, the new forms must be included in your inventory. Before printing, therefore, new forms should be submitted to you for review so that you can make sure that (1) your written standards are met and (2) you can include them in the computer system. This means you will be giving the form either a new number or adding a revision date to a revised form. It is up to you to notify users that a revision is being printed.

When writing your standards, work closely with Purchasing and/or your in-plant print shop to ensure that all company policies are being followed and that everyone can live with the standards. Purchasing buyers are generally as anxious as you are to cut costs and improve quality.

Finally, by all means track the savings and improved service this program generates. Management will be suitably impressed.

Chapter 11

Image-Reduction Options

Several times in this book I have discussed the option of image reduction. And I can make a safe bet that before you began the evaluation, or perhaps during it, someone in management urged you to "forget the evaluation and just tell us what we should microfilm."

The evaluation gave you a pretty good idea of where volume bottle-necks or security problems lie. These may be symptoms of deeper problems, or they may be made-to-order opportunities for image reduction.

During the evaluation you also began to realize how various departments relate to one another:

- Purchasing awaits the requisitions from Materials Management or department heads.
- Accounts Payable pays bills approved by Accounting, which in turn awaits notice from Materials Management that the goods have been received.
- Operations notifies Sales that goods ordered by clients have been shipped; Marketing notifies Operations of modifications required by Sales.

So when you come across a record series suitable for imaging, you will know who the potential users are, even have some idea of how they will want to use the data. Knowing such needs will lead you to specific equip-ment and technologies—for example, networking of electronic image-viewing stations or centralization of imaging tasks.

The point is that during the evaluation, you have gathered much of the information you will need for any study of electronic imaging or microfilm options. You can feel fairly safe in recommending that a study of specific record series will yield huge savings in space, time, and dollars.

Even if your evaluation only points out the same areas that manage-ment has been mentioning, you will better understand the ramifications of the project. So no blushing or apologizing. Your records management program is built on a solid foundation.

Assessing Records for Image Reduction

Certain record series are better candidates than others for image reduction:

• *Accounts payable.* All the supporting documentation such as vouchers, purchase orders, receiving memos, quality assurance tests, vendor brochures, guarantees, warranties and check payment transfers take up volumes of room.

• *Personnel files.* Very often a company's personnel files take up more room than its sales records. This is because employees work for a company for a long period and many things happen during that period—promotions, disciplinary actions, savings plans, stock option plans, reviews, and so on. In addition, the records are usually kept for several years after termination. Is it any wonder that personnel staff are always asking for more space?

• Purchase orders. Purchase orders are usually kept for five or six years after the transaction is completed. And a good deal of the data accompanying the purchase order are the same as in the accounts payable packet.

• *Freight records.* Freight records include manifests, bills of lading, claims, certificate of insurance (from the trucker), packing slip copies, packing slips, and other assorted items.

These are examples of current data—that is, information necessary to those working on current tasks and problems. Long-term storage records that are also likely candidates are:

• Corporation documents
• Income tax returns and supporting documents
• Council minutes
• Agenda packets
• Legal cases, settled
• Patents, formulas, designs
• Benchmark studies, reports, plans

Because almost every company has personnel files, let's work through an optical disk system for personnel records.

Optical disks look just like CDs. The difference is that *you* create the image.

The blank optical disk is inserted into a 486 PC. The document is fed into a scanner (similar to some photocopying devices) and the image of the document is digitized. The digitized image goes to what is called a streamer tape, which allows you to see on your PC screen what you have just imaged. If you are satisfied with the images (because generally the day's routine quantity is scanned before viewing), they are embedded on the disk. It is usually during the viewing process that the index to the records on the disk is created. The workstation operator keys in the required identifying data. Often the operator works from paper, but more often he works from the image on the screen, using the same PC upon which the disk resides.

When the disk is full and the index is complete, the original documents may be stored off-site for backup. An option is to duplicate the disk and store it off-site. Then the paper may be destroyed.

Your company's need will dictate which is better for you. It's nice to know that the streamer tape acts as a temporary backup while the disk is being filled.

The first step is to flowchart all incoming, outgoing, and filed records. Omitting the processing details for now, your chart could look something like Exhibit 11-1.

With an optical disk system in place, the incoming mail would be imaged and sent electronically through networked PCs to various departments. Each department would receive only its necessary records and Personnel would have the complete file on disk. The paper file might be destroyed or sent to off-site storage for a short period, just to be sure the optical disk system is performing accurately. (You can't be too rich, too thin, or too careful.)

Since personnel files are vital records, a duplicate disk could be stored off-site as a backup. The duplicate is made when the disk is full. But most optical disk systems produce what is called a streamer tape, which has double uses:

1. The streamer tape is used to verify the image captured so the operator can view it before it is encoded on the disk.
2. The streamer tape acts as a backup source (like a video tape) until the disk is full.

With this system in place, the flowchart might look something like Exhibit 11-2.

The optical disk may reside on networked PCs for access by depart-

Exhibit 11-1. Flowchart for current records system.

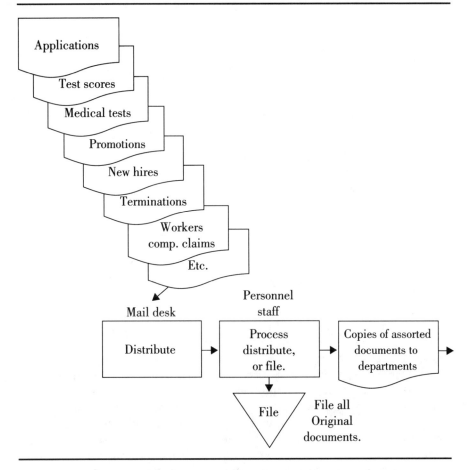

ments, or multiple disks may be held in a "juke box" until called for by users.

CD-ROM works the same way as optical disk. The main difference is that the encoded image is burned onto the CD-ROM surface, thus ensuring permanency of the image. A flowchart using CD-ROM technology would look the same as that for optical disk except for one final step. When sufficient images have been scanned to complete a CD-ROM, the streamer tape is sent to a service bureau, which burns the images onto the disk. The burning device currently costs about $10,000. Most companies using CD-ROM today are also using service bureaus. The service bureau also will make

Exhibit 11-2. Flowchart for optical disk application.

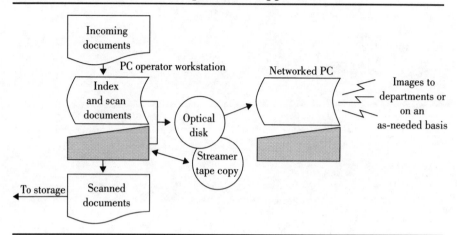

copies as needed. The burning process costs about $200, although this price may drop suddenly if more service bureaus decide to offer the service, or if the equipment drops in price.

How do optical disk and CD-ROM improve records retention? Generally speaking, if a record must be kept seven years or more, it is cost-effective to store the record on disk.

Much has been written about microfilm as an image reduction method. For many years it was our *only* method of getting rid of vast amounts of paper. Today, microfilm vendors are able to network viewing stations and offer many of the same advantages as the disks. When you research costs, one-time and ongoing, you will be able to reach a decision on which image reduction method is best for your company. One important consideration is the investment your company may have already made in microfilm. Most microforms can be converted to disk, but it's pricey. Be sure of all your numbers before making your proposals.

So permanent and many long-term-storage record series are good candidates for electronic imaging.

There are pitfalls, however, in even these seemingly effective means of image reduction. Let's take closed medical files, for example. When a patient hasn't been seen by a health-care facility for seven years, in many states that record may be destroyed. Few health-care facilities, however, exercise that option, preferring to keep such records forever. (And building ever larger records centers to house them.)

So why not put these records on disk in the first place? After all, with careful indexing the file can be pulled together on the PC monitor in the blink of an eye. The problem is that many doctors want to have that file folder in their hands when they see a patient.

"OK, then," you say, "how about when the file is closed?"

But how do we know when the file is closed? Obviously, when a patient dies the medical portion is certainly closed—if the staff is aware of the death. But often a patient moves out of town and does not notify the medical facility. Or the patient changes doctors and never notifies the office.

"Well, suppose we image only those files that have seen no action for seven years?"

Yes, this is an option. But why spend money imaging records that could, and probably should, be destroyed?

Staff members who have grown into professional careers based on the paper trail they've generated are often loath to see that precious paper disappear onto film or a disk. My advice to you is to bring these folks to an imaging demonstration and explain the benefits—to them and to the company. A good resource is the annual conference of the Association of Imaging and Information Managers (AIIM).

Those who have been familiar with video games and computer instruction since the second grade will welcome your proposals eagerly and urge you on to higher and more advanced technologies.

Getting Cost Estimates

Most vendors of big-name equipment will study your image-reduction needs at no cost; generally speaking, I have found their numbers relating to volume of records to be processed to be reliable. Where vendors have failed me is their representation of "through-put." That is how long it takes to scan and index a document. As you can surmise, this is indeed a big factor. If you underestimate the through-put time, you will understaff the system and create a bottleneck of documents waiting for processing.

Since the imaging system is not cheap, and if things go badly you'll have a bunch of people standing around saying, "I told you so," may I suggest two ways to avoid leaping on a slow boat to China?

1. *Ask the vendor to do a feasibility study.* Follow him around *every* step of the way—and I mean *every*. Do not let him out of your sight. Ask questions like:

"How did you arrive at that figure?"

"How do I program or change the index?"

"Will you agree to a pilot program while we try out the system for a week or two?"

"Will you help us to create the index?"

"What kind of training will you provide?"

"What is your after-care program?"

If you are satisfied with the answers to your other questions, you probably have a good vendor.

2. *Call in a consultant* (after obtaining approval for the expenditure) to go over the same ground. Such a study could cost from $6,000 to $18,000 or more, depending on the number of departments to be studied, the complexity of hardware and software required, and the consultant's fee schedule.

Somewhere between the vendor's proposal and the consultant's recommendations the most appropriate path will appear.

Believing, as always, that a picture is worth a thousand words, I refer to a typical study I made to determine the feasibility of converting a very large series of files to electronic imaging. The study was performed by a consultant because the client was not happy with some vendor-sponsored studies that had been made. You will find it in Appendix C.

Whichever image-reduction method you follow, never lose sight of the records index. This item is the difference between success and your trip to the Orient. At minimum, the index must contain:

☐ File identification number
☐ Title of the document
☐ Date of the document

Be sure to define the date—is it date received, date processed, or date of origination, or something else altogether?

It is after the minimum data are determined that the squeeze sets in: How much more data are enough and when do you have so much that data entry is slowing down the whole process?

As you can see from page 7 of the sample study (see Appendix C), in a meeting it was agreed to add two more items to the index. This brought the total possible keystrokes to 174, not counting the password to sign on. If you type or use a computer keyboard, you know that 174 keystrokes represent serious time to index each document. So when you consider the labor involved in processing the daily volume of work, cost-justification becomes critical.

The sample study has a bare-bones type of index. If you are contemplating a system that will provide management with information from several departments, your index may include several more items, such as:

☐ Location
☐ Custodian
☐ Customer or product name

These all require a certain amount of updating.

In conclusion, none of the above advice is intended to dissuade you from optical disk or CD-ROM. Absolutely not! One of the pure joys of being a records manager is in recognizing the worth of new technology and applying that technology successfully to lick a nagging and costly problem.

Chapter 12

The World-Class Records Manager

It's graduation day. Congratulations!

Are *you* happy with your progress? Are you ready to take your place in the sun as a world-class records manager?

Do you remember when I suggested you develop your own five-year plan? Have you made progress? Do you want to make some revisions?

First, review the organization chart for your unit. Do you still have the same boss as when you started? Has *your* title changed? Have you added staff? If so, draw boxes for these additions firmly on the chart and list the duties you expect each assistant to perform.

Do you have plans for future programs, studies, or services? If so, put those plans in dotted boxes (if they are indeed new), with the duties listed below.

Now let's talk about your own development. I hope by now you have joined a chapter of the Association of Records Managers and Administrators (ARMA). Perhaps you are studying to pass your Certified Records Management (CRM) tests. I sincerely hope so.

Remember your company's mission statement and your pledge to help in reaching the goals listed in it. And also remember that even though you are the master of all you survey in the records center, the records belong to the company, not to you.

You are definitely ready to run your own records management unit. For additional advice, I suggest you read *Records Management* by Susan Z. Diamond (AMACOM) for guidance in organizing your operation.

Keep up with new technologies. Improve your written procedures. Help all you can with your company's disaster recovery plan. With each effort, you will gain knowledge and confidence.

Appendixes

Appendix A

Sample Records Management Evaluation

The following report is an example of a completed Records Management Evaluation, which took place in 1994 in the City Hall office of a small southeastern U.S. city.

RECORDS

MANAGEMENT

EVALUATION

CITY OF OCALA
JANUARY 31, 1994

Reprinted with permission.

RECORDS MANAGEMENT, INC.
4829 N. W. 75th. AVE.
OCALA, FL. 34482
(904) 620-8662
Fax 629-4467

January 31,1994

Ms. Janet Tutt
Assistant to the City Manager
City of Ocala
Ocala, Florida

Dear Ms. Tutt,

RECORDS MANAGEMENT, INC., is pleased to present today
the results of the Records Management Evaluation completed
for the City of Ocala.

We want, especially, to thank you, Janet, for your
total cooperation and excellent hospitality. As a result
we were able to interview 52 employees which we believe
provides a fair sample.

During the course of the evaluation we received 131
pointed comments and suggestions. These, along with the
statistical data gathered and our recommendations should
enable the City of Ocala management to make decisions
regarding a records management program. It is our opinion
the staff will welcome and support such decisions.

We have truly enjoyed the opportunity to conduct this
study and we look forward to working with all City of
Ocala staff members in the future.

Sincerely,

Gloria J. Gold, C.R.M.
RECORDS MANAGEMENT, INC.

Lee Barnard, President
RECORDS MANAGEMENT, INC.

RECODS MANAGEMENT EVALUATION
CITY OF OCALA

Table of Contents

INTRODUCTION

RECORDS MANAGEMENT, INC., conducted a Records Management
Evaluation for the City of Ocala, Florida, January 3,4, and
5, 1994.

Ms. Janet Tutt, Assistant to the City Manager and Ms. Mary
Gorgone, Supervisor of Central Services, coordinated the
study for the City. The study team interviewed 52 staff
members during the evaluation. The purpose of the evaluation
was to develop current costs of handling records for the
City of Ocala and to determine issues of concern in records
retention and safety, filing, storage and image reduction.

Two of the 52 staff members interviewed have been employed by
the City of Ocala less than one year:
>   Virginia Howell - Housing & Sanitation
>   Cindy Bedgood   - Substance Abuse Prevention

Response from the 52 staff members was candid and well
thought out and should receive careful consideration from
management.

The departments included in the evaluation study are:

Internal Auditor	Human Resources	Electric
City Manager Off.	Public Works	Downtowm Dev.
Planning	Risk Mangement	Recreation & Parks
Engineering	Housing &	C.D.B.G.
Finance	Sanitation	M.I.S.
Purchasing	Zoning	Substance Abuse
Budget	Building	Fleet Management
City Clerk	Water & Sewer	City Clinic
Fire Department	U.B.O.	Traffic
Payroll	City Attorney	Library

All computations, calculations and projections used are
developed from data supplied in interviews. Standard statistics recommended by both the Dartnell Institute for
Business Research, Chicago, Illinois, and the Association
of Records Managers and Administrators have been used.

Records Management Evaluation team members were: Lee
Barnard, President, Gloria Gold, CRM, and Marcia Swolsky,
Records Analyst.

CITY OF OCALA

RECORDS MANAGEMENT EVALUATION

FINDINGS

VOLUME

In the offices of departments studied, in closets, under
desks, and in the basement, the current volume of paper
records, microfilm and micro-fiche is 14,618 linear feet. If
stacked side by side,these records would reach from Ocala
City Hall to the Municipal Golf Course.

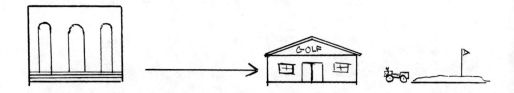

Furthermore, at an annual growth rate of 15%, the City
will have twice the current amount of records by 1999.
The records will then be more than five and one-half miles
long and reach from City Hall to Silver Springs Attraction.

SPACE COSTS

The 14,618 linear feet of records occupy 9,202 square feet
of office and storage space in City Hall,the Municipal
Complex and other areas.

At $18.00 per square foot for office space in City Hall
and nearby buildings, and at $5.50 per square foot for all
the other areas, City of Ocala records occupy space costing
$130,186.00 per year. By 1999, this cost will have doubled
to $261,851.00 per year.

EQUIPMENT COSTS

The study team assumed that all currently owned file cabinets
were fully depreciated. It further assumed, and was confirmed
that the City depreciates fixed assets over a ten year
period. In the following graph the depreciated figure, or
one-fifth of the total cost was used for each year.

Nevertheless, when cabinets are purchased, the cash outlay
is substantial. Over the next ten years, assuming a 15%
growth in records volume, 400 additional cabinets will be
required to hold files.

Those cabinets will cost an average of $18,000 a year in
cash. And at least as serious, they will require an
additional 3300 square feet of space. Or about the size
of the basement area holding records and supplies.

PERSONNEL COSTS

RECORDS MANAGEMENT, INC., staff classified personnel who
file, retrieve files or search for files as senior management, mid-management, or clerical support.

Based on the percentage of time the 52 staff members we
interviewed attributed to these tasks (as well as the time
of others similarly involved), the current costs for
personnel handling files is:

$429,874.00 per year

Once again, this figure includes personnel in all offices
we studied.

Because the current volume of records is so high, the
anticipated 15% increase is correspondingly high. The
average annual increase (for each of the next five (5)
years) in staff time devoted to filing and retrieving
information will be:

$85,975.00

This is the equivalent to adding four new clerical support
employees per year.

No salary increases of any kind are included in this figure
nor was office space for additional staff a consideration.

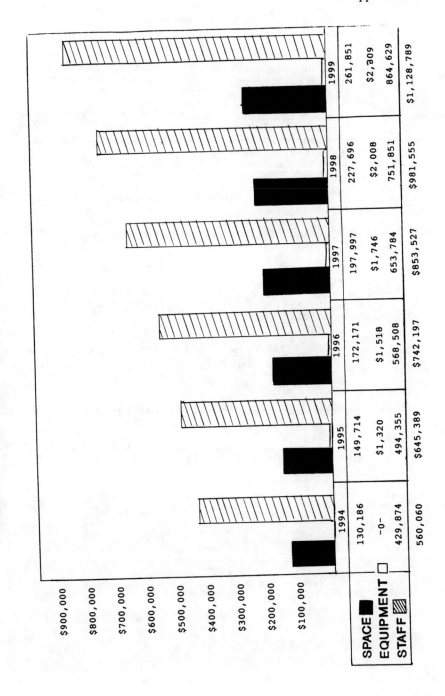

RECORD COSTS: CURRENT AND PROJECTED

	1994	1995	1996	1997	1998	1999
SPACE	130,186	149,714	172,171	197,997	227,696	261,851
EQUIPMENT	-0-	$1,320	$1,518	$1,746	$2,008	$2,309
STAFF	429,874	494,355	568,508	653,784	751,851	864,629
	560,060	$645,389	$742,197	$853,527	$981,555	$1,128,789

FORMULA FOR COMPUTING CURRENT AND PROJECTED

RECORDS HANDLING COSTS

Square footage costs are computed as follows:

City Hall	–	$18.00 per square foot
City Complex	–	$ 5.50 per square foot

Cabinets and other shelving were computed as we found them:

Filing Equipment:

Cabinets/Units	Linear Feet	Square Feet
2-Drawer Vertical	4	9
3-Drawer Vertical	6	9
4-Drawer Vertical	8	9
5-Drawer Vertical	10	9
2-Drawer Lateral	6	7.5
3-Drawer Lateral	9	7.5
4-Drawer Lateral	12	7.5
5-Drawer Lateral	15	7.5
Shelving Units		2.5 x ____ ft.
Shelving Units		2.5 x ____ ft.
Shelving Units		2.5 x ____ ft.

Benchmarks

Shelving	=	2.5 sq. ft. x ln. ft. of one shelf (3-foot long shelf unit = 7.5 sq. ft.)
Bankers Boxes, lg.	=	2 linear feet
Records Boxes, std.	=	12" linear,
Check Boxes	=	Measure, 2 to 3 linear feet
Map Cabinets	=	16 sq. ft.
Stack-on Steel	=	Same as vertical cabinets
Tubs	=	3 sq. ft.

New space was computed at either $18.00 per square foot or $5.50 per square foot.
New cabinets were presumed to be six (6) drawer lateral cabinets holding 18 linear feet of records and occupying 7.5 square feet. Cabinets cost was computed at $ 200.00 each with a five (10) year depreciation. Only 1/5 of the cost was used per year. We assumed current cabinets, those now on the floor, are fully depreciated.

(7)

Current salary benchmarks used were (including fringe):

>   Senior Management   - $47,022 per year
>   Middle Management   - $30,934 per year
>   Clerical,Secretarial - $20,756 per year

Association of Records Managers and Administrators International estimates that twelve (12) file cabinets require
one (1) staff person. RECORDS MANAGEMENT, INC. computes
at twenty-one (21) cabinets per full-time employee, allowing
for stored materials.

Projections were based on 15% average increase in volume.
No allowance has been made for salary adjustments. Figure
1 does not include space costs for housing additional
employees necessary to meet volume increase.

RECORDS INVENTORY, RETENTION AND DISPOSAL OF RECORDS

Costs of space, equipment and personnel are fairly easy to identify. Much harder is the cost of losing a file. Or worse, losing the confidence of the public.

Another unpredictable cost is that of having records on hand too long. Administrative need is one thing. Legal vulnerability is another.

The study team mandate was to inventory every record series in City Hall, offices and basement. That work has been completed. When the data has been computerized, listings will be run so that all those who manage records may make corrections, additions and/or deletions.

However, 10 departments were not included in the mandate. In order to achieve City-wide savings, the records of all departments should be included. This will provide a single, uniform system which then can be used to govern costs on an equitable basis.

Two other facts are critical to the argument for a total inventory system - one that includes all departments:

- Most staff members will not take responsibility for disposing of records without specific directions and appropriate approvals.

- A retention schedule is obsolete in 30 days if it is not based on a detailed, specific records inventory and legal citations.

For these reasons,an official and complete organization-wide records retention schedule is cost effective. The cornerstone of the records retention schedule is the records inventory. The benefits of a retention schedule are achieved through an inventory because:

A detailed records inventory has not been taken for the offices outside City Hall as far as we could determine.

Of the records observed in storage and on the floor in filing cabinets, approximately 30% to 40% may be eligible for disposal.

(9)

Having completed the inventory and retention schedule
for City Hall, we can now verify that 60% of records in
the basement can be disposed of in 1994. About 30% of
office records can be disposed of in 1994.

Of the records observed in storage and on the floor in
filing cabinets, approximately 30% to 40% may be
eligible for disposal.

31% of staff members interviewed identified records
retention and corresponding lack of space as their
key needs.

56% of staff members interviewed said they did not
have a written retention schedule.

**44% of staff members interviewed said they have <u>NEVER</u>
disposed of any records.**

25% were unaware of any retention schedule but did
dispose of records.

31% of staff members interviewed reported they had a
schedule and have disposed of records according to
schedule.

15% of those interviewed were concerned about security
of vital records.

Several staff members interviewed stated specifically that
an offical and complete retention schedule would avoid
endless duplication, shorten retrieval time from
various departments, and relieve managers of responsibility
in disposing records.

There is about a 50 - 50 split on whether or not the City
of Ocala has an official retention schedule. Of those who
have a schedule, approximately half have not disposed of
records. Of those who have no schedule, half had disposed
of records anyway.

(10)

DO WE OR DO WE NOT HAVE
A RETENTION SCHEDULE?

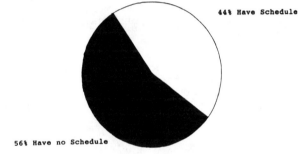

44% Have Schedule

56% Have no Schedule

RETENTION SCHEDULES

RECORDS MANAGEMENT, INC.

Figure 2

SECURITY OF VITAL RECORDS

Vital records, those records necessary for the organization to recover within 24 hours after suffering a
disaster, are considered adequately protected only
when backed up off-site.

23 staff members stated they held vital records, only
8 of these said they had sufficient back up.

65% had no off-site back up for vital records

The risk is very evident for some records series.For
example, licenses, contracts, original legal documents,
payroll, zoning, incident reports and historical
records.

Security of vital records is an important part of an
organization's disaster recovery program. The records
inventory is an opportunity to identify all of the vital
records and provide a recommended backup medium and frequency
for each. Without a records inventory, some vital records
series could inadvertently be overlooked.

An effective vital records program actually reduces
other business costs. Planning time for a disaster recovery plan, for example, can be reduced by one-third.
Records Management, Inc. clients have saved tens of thousands
of annual insurance premium dollars as a result of such
planning.

Backup procedures for vital records which provide image
reduction can reduce space costs by 98% and retrieval
time by more than 50%.

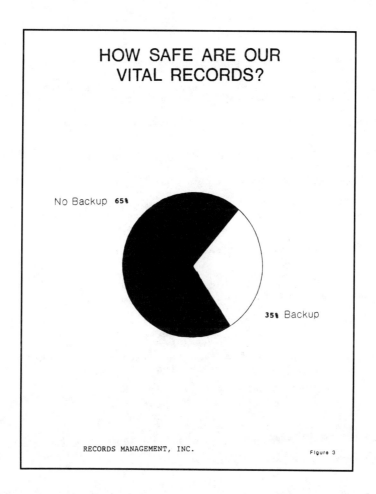

HOW SAFE ARE OUR VITAL RECORDS?

No Backup **65%**

35% Backup

RECORDS MANAGEMENT, INC.

Figure 3

FILING AND RETRIEVAL

In a recent University of Minnesota survey of the nation's
Information Systems managers, 94% stated that achieving
the competitive edge for their company was a major
concern, preceded only by stategic planning.

- The problem is one of timeliness in response to
  clientele.

- 100% of the City of Ocala staff agreed that
  filing, tracking, retrieval and storing records
  is a major problem.

- In all, 131 comments and suggestions were offered by
  those interviewed. 56 comments concerned filing, retrieving, tracking and storing records.

- **The major problem is retrieving the records stored
  in the <u>basement.</u>**

- Records and information systems effectiveness,
  according to users, was gauged as follows:

  <u>QUESTION:</u> In summary, would you say that the way
           in which files and other information
           are filed, stored and retrieved in the
           City of Ocala is satisfactory, unsatis-
           factory, or something in between ?

           12 responded satisfactory
            7 responded unsatisfactory
           14 responded in-between

<u>64% reported information handling less than satisfactory</u>

- At the same time, 36% said specifically, " Everything
  is O.K.

- This statistic is particularly telling because staff
  members generally are loathe to comment negatively
  to strangers regarding systems now in place.

(14)

[cartoon, page 15, not shown]

IMAGE REDUCTION

- **91% of those interviewed emphatically stated that the
  microfilm now in use is unsatisfactory.** In addition
  these same people want image reduction because of the
  benefits of space savings and retrieval time.

- Following is a broad-brush listing of some of the records
  series which may have the potential for good image
  reduction systems. The study team did not interview
  all staff members so it is entirely possible other
  applications are equally appropriate.

- It should be noted that although it appears that one-
  third of space now used to house records could be
  eliminated through use of image reduction, each series
  should be justified individually. If the retention
  period is less than 7 years, it may not be economically
  feasible to change media. More detail on imaging will
  follow later in the report.

Almost 100% dissastifaction with microfilm and micro-
fische. Even so, custodians have recognized the need
to do something to conserve space. Listed below are
the records series which appear to be image reduction
candidates:

> Audits
> Engineering originals, as - builts, changes
> Survey Books
> Final Budgets
> City Clerk's Permanent Documents
> * Purchase Orders
> Payroll Registers
> Adjusted Journal Entries
> Risk Management Contracts, Policies
> Zoning Plans
> City Agreements
> Grant Documents, State and Federal
> * License Applications
> Test Results
> Park Plans
> CDBG Federal Audits
> Patient Records
> MPO Documents
> Permanent Library Documents
> Electric Energy Audits and Reports
> * Meter Tests
> * Old Computer Print-Out (various)
> City Council Minutes
> City Council Agenda Packets

* Depending upon usage

(17)

WHAT THEY ARE SAYING

In undertaking the evaluation survey, City of Ocala management requested the study team ascertain issues which are of concern to the staff. Following are a few comments and suggestions.

" We need an index to contents of boxes "

" Boxes are too heavy and high to get "

" We have lots of duplication '

" We need an emergency recovery plan "

" We have a tendency to cling to things "

" Several of us are packrats - largely due to experience "

" Need more filing space "

" Wish we did not have to store in basement - nobody wants to go down there - too many critters down there "

" Would like to know what should and shouldn't be filmed "

" We all hate the basement - people would use it if it were lighted better, clean and carpeted "

" Staff does not understand how to deal with records "

" Previous filming was very poor "

" Need to be better organized in the storage department so we can retrieve better and faster "

" Film has to be pieced together for the big stuff "

" Need retention and disposal schedule "

" Now finding old microfilm not usable "

" Security in basement is bad - but who would go down there anyway ? "

(18)

WHAT CITY OF OCALA PERSONNEL CONSIDER AS REAL
RECORDS MANAGEMENT AND INFORMATION HANDLING NEEDS

An inventory, retention and disposal system	5
Reorganize basement storage	30
Image reduction	29
Forms management	12
Filing Systems	30
Fax between offices and City Hall	1
Security of sensitive files	18
Miscellaneous	17
TOTAL NUMBER OF RESPONSES	131

(19)

"Mistakes in Records Management
are paid for in
the legal department."

CITY OF OCALA

5 - STEP

COMPREHENSIVE

RECORDS

PROGRAM

Proposed by

RECORDS MANAGEMENT, INC.

January 31, 1994

5 - STEPS

I.   Complete the records inventory to include all City of Ocala offices.

II.   Dispose of outdated, obsolete, and redundant records and microfilm.

III.   Reorganize basement storage at City Hall.

IV.   Stop microfilming records and start to store records on optical disk.

V.   Provide for on-going maintenance of records program.

(21)

RECOMMENDATIONS

I. Complete the records inventory for the remainder

of the City of Ocala offices:

> Engineering
> Electric and UBO
> Purchasing
> Planning
> Risk Management
> Fire
> Recreation and Parks
> Water and Sewer
> Public Works
> Fleet Management

The inventory, retention schedule and disposal program
is the best cost cutting and cost containment method
available to government agencies.

Approximately 40% of paper records in the above offices
may be disposed of once the inventory is complete. Another
30% will either be stored in low cost, long term storage or
reduced in volume by imaging.

Tasks involved in recommendation I:

1. Identify all the records series, or types of
   records each off-site agency has currently.

2. Detail where each is located, in offices and
   in storage.

3. Set retention periods according to statutes,
   regulations and administrative needs.

4. Shorten retention period for duplicate series.

5. Identify vital records, how they should be
   backed-up and how frequently.

6. Specify current and anticipated volume of records
   to allow adequate planning for storage.

It should be noted that these are the same steps already
taken for offices and storage in City Hall. The following
steps are those that will be taken to complete the City
Hall inventory.

(22)

Software provided by Records Management, Inc. will
generate the following reports:

- A list of records eligible for disposal by
  department.

- Lists of records disposed.

- Reports of all records, where located, which
  are the "copy of record", which are vital and
  many other reports as necessary.

RECORDS MANAGEMENT, INC., leaves written procedures
and trained personnel in place after a system is
installed to enable the client to realize the maximum
benefits of the program. The procedures manual is
written in playscript format and at least two staff
members from each location are trained in all phases
of the manual.

Written procedures provide training for new employees
and reduces questions and discrepancies related to the
program.

A two hour session explaining to all staff members the
objectives of the inventory and retention system, how
it will be maintained, the various uses of the system
and the benefits.

COSTS FOR RECOMMENDATION I

Total Inventory and Retention Program for all departments

outside of City Hall including software, training, procedures

and initial disposal: **$10,260.00**

SAVINGS: Approximately $8,800.00 per year in space
Approximately $18,000.00 per year in equipment *

TOTAL SAVINGS PER YEAR - $26,800.00

* includes all City Hall offices. The next page will
  provide an idea of the inventory detail.

(23)

ADDITIONAL BENEFITS

Inventory, Retention, Vital Records Program

A)   Annually, the system automatically produces a list of
     records eligible for disposal so that the decision
     process for disposal is shortened and future volume
     can be controlled. Less than 5% versus the projected
     15%.

B)   The City will be able to routinely dispose of records
     according to an official schedule so that staff members
     will not need to worry about liability or
     responsibility.

C)   The automated system and written procedures will add to
     the efficiency and consistency of the system.

D)   Managers will be advised in writing when records are
     eligible for disposal. In unusual cases the system may
     by-pass records disposal if required.

E)   Record series will be tracked from filing through
     disposal, whatever the location, ownership or
     medium.

F)   Vital records, throughout the City, will be
     identified so that almost one-third of a city-wide
     Disaster Recovery Program is completed.

II.   Dispose of obsolete, outdated and redundant

records and microfilm.

Routine disposal which follows an approved written
retention schedule is management's cheapest and very best
cost containment tool.

60% of the records presently stored in the basement have long
exceeded their legal and administrative needs.

A listing, generated from the inventory system, should
be submitted to the State Records and Archives requesting
disposal.

When the inventory, retention and program modifications
are completed, a day or days should be set aside to
dispose of all records which are eligible for disposal.
The computer system will generate a report for managers
to review before the disposal takes place. RECORDS
MANAGEMENT, INC. staff will supervise the disposal process
or be on-site for guidance.

COSTS FOR RECOMMENDATION II

- Staff time to dispose of records

- Small reward for participants, e.g. desk plant or

T-shirt.

(25)

RECORDS ELIGIBLE FOR DISPOSAL

Basement Summary

    Total Boxes   1,491

Boxes Eligible For Disposal

1994	891 (60%)
1995	59
1996	36
1997	39
1998	22
1999	13
2000 +	301

Boxes of Permanent Records   130

Office Summary

    Approximately 30% of records in City Hall offices could be disposed in 1994

Basement Notes: If permanent, Vital and records which must be kept more than 10 years were placed on optical disk, only 169 boxes would be left to shelve. This would represent a space reduction of 88%.

(26)

BENEFITS

- Annual Disposal

- Growth of space occupied by records will increase
  less than 5% annually versus 15% growth now anticipated.
- Dollar amounts saved are included in Recommendation I.

III. Reorganize basement storage into City Records Center

    Design and organize a records center for the City of Ocala.

Tasks involved in Recommendation III:

1) Design a protected environment for inactive records and backup for current vital records.

2) Develop an automated retrieval and indexing system which provides routine records eligible for disposal Reports for managers' approval, in conjunction with inventory and retention system.

3) Develop a simplified, comprehensive box numbering and file indexing system to interact with filing system used in City Hall Offices.

4) Design the center, select security system, shelving, other hardware and related items.

5) Conduct two-hour orientation session for all users; provide on-going briefing data for department managers.

6) Prepare written procedures manual for records storage operation and users' needs; provide training for at least two staff members.

7) Develop conversion plan.

8) Install automated records center management software system.

9) Supervise labeling, indexing (as needed), shelving and recording of all items.

10) Provide reports to all users.

Records Storage Center Costs - $8,400.00 *

* This does not include costs of remodeling or equipment or actual conversion

YEARLY COSTS SAVINGS - $26,000.00 *

* Derived from savings in filing time and space

(28)

BENEFITS

Records   Center

A.   All inactive records centrally located, indexed, in a
     secure environment.

B.   Fully automated system will be compatible with that used
     in inventory, retention and filing systems.

C.   Responsibility for filing and retrieving will be given
     to the Records Clerk, Central Services, relieving
     managers of the necessity to go in search of records.

D.   Personnel time savings will be in excess of $25,000.00
     per year.

E.   All users will receive reports of their records
     currently in storage and the location of each.

F.   Written procedures and trained staff will be in place
     to maintain the system and to orient new users.

G.   Records Clerk time required should be less than
     one-half time (for all systems proposed).

H.   Vital records can be backed up in a routine and
     secure manner, delivered and/or rotated by Records
     Clerk as need arises.

I.   Special deliveries (fax) and other services may be
     added as needs are identified.

J.   On-going audit and supervision available from RECORDS
     MANAGEMENT, INC. on an annual retainer.

K.   The bottom line is this proposal will make the records
     center user happy, develop a great reputation for
     Central Services, and provide security for Vital
     records.

(29)

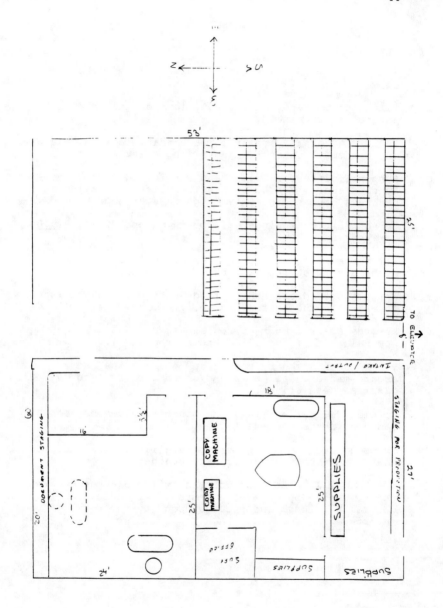

IV. Discontinue microfilming documents and start

using optical disk for image reduction.

RECORDS MANAGEMENT, INC., staff reviewed the microfilming program as it currently exists in the City
of Ocala.

FINDINGS

1. Fifty-five (55) record series have been microfilmed
in whole or in part at a cost of $81,375. Of these,
approximately thirty (30) have a retention period of
less than five (5) years. These series should not have
been microfilmed.

    Examples of records which **should** **not** have been filmed:

		RETENTION
13 rolls	Personnel prior to 1971	4 years after termination
15 rolls	Pay and Time Cards	2 years
5 rolls	Property Tax receipts	When superceded
8 rolls	Occupational Licenses,1968	1 year after expiration
125 rolls	Accounts Payable	5 years (max.)
9 rolls	Daily Correspondence	3 - 4 years
102 rolls	Building Permits (old)	1 year after expiration 5 years (max.)
11 rolls	Monthly Financial Statements 1975-1979	2 years

2. The City of Ocala owns ten (10) micrographic readers
and readers/printers, in various stages of disrepair.
Not all of the printers print, and at least one (1)
reader does not read. The following items have limited
usefulness:

    Finance - a reader that should be surplus.
    City Clerks Office - can be used for reading only.

(31)

3.   In addition, The City of Ocala owns a system for
      notching microfiche called <u>Retrex.</u> In this system
      each fiche is placed into a mylar jacket topped by
      a metal bar. A notching mechanism is fitted over the
      metal bar and one digit by one digit, the mechanism
      cuts the index number into the metal bar. The film is
      then viewed to ensure that the correct number is above
      the correct film.
      The object of the system is to speed retrieval. This
      is accomplished by setting the "finder" to a specific
      number and then moving the "finder" over the packed
      drawer. The selected "fiche" will jump up about 1/4"
      and then be pulled out of the drawer. The fiche need
      not be replaced in sequence, so long as it is in the
      correct drawer. The "finder" will find it.
      Although this is a labor intensive system, as well as
      being expensive, it must be noted that the staff is
      satisfied with it's performance.

Drawbacks to the system are obvious:

1.   The notching is labor intensive and expensive. Each
      jacket costs approximately $1.00.

2.   Most agencies with hundreds of thousands of fiche, use
      color coding stripes and file them numerically in fiche
      cabinets or rotating power files. In the latter instance
      pushing buttons to correspond to the index number will
      bring tray, or carrier, to arm level. On certain models
      a light beam points to the correct fiche desired. An
      outcard is used when a fiche is removed.

3.   The current backlog of microfilm awaiting notching
      appears to exceed supplies in stock. However, it must be
      said that the agencies using the system, Electrical
      Engineering in particular, are very satisfied with
      the system.

4.   The greatest difficulty is that the group of agencies
      which has the greatest need for image reduction - those
      with maps, plans,blueprints, are not helped under the
      current system. Their documents have been filmed but to
      reproduce a hard copy they must be satisfied with either
      a 81/2" x 11" copy of an "E" size drawing or 6 to 8
      sections of an "E" size drawing pieced together. In both
      cases scale and detail are lost.

5. Optical disk will print a "C" size drawing (11" x 17")
   clearly and to scale. We will explore the possibilities
   of imaging the larger drawing sizes. However, the
   Engineering staff has said that "C" size prints would
   be acceptable.

(32)

IMAGE RECOMMENDATIONS

1. **Stop microfilming.** The system is pleasing no one.
    Department-by-department design the imaging
    system for each record series which meets the
    following criteria:

    A. Retention is ten (10) years or longer.

    B. Record is vital and imaging is better, faster,
       cheaper than any other method of duplication.

    C. Record is created in computer and can be placed
       on optical disk (Computer Output To Laser Disk),
       by-passing paper totally.
       Record series in this category would be payroll
       registers and annual financial statements. The
       cost of paper saved by this system will pay a
       substantial portion of the conversion costs.
       Those systems which are currently on microfilm,
       e.g. Council agenda packets and minutes, should
       transfer to disk at the approved cut-off date
       (which may have already passed).

RECORDS MANAGEMENT, INC. will contact a vendor to provide
system needs and cost figures for an optical disk system.
There is no additional cost for this service.The study will:

1. Does the cost of image reduction fall within the
   existing budget, or is it a plan for a later date ?

2. Explore the possibilities of cooperative imaging
   using facilities of other governmental bodies.

3. Determine if other governmental units can be used
   to provide back up in the event of a natural or
   man-made disaster.

From this study, City of Ocala management can then decide
whether or not to budget for hardware and software. A
basic optical disk system requires a 486 personal computer,
a laser printer and a scanner.

Beyond the hardware, the software requirements are determined
by the user's needs.

Costs for Recommendation IV. - $0.00 until hardware

and software are selected.

(33)

BENEFITS

- Image technology is computer oriented and therefore more user friendly than microfilm.

- Control over quality and security are based firmly in the user's hands.

- Optical disk systems can be networked to users if required.

- Optical disk is being accepted as an information tool of the next century.

V.   Provide on-going maintenance of City of Ocala's

Comprehensive Records Management Program.

    A.   MIS Department will <u>loan</u> Central Services
    a personal computer on which to capture the
    inventory data , generate disposal lists, and
    list of Vital records.

    B.   R.M.I., will provide training for custodians
    to correct inventory listings and add/change
    inventory items.

    C.   R.M.I., will provide an optical disk study to
    determine the costs to change imaging technologies
    from microfilm to optical disk.

    D.   R.M.I. will assist in the annual disposal day.

    E.   R.M.I. will dedicate two days per month, on-site
    to:

        1. Implement new filing systems.

        2. Monitor inventory, records center and
           optical disk systems.

        3. Supervise annual disposal process.

        4. Strive to reduce records handling costs.

        5. Assist in acquisition, manage installation
           of optical disk system, design the index,
           and manage the pilot program if required.

Cost: $9600.00 per year

(35)

BENEFITS

A.   R.M.I. will provide expert staff specifically
     experienced in the proposed projects.

B.   No "fringe" benefits to provide.

C.   Contract may be cancelled upon thirty (30) days
     written notice by either party.

D.   Total amount is less than one-fourth the cost of
     similarly qualified personnel in a full-time
     position.

E.   **The program will succeed because R.M.I. will not
     let it fail.**

SUMMARY OF RECOMMENDATIONS

		Cost		Savings
I.	Inventory, Retention Disposal System for balance of City Hall offices	**$10,800**		**$25,000** yr.
II.	Dispose of old Records	-0-		Included in #1 above
III.	Records Center for all City Hall Offices	**$8,400** $30,000 $15,000	RMI Equip. Remodel	**$25,000** yr.
	TOTAL	**$53,400**		
		$4,700	On-going Cost (part time clerk)	
IV.	Optical Disk Study	-0-		Unknown
V.	RECORDS MANAGEMENT Retainer	$9,600 yr.		$24,000
	TOTAL SAVINGS			**$81,400**

FIVE YEAR PROJECTIONS

Year	One-time	On-going	Net Savings
1	$64,000	$14,300	$2,900
2	–	$14,300	$67,100
3	–	$14,300	$67,100
4	–	$14,300	$67,100
5	–	$14,300	$67,100
	TOTAL SAVINGS		**$271,300**

* Savings based on $40,000 Records Manager

(37)

CITY OF OCALA
ACTION PLAN

Activity/Week   1   2   3   4   5   6   7   8   9   10   11

I. Inventory   _____

    Retention   _____

    Approval   _____

    Procedures   _____

II. Disposal   ___

III. Records Center

    Center Design   _____

    Approvals   _____

    Procedures   _____

    Training   ___

IV. Optical Disk   _____

V. Retainer   _____▷

(38)

RECORDS INVENTORY DATA COLLECTION FORM

Facility   Division   Department   Shared

`C` `H` ☐ ☐ ☐   ☐ ☐ ☐ ☐ ☐   ☐ ☐ ☐ ☐ ☐   ☐

Custodian Position   Custodian Name

☐ ☐ ☐ ☐ ☐ ☐ ☐ ☐ ☐ ☐   ☐ ☐ ☐ ☐ ☐ ☐ ☐ ☐ ☐ ☐

Record Series Title

☐ ☐
☐ ☐

Record Series Description

☐ ☐
☐ ☐

Media   COR   If NO, who maintains Copy of Record?

☐ ☐   ☐   _____

            Date Range On-Site   Volume (Ln Ft)

☐ ☐ ☐ ☐ ☐ ☐   Thru ☐ ☐ ☐ ☐ ☐ ☐   ☐ ☐ ☐ ☐ ☐

            Date Range Off-Site   Volume (Cu Ft)

☐ ☐ ☐ ☐ ☐ ☐   Thru ☐ ☐ ☐ ☐ ☐ ☐   ☐ ☐ ☐ ☐ ☐

Storage Location: _____

Frequency   Privacy/Secured   Vital/Backup

☐   ☐ ☐   `N` ☐

Filing Sequence: (alpha/numeric/chronological/subject)

Retention:
Years   Instructions   Office   Storage   Offsite

☐ ☐   ☐ ☐ ☐   ☐ ☐ ☐   ☐ ☐ ☐   ☐ ☐ ☐

Governing Authority   _____
                                                  _____
☐ ☐ ☐ ☐ ☐ ☐ ☐ ☐ ☐ ☐ ☐ ☐ ☐ ☐   ☐ ☐ ☐ ☐ ☐   _____
                                                  _____

Appendix B

Procedures for Developing a Records Retention Schedule

The following is a set of procedures for a retention schedule that you may adopt, modify, or disregard. It has been developed over the years to make sure that enough eyes have looked at the retention schedule and that all managers are brought into the process. It also is distributed to each manager for reference.

Reprinted with permission.

TABLE OF CONTENTS

I. RIDS: System Description

RIDS is the name of the filing system developed by Records Management, Inc. for its clients.

The purpose of RIDS is to allow users to file and retrieve records, regardless of media,, in the most time-efficient method.

The numbered files and identifying data for each are recorded on the client's computer.   In addition to the total search capabilities, RIDS generates the attached reports.

RIDS allows the users to maintain the system with a minimum of effort and at the same time produces these cost-saving benefits:

    * Annual disposal of obsolete records

    * Elimination of duplicate/redundant files

    * Cost-avoidance of additional filing cabinets, floor space
      and staff.

    * Staff members have immediate knowledge of what is in their
      files and can see at a glance records, and <u>related</u>
      <u>information</u>, which may be located elsewhere in the office.

II. SCOPE

RIDS is designed to record both File Series and individual file folders. This is important because RIDS can be used as an index to specific records and as an inventory of all records series within a company or agency. No longer is it necessary to question whether an item belongs in the Records Inventory or in the Index to Files. Records Series such as personnel files and invoices can be indexed on the same system as file folders such as Airport Study 1965, etc.

In addition, every field can be searched. Both the Title Field and the Description Field can accommodate up to 50 characters, and the Governing Authority Field holds 40 characters.

To conduct a search, press Control S. Move cursor to field you wish to search. Type in the information you wish to search. Then press F10. The computer will search the file field and tag all records meeting the search criteria. This tagged list can be viewed on the screen, saved on a disk or printed.

All critical fields generate reports. These reports are:

> List of Vital Records
> List of Records Eligible for Imaging
> List of Records Eligible for Disposal by Year
> List of Records Disposed
> List of Records by Custodian

RIDS allows the users to maintain the system with a minimum of effort and at the same time produces these cost savings benefits:

* Annual disposal of obsolete records

* Elimination of duplicate/redundant files

* Cost avoidance of additional filing cabinets, floor space and staff.

* Staff members have immediate knowledge of what information is in their files and can quickly see records, and related information, which may be located elsewhere in the office.

The following page is a sample of the screen format for RIDS.

RECORDS INVENTORY DATA COLLECTION FORM

Facility	Division	Department	Image Reduction

Facility: C H
Division: C K
Department: C o m m
Image Reduction: [ ]

Custodian Name

L A N N O N   K
F I A L A   J

Record Series Title

B U D G E T   B O O K S .

Record Series Description

Media
0 6

COR
[X]

If NO, who maintains Copy of Record?

Date Range On-Site
1 9 8 5   Thru   1 9 9 2

Volume (Ln Ft)
[ ][ ][ ]-[ ]

Date Range Off-Site
Thru

BOX #

Storage Location: ~~VAULT~~ /OFF

Frequency
[ ]

Privacy/Secured
[ ][ ]

Vital/Backup
[ ][ ]

Retention:

Years	Instructions	Office	Storage	Offsite
'	P E R	A C T		

Governing Authority
G R S L G   #   2 1 .

Dispose
PERM

IV. DESCRIPTION OF FIELDS

The ability to Add, Delete and Change a record is controlled through the menu, under RIDS MAINTENANCE.

FIELD	# OF CHARACTERS	ALPHABETICAL or NUMERICAL	FIELD DESCRIPTION
File #	(8)	A/N	File folder identification number made up of 3 letter department abbreviation followed by a dash and 4-digit file number in each sequential order. Each department's files begin with 1, as in AAA-1. This allows each department to have as many as 9999 individual file folders.
Facility	(5)	A/N	Number of building or room number in which record is located.
Division	(5)	A/N	Name of the division owning the record.
Department	(5)	A/N	Name of department owning the record.
Image Reduction	(1)	A	Indicates if this is a potential imaging application: Y if yes, System will default to N if not filled with a Y.
Custodian Name	(10)	A	Last name and first initial of person holding the record, regardless of storage location.
Title	(40)	A/N	The full title of the file folder. May contain the range of dates, as in 1944 - 1989.

Description   (40)   A/N   Contains descriptive data, key
                                     words, phrases, authors, places,
                                     dates, any data which will aid in
                                     searching for this and/or other
                                     similar files.

FIELD	# of CHARACTERS	ALPHABETICAL or NUMERIC	DESCRIPTION of FIELD

Media   (2)   (N)   A code which stands for the
various

types of media on which the record
is recorded. The user may find the
same record on paper and microfilm
and then can decide which will be
most useful.

The code is:

01 Paper 8 1/2 x 11

02 Paper 8 1/2 x 14

03 Microfiche

04 Microfilm Roll

05 Computer Printout

06 Drawings, maps, plans

07 - 10 Left blank for your own use

11 Bound books

12 Checks

13 Half sheets

14 Post binder

15 Mixed media (several media in one
    folder)

16 Tapes

17 Photos and negatives

18 Disks

| COR | (1) | Y | Copy of record. This does not necessarily mean the original record. It means the copy in question is the official copy and must be retained |

᛭ ᛫

for the full and legal and administrative period. Other copies of this record may be disposed when their administrative need is satisfied, the data is obsolete or has been superseded.

| Volume | (5) | N | Linear feet of record, usually captured in storage area. Used for planning for a records center or for the use of commercial storage space. |

| Date range Off Site | (4 - 4) | N | The years of this record stored off-site. |

| Box # | (5) | A/N | The number of the box stored in internal storage, eg. Basement, closet, conference room. |

| Off-site storage location | (10) | A/N | The number given by the commercial records center. |

| Frequency | (2) | A | The abbreviation for how often the the record is produced: |

Mo = Monthly

WK = Weekly

DA = Daily

QT = Quarterly

AN = Annually

SA = Semi-Annually

BI = Biennially

| Privacy | (1) | A | Is this record private or |

confidential? Y indicates yes, system
will default to N if record is a
public record.

Secured	(1)	A	Y indicates yes, record is secured. System will default if record is not secured.
Vital	(1)	A	Y indicates yes, record is essential to the organization's recovery within 24 hours following a disaster, or is of great historical value, or represents a large investment in an important record not likely to be re-done were it to be destroyed. System will default to N if record is not vital.
Backup	(1)	A	Y indicates record is backed up off-site. System will default to N if record is not backed up off-site.
Retention Years.	(2)	N	The number of years the record must be kept.
Instructions	(3)	A/N	Indicates when the record is eligible for the disposal:

ATC   After the last transaction
(which may be an audit) is complete.

ACT   While active

LOP   Life of Property

LOS   Life of Structure

AEX   After Expiration

OBS   When Obsolete

SUP   When Superseded

DAM   Dispose after Microfilming, or
imaging

.PER   Permanent

TER   After Termination
REV   Review Before Disposing

Office, Storage
Off-site
            (3)   A/N   Breakdown   the   years   and   the
                                   instructions for each location
                                   during the life of the record.

Governing Authority
            (40)   A/N   The legal or administrative citation
                                   used   to   back   up   the   retention
                                   assigned:

                                   GRSLG - General Record Schedule
                                   Local Government (State of Florida
                                   Records Management Program)

                                   GRSEL - General Records, Schedule,
                                   Elections

                                   GRSLG B & Z - General Records
                                   Schedule, Building and Zoning

                                   CFR - Code of Federal Regulations

                                   GRS-FED - General Records Schedule
                                   for Government and Business, National
                                   Archives and Records

                                   DARTNELL - Dartnell Institute of
                                   Business Research

                                   NABAC - National Association of Bank
                                   Auditors and Controllers.

Dispose   (4)   A/N   Year   in   which   record   may   be
                                   disposed, or   Instruction   for
                                   disposing when certain   conditions
                                   have been met, as in LOP, PER, or
                                   SUP.

Disposed   (1)   A   Indicates record for this year has
                                   been disposed. System manager will
                                   run the list of disposed records.
                                   This is a Vital Record. Then the
                                   System Manager must   reset   the
                                   disposal date for the following year,

providing the record is continuing,
as in Purchase orders,and eliminate
the Disposed "Y".
If the record is not continuing, the
system Manager may leave the record
intact after the Disposed List
has been generated.

V. SYSTEM LISTINGS:

The RIDS System generates many different types of reports.
The following is a list of the RIDS Reports:

> Master Listing - All Files
> Custodian Listing
> Disposal Listing
> Vital Records Listing
> Image Application Listing
> Yearly Disposal Listing
> Master Listing - Quick List
> Custodian Listing - Quick List
> Numeric Master Listing
> Off- site Storage Listing

The (2) Quick List Reports are the same file lists as the Master
and Custodian - All, only without as much data shown on the screen.

The following pages are examples of the Reports.

```
Run Date:  5/04/94              Master Listing - All                Page  14
Run Time: 12:11AM            Alphabetical by Record Title
```

===

```
Id#: 0000247
BLANK                                        Div:        Dept:
                                             Cust Name:
Media:    -                         Privacy: N   Vital: N   Backup: N
Date Range  On-Site:   /  /    thru   /  /
Date Range Off-Site:   /  /    thru   /  /
Storage Location:      -
-------------------------------Retention-------------------------------------
Years:      Instructions:    -
Office:        Storage:       Offsite:      Dispose:    0 Disposed: N
Governing Authority:
```

===

```
Id#: 0000248
BLANK                                        Div:        Dept:
                                             Cust Name:
Media:    -                         Privacy: N   Vital: N   Backup: N
Date Range  On-Site:   /  /    thru   /  /
Date Range Off-Site:   /  /    thru   /  /
Storage Location:      -
-------------------------------Retention-------------------------------------
Years:      Instructions:    -
Office:        Storage:       Offsite:      Dispose:    0 Disposed: N
Governing Authority:
```

===

```
Id#: 0000249
BLANK                                        Div:        Dept:
                                             Cust Name:
Media:    -                         Privacy: N   Vital: N   Backup: N
Date Range  On-Site:   /  /    thru   /  /
Date Range Off-Site:   /  /    thru   /  /
Storage Location:      -
-------------------------------Retention-------------------------------------
Years:      Instructions:    -
Office:        Storage:       Offsite:      Dispose:    0 Disposed: N
Governing Authority:
```

===

```
Id#: 0000250
BLANK                                        Div:        Dept:
                                             Cust Name:
Media:    -                         Privacy: N   Vital: N   Backup: N
Date Range  On-Site:   /  /    thru   /  /
Date Range Off-Site:   /  /    thru   /  /
Storage Location:      -
-------------------------------Retention-------------------------------------
Years:      Instructions:    -
Office:        Storage:       Offsite:      Dispose:    0 Disposed: N
Governing Authority:
```

===

Record Series Title	Custodian
1 COMM LONG FILES MAY 1988	LANNON
2 CITY COMM METTINGS	LANNON
3 COMM LONGS FILES	LANNON
4 CONTRACT FILES	LANNON
5 CITY COMM MINUTE PAPERS	LANNON
6 CITY COMM MINUTE PAPERS	LANNON
'7 CITY COMM MINUTE PAPERS	NANNON
)8 CLERK BUDGET 91-92	LANNON
)9 COMMITTIES 1986	LANNON
_0 PHYSCIAL INVENTORY 83-87	LANNON
11 CITY COMM FILES	LANNON
12 CHART OF ACCOUNTS	LANNON
13 ELECTIONS QUAL. AND REPORTS 1970-1977	LANNON
14 CITIZEN'S LETTERS	LANNON
15 CLERK SUBJECT FILES	LANNON
16 COMM STUDIES MICROFILMED	LANNON
17 COMM AGENDA PACKETS MICROFILMED	LANNON
18 COMM AGENDA PACKETS MICROFILMED	LANNON
19 ABSENTEE BALLOTS AND RELATED ITEMS 1976-77	LANNON
20 C/GARY JUNIOR C/LISLE GRACE AND SYDNEY KNIGHT FILE	LANNON
'21 COMM MINUTE PAPERS 1-5-76 - 6-28-76	LANNON
'22 COMM MINUTE PAPERS 6-2-75 - 12-17-75	LANNON
)23 COMM MINUTE PAPERS SEPTEMBER 74 - MAY 75	LANNON
)24 COMM MINUTE PAPERS 1-3-77 - 4-25-77	LANNON
)25 TELEPHONE MESSAGE PADS 85-87	LANNON
)26 COMM FILES 1982-1984	LANNON
)27 COMM MINUTE PAPERS MAY-77 - AUGUST-77	LANNON
)28 CITY WORKSHOPS AND STUDIES 86-87	LANNON
)29 COMM CORRESPONDENCE 1977	LANNON
030 COMM METTINGS 78-84 COMM FILES	LANNON
031 COMM FILES TELEPHONE MESSAGES 1984	LANNON
032 COMM CORRESPONDENCE 1976	LANNON
033 COMM FILES SUBJECT FILES 1980	LANNON
034 COMM CORRESPONDENCE 77-79	LANNON
035 COMM SUBJECT FILES 1977-1980	LANNON
036 COMM MINUTE PAPERS 1-6-86 - 3-17-86	LANNON
037 CLERK CONTRACT FILES 1979 2 BOXES	LANNON
'038 CLERK CONTRACT FILES 1980	LANNON
)039 CLERK CONTRACT FILES A-C 1975-77	LANNON
)040 CLERK CONTRACT FILES K-P 1975-77	LANNON
')041 COMMITIES AND TASKFORCE 1980-83	LANNON
)042 BOARDS AND COMMITTIES FILES 1985	LANNON
)043 COMM CONTRACT FILES 1980	LANNON
)044 CLERK SUBJECT FILES 1974-1977	LANNON
)045 COMM CORRESPENDENCE 75-77	LANNON
0046 MISC FILES 1977-1982	LANNON
)047 CLERK SUBJECT FILES 1970-1984	LANNON
0048 OPERATIONS COMMITTIE 1985	LANNON
0049 CLERK'S SUBJECT FILES 81-82	LANNON
0050 COMM MISC FILES	LANNON
0051 COMM MISC FILES 1983	LANNON
'0052 COMM CITIZEN'S FILES 82-83	LANNON
'0053 BOARDS AND COMMITTIES 1974	LANNON

Custodian	Record Series Title	File#	MD	V/BU
LANNON	1982 INDICES	0000158	1	Y/N
LANNON	1985 INDICES	0000159	1	Y/N
LANNON	1986 INDICES	0000160	1	Y/N
LANNON	BUILDING CODE STANDARDS	0000189	11	Y/N
LANNON	CEMETERY DEEDS	0000317	1	Y/N
LANNON	CODE OF ORDINANCES 1980 - 1992	0000225	1	Y/N
LANNON	CODE SUPPLEMENT FILE 1990	0000223	1	Y/N
LANNON	COMM AGENDA PACKETS MICROFILMED	0000017	2	Y/Y
LANNON	COMM AGENDA PACKETS MICROFILMED	0000018	2	Y/Y
LANNON	CONTRACT INDEX 1 INDEX BOX	0000205	13	Y/N
LANNON	DEERHAVEN STATION	0000149	11	Y/N
LANNON	EASEMENT FILES	0000182	1	Y/N
LANNON	FINANCIAL DISCLOSURE FORMS	0000177	1	Y/N
LANNON	FINANCIAL DISCLOSURE FORMS	0000178	1	Y/N
LANNON	KANAPAHA WASTE WATER TREATMENT PLANT	0000195	15	Y/N
LANNON	LAND DEVELOPMENT CODE	0000130	11	Y/N
LANNON	LAND USE AND ADDRESS	0000132	15	Y/N
LANNON	MAPS	0000136	11	Y/N
LANNON	MINUTE BOOKS	0000157	11	Y/N
LANNON	MINUTE INDEX BOOKS	0000174	11	Y/N
LANNON	MINUTES-CITY COMM	0000164	11	Y/N
LANNON	NOTARY PUBLIC CERTIFICATE	0000139	1	Y/N
LANNON	ORDINANCE BOOKS	0000137	11	Y/N
LANNON	ORDINANCE BOOKS-3	0000183	11	Y/N
LANNON	ORDINANCE-COMPREHENSIVE DATA ANALYSIS	0000131	1	Y/N
LANNON	ORDINANCES	0000192	15	Y/N
LANNON	ORDINANCES	0000309	1	Y/N
LANNON	PENSION FUND	0000185	1	Y/N
LANNON	PERSONNEL FILES	0000180	1	Y/N
·LANNON	PERSONNEL RECORDS	0000311	1	Y/N
LANNON	REGULATIONS-LAND DEV FOR COLLEGE PARK	0000133	1	Y/N
LANNON	RESOLUTION BOOK	0000184	11	Y/N
LANNON	RESOLUTION BOOKS	0000173	11	Y/N
LANNON	SPECIAL LIEN BOOK RESOLUTION R-92-14	0000202	1	Y/N
LANNON	UTILITIES SYSTEM REVENUE BONDS	0000170	11	Y/N
LANNON	ZONING CODE	0000187	15	Y/N

Custodian Record Count: 36

```
Run Date:  5/19/94          Custodian Listing - Tagged              Page   1
Run Time: 12:11AM      Division/Department/Custodian Name
================================================================================

                   ** Division:      /Department: CC    **

                   ** Custodian Name: FIALA      **

Id#: 0000377
MEMBERSHIP LISTS INDIVIDUAL                    Div:       Dept: CC
BOARDS AND COMMITTIEES  1988-1990              Copy of Record: Y
Media:  1-8 1/2" X 11" PAPER                Privacy: N  Vital: N   Backup: N
Date Range  On-Site:    / /    thru    / /
Date Range Off-Site:    / /    thru    / /
Storage Location: OFF  -
------------------------------------Retention-----------------------------------
Years:  2  Instructions:     -
Office:      Storage:       Offsite:      Dispose: 1994 Disposed: N
Governing Authority: GRSEL#20
================================================================================

Id#: 0000410
NEWSPAPER ARTICLES                             Div:       Dept: CC
POSITION SELECTION                             Copy of Record: Y
Media:  1-8 1/2" X 11" PAPER                Privacy: N  Vital: N   Backup: N
Date Range  On-Site:    / /    thru    / /
Date Range Off-Site:    / /    thru    / /
Storage Location: OFF  -
------------------------------------Retention-----------------------------------
Years:  1  Instructions:     -
Office:      Storage:       Offsite:      Dispose: 1994 Disposed: N
Governing Authority: GRSLG#166
================================================================================

Id#: 0000419
SCHEDULED EVENTS                               Div:       Dept: CC
CHECK LISTS FOR DUTIES AND FUNCTIONS 1990      Copy of Record: Y
Media:  1-8 1/2" X 11" PAPER                Privacy: N  Vital: N   Backup: N
Date Range  On-Site:    / /    thru    / /
Date Range Off-Site:    / /    thru    / /
Storage Location: OFF  -
------------------------------------Retention-----------------------------------
Years:  3  Instructions:     -
Office:      Storage:       Offsite:      Dispose: 1994 Disposed: N
Governing Authority: GRSLG#176
================================================================================

                   Total Records Printed:       3
```

VI. HOW TO FIND A FILE IN THE PC

1. Go to main menu, select RIDS, Press enter

2. RIDS Main Menu will appear on screen

3. Select Maintenance Menu, Press enter

4. Maintenance Menu will appear on screen

5. Select Rids Maintenance, Press enter

6. List of Files will appear on screen

7. Press Control S, Rids Form will appear on screen

8. Press Control S again for different criteria to search by.

9. Move cursor to field to be searched

10. Enter search information, Press F10

11. Move cursor to Select, Press enter

12. Computer will search files and tag those files which match the search criteria.

13. Then press search on next screen

14. Press yes and enter and the first tagged file will appear

15. Press ESC to return to Master File List

16. Press PgDn to view entire File Title List until desired File is found

VII. HOW TO ADD A FILE

System Manager:

RIDS is based on database software and runs on the Office Manager's PC. Only the Office Manager may add, change or delete a file.

RIDS is menu-driven and will be found in the Directory under RIDS.

Steps to access RIDS:

1. Go to MS-DOS Main Menu

2. Select RIDS, press enter

3. Select Maintenance Menu, press enter.

4. Select RIDS Maintenance, press enter, Master Title List will appear

5. Press Insert, the next available File Identification Form will appear on screen

6. Enter new file #, name, etc., when form is completed press F10 for file to be entered into RIDS File Directory

7. Screen will now show the Master Title List. Press Insert for next File Information Form.

VIII. HOW TO CHANGE A FILE

1. Follow steps 1 thru 4 in Section VII

2. Enter File ID # and press enter; File will appear on screen.
   Change file information as required; Press F10 for changes to be saved in the File Directory.

IX. HOW TO DELETE A FILE

1. Follow steps 1 thru 4 in Section VII

2. Enter File ID # and press enter; File will appear on screen. Review file, press ESC. to return to Master List. Move cursor down to desired file, press Delete. File will again appear on screen; Press enter to delete file. Press Y or N to complete procedure.

X. HOW TO BACK-UP DATA ON A DISK

1. Go to main RIDS Maintenance Menu

2. Move cursor to Utility Menu, then press enter

3. Move cursor to Back-up Data Files

4. Insert disk into computer and press enter.
   Computer will store RIDS data on disk.

XI   ANNUAL DISPOSAL or D-DAY

Once a year, preferably after the annual audit is complete, the following steps should be taken:

<u>Who</u>	<u>Step Number</u>	<u>Action</u>
System Manager	1.	Designate Disposal Day and inform staff
	2.	Print list of records, alphabetical with custodian
	3.	Highlight each title whose disposal date equals the current year
	4.	Distribute lists by custodian
<u>Custodian</u>		
	5.	Go thru your list of highlighted titles to determine if file may be disposed
	6.	If file is in your office and may be disposed, mark the entry with a Y after Disposal Date and circle the file number so it may be removed from the master list.
		OR
	7.	If file may be disposed but is in the storeroom or off-site storage, circle the file number and the Office Manager will see that the file is disposed of properly
		OR
	8.	If for any reason you are not wiling to dispose of the file at this time, mark the entry with an <u>N and CIRCLE THE FILE NUMBER</u> (Note: You will be notified the following year that this file is once again eligible for disposal.

Appendix C

Feasiblity Study for Optical Disk Image Reduction

MINNEAPOLIS, MINNESOTA

HUMAN RESOURCES DIVISION

OPTICAL DISK FEASIBILITY STUDY

January 24, 19___

_____, Director
Human Resources Division
_____
_____

Dear _____:

We are pleased to present this morning our recommendations concerning optical disk as a storage medium for Human Resources records.

We hope the following pages and the demonstrations today will answer your questions regarding optical disk and that the savings and other benefits will justify the recommendations we are making.

Please consider that this is only the beginning of the process and that we look forward to assisting you in any way possible.

Thank you for the confidence you have expressed in us and the opportunity to make this study. We look forward to working with you and your staff on this exciting project.

Sincerely,

Gloria Gold, CRM
Vice President

GG/dt
Enclosure

TABLE OF CONTENTS

Current Situation

Human Resources, a division of _____, requires total
security of documents because of the confidentiality of most of the
records. In addition, because of the nature of the company product,
management has taken the position that personnel files must be kept
permanently. There are employee health and safety considerations in
this decision and, at the moment, it does not appear this is likely to
change.

The bottom line, therefore, is that records volume will continue
to increase. Not only is the increase due to turnover in
positions, and new hirings, but also because the paperwork per
employee is increasing.

Human Resources, at the same time, is performing many functions
not formerly associated with personnel management. This often
requires special staff talents, private areas for conferences,
and room to plan and develop new programs to meet new needs.

The current space is totally inadequate to meet the on-going
challenges, but the staff is coping in the hope of finding relief
in the new quarters. Unfortunately, no more space is going to be
allotted and the location of the space makes expansion unlikely.

The possibility of storing some, or many, records on optical disk
was raised and a study approved to determine cost savings and
benefits, if any.

Findings

- Human Resources offices contain more than 400,000 paper records.

- The survey team estimates that Human Resources is currently holding about 164.5 linear feet of records which could be placed on optical disk.

- An additional 50 feet of active personnel records and other file series may be placed on disk at a later date. Our study focuses on the 164.5 feet of records suitable for disk storage.

- The 164.5 feet of records occupy approximately 100 square feet of office and file room space.

- Based on new building costs, the space to house these records will cost, at a minimum, $7,000 a year.

- Computed at a 15% annual increase, the national average, space costs will double in five years.

- Space costs, in fact, over the next five years, and including 1988, will amount to almost $50,000.

- Human Resources is alloted less space in the new building than in their present offices.

- The space occupied by records stored in private offices and reception areas would be available for other uses if the identified records were stored on disks.

- On optical disks these records, which now occupy 100 square feet, would occupy about 4 linear inches. (The workstation would be accommodated on a desk.)

- Filing equipment is currently at capacity. Any increase in volume will require additional files and/or shelving.

- Microfilm, which was used previously as a means of reducing volume, has not proved to be effective.

- Human Resources does not, currently, have a complete files index.

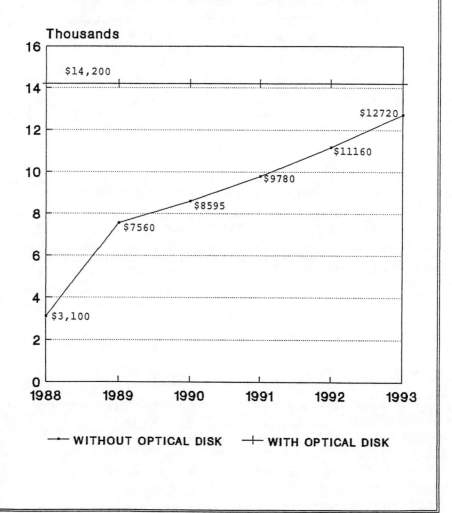

PROJECTED COSTS
SPACE, EQUIP, SUPPLIES

Conclusions

• Optical disk would be an efficient medium on which to store inactive, semi-active and historical Human Resources records.

• Retrieval would be speedy, files could not be misplaced or contents separated. Security would be more complete than today's methods.

• Converting identified records to disk would free up space in the new quarters to allow for future expansion of services by the Division.

• Meanwhile the space could be used more efficiently in offices and reception areas.

• Based on space and equipment costs avoided over the next five years, the optical disk system costs less than $4,000 per year.

HUMAN RESOURCES

RECORDS SERIES SUITABLE FOR OPTICAL DISK

Personnel Records-Inactive

File Series	Volume (in feet)
Terminated Personnel Files	19
Terminated Personnel (3x5 cards)	4.5
Apprenticeship Records-MN office	3
Apprentriceship Files-L.J.	1.5
Drivers, by Name, Employee Number	1.5
Employee Rosters	3
Seniority Records	2 (legal si ǝ)
Performance Appraisals	9
Job Postings	6
Position Requisitions	3
Job Descriptions-old	1.5
	54

Estimated 81,000 images
Equivalent to 1 disk

Career/Position Improvement

File Series	Volume (in feet)
Testing	3
Advertising Records	1.5
Training Records	1.5
Service Award Files	3
Safety Awards	1.5
Training Requests and Sign-offs	2
	12.5 ft = 1 cabinet

Estimated 18,750 images
Equivalent to 1/4 disk

Compensation/Benefits

File Series	Volume (in feet)
401K	2
Union/Salary Increases	1
NRECA: Pension, ERISA	4
NRECA: Pension (Death Claims)	12 (legal)
NRECA: Salary Reports for Pension	.5
Vacation/Sick Leave-Annual	3
Pre-retirement Files	.5
Compensation Records	9
IRS Files	2
LTD	5
Audiograms/X-Rays	7.5
Health Insurance History	5
Deferred Compensation	1
COBRA	1
Old Health Insurance Claims	6
Workers Compensation Files	4
Old Salary Records	5.5
Labor Negotiations	7
Union Dues-Correspondence	3
	79

Estimated 118,500 images
Equivalent to 2 disks

Historical/Reference/Resources

File Series	Volume (in feet)
Financial Planning	2
EEO Reports	1
United Way	1
Dept of Labor Records	4
Business Ethics Reports	1.5
Fitness for Duty	3.5
Salary Administration Manual	2
	19

Estimated 28,500 images
Equivalent to 1/2 disk

HUMAN RESOURCES

INDEX FIELDS

(25)   Employee Name __ __ __ __ __ __ __ __ __ __ __ __ __ __ __
                      __ __ __ __ __ __ __ __ __ __

(4)   Employee id # __ __ __ __

(7)   Document Type __ __ __ __ __ __ __ __

(8)   Document Date __ __ __ __ __ __ __

(100) Document Desc _____
                     _____
                     _____

(3)   Privacy Code __ __ __

(15)   Cross-reference
       to Maiden Name __ __ __ __ __ __ __ __ __ __

Passwords are needed.

(10) position ⎫ add to index for each employee

(2) doc page # ⎭ use only for multi-page documents

OPTICAL DISK OPTIONS

OPTION I

Install the least costly stand-alone optical disk system available.

- 5 1/4 inch disks, holding 12,000-15,000 images

- Stand-alone, self-contained system

- 800 mg MAXTOR Optical Disk Drive

- SCSI Interface

- Maintenance and support

- Upgradeable to receive juke box, if needed

- Disks to cost about $150 each

Estimated Cost: $43,000

PROS

- Low-end cost of technology

- Can be justified on space savings alone

- Cost of disks is much lower than 12 inch disks

CONS

- Concern that 5 1/4 inch disk may not be the company standard

- Will need between 10 & 12 disks versus 3 or 4 12 inch disks

OPTION II

Install a medium-priced stand-alone optical disk system.

- 12 inch disks holding about 100,000 images each

- 1.2 gbt optical disk drive

- 160 mg hard disk drive

- Support, maintenance as in Option I

- Upgradeable to network system, if required

- Disks to cost about $800 each

Estimated Cost: $67,000

PROS

- Compatible with other 12 inch disk systems DPC is likely to buy in the future

- Much less need for changing disks as more data resides on each disk

- Many good systems available at this price

CONS

- Cost of disks is higher, but so is capacity

- Initial outlay cannot be justified on space savings alone

OPTION III

Install a medium priced optical disk system in Accounts Payable networked to Human Resources.

- 12 inch disks, holding 100,000 images each

- Workstation (PC), scanner and laser jet printer to reside in Human Resources

- Record Server, image server and 12 inch optical disk drive to reside in Accounts Payable

- Optical disk drive to be totally dedicated to Human Resources, totally secured

Estimated Cost: $30,000-40,000

PROS

- Lower initial investment

- System is totally secure

- Configuration is compatible with other DPC plans/ concepts

CONS

- A/P will have to bear the networking cost of more than $107,000 - chiefly because of the software portion of the cost

- Control of disks is in another department

- System may be more expensive to upgrade in the future

Image Search Network Schematic

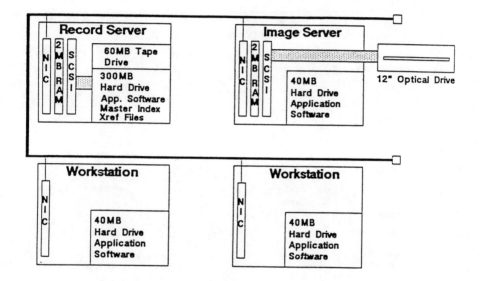

RECOMMENDATIONS

- After considering all the options, pros and cons, it is our opinion that Option II, in the long run, is the most economical, most efficient choice.

Rationale:
1) Option II allows DPC to bid out two identical systems, leading, hopefully, to a better pricing structure.

2) Option II places the cost evenly on the users.

3) The system can be turned over to another DPC user should Human Resources go on to a higher version of the technology.

4) Even though a network can easily provide essential security, the in-house system is totally under control of users and equally important, flexible to use at any time during the working and non-working day.

5) Having two identical systems, DPC has a back up for each under emergency conditions.

6) The benefits cited above are worth the annual difference of less than $4,000 a year.

- No changes are recommended, or needed, in staff classifications. The proposed system deals with inactive and reference data rather than the highly active current files. When and if active files are brought into the picture, workflow will be seriously involved and consideration may be given to classifications at that time. The consultant team has confidence that Human Resources is up to the challenge of the new technology.

- Workflow dealing with the records on optical disk will change only slightly. Figure 3 deals with the workflow concept, although these may be altered as additional needs are explored.

- The optical disk system could be placed in the open office area along the lines of figure 4. This would allow easy access for all users and place the optical disk by one staff person who could be the primary operator.

OPTICAL DISK FEATURES

The features/requirements we have included are identical to the those included in the Accounts Payable study. This is to provide standard features to facilitate identical systems. These systems could be bid out together to ensure backups for each system, possible lower price structure, and similar service agreements.

The Human Resources system would require password capability which may not be required by the Accounts Payable system. If Accounts Payable is in agreement, that could be added to the Accounts Payable specifications.

OPTICAL DISK FEATURES

General

- Must accommodate downloading from mainframe to create static file to eliminate excessive data entry

- 12" Optical Drive and Disk

- System will have a 90-day acceptance period before warranty goes into effect

- System will have a 6-month warranty on parts and labor.

- Cost figures to be supplieed for:

  -- outright purchase
  -- lease/purchase buyout 3 year
  -- lease - 3 year

- Service will be same day if called before 9 am, before noon of next day if called after 9 am

- Service will include immediate replacement components if repairs cannot be made same day as service

- Vendor should provide priority parts ordering available on an overnight/next day basis

- System must provide note pad or electronic messaging capability for security

- Image output quality must comply with ISO standard FAX 4

- Training of staff will take place on site on the delivered equipment. Training must be included in system pricing to include supervisor, key operators, and casual users.

  -- provide user manuals (user readable/friendly)
  -- assistance in creating user-defined screens as required by Human Resources Optical Disk Index. Vendor must provide report generating capability for Human Resources management.

- System must have capability to add multiple 12 " optical disk drives and additional hard disk storage if required at a later date

- If the successful vendor delivers equipment which in any way fails to meet specifications, a full and immediate refund will be forthcoming from the vendor, plus the cost-to-date calculated by _____, for converting, training of staff and costs to the company incurred as a result of the optical disk failure.

- Availability of Support Center #800 hotline to address hardware and software analysis is a must which initiates service calls directly to vendor.

- Vendor must specify average mean time between failure statistics for system components to minimize customer downtime pertaining to hardware and software.

- Vendor must provide bench mark parameters that will be consistent throughout total system. The capabilities must be agreeable with customers ongoing needs, i.e. indexing, print quality, software functions, etc.

- Vendor must be able to physically support both present and future optical L.A.N. system configurations to ensure vendor's company committment to industry.

- Average downtime of more than four hours a month in the first six months will be considered unacceptable.

- Average downtime of more than two hours per month in the next 18 months will be considered unacceptable.

Specific

- Hardware will include, but not be limited to:

    (1)   12" optical disk drive

    (1)   300 DPI laser printer

    (1)   Workstation - P.C. IBM compatible

          70 mb hard drive
          1.2 mb floppy drive
          15" high resolution monitor
          application software
          IBM DOS 3.3
          streamer tape drive

    (1)   300 DPI scanner

● Features will be stated by the bidding vendors and rated by
  the buyers. Among them may be:

               Facsimile transmission
               Automatic feed
               Windows
               Zoom capability
               Software features:
                    Unlimited record size
                    Fast search fields
                    Multiple field audits
                    Special reports
                    "And" or "Or" logic.
                    Batch searches
                    Sort sequence
                    Imaging cashing
               Reports
               Optical disk back-up

HUMAN RESOURCES
TERMINATED EMPLOYEE RECORDS
PROPOSED WORKFLOW

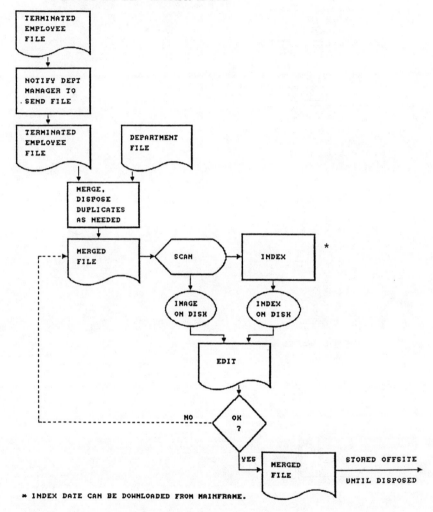

* INDEX DATE CAN BE DOWNLOADED FROM MAINFRAME.

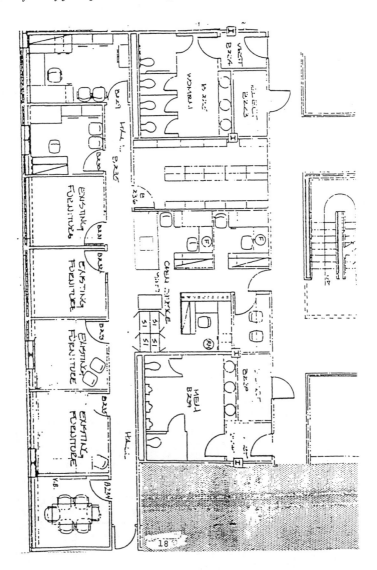

BENEFITS

● Space:

  Based on projected annual increases of 15% and the $60 per square foot cost in the new buildings, the costs for storing the inactive Human Resources records in paper form will be:

Year	Square Feet	Cost
1988	100	$3,000 (current costs)
1989	115	6,900 (new building costs)
1990	132.25	7,935
1991	152	9,120
1992	175	10,500
1993	201	12,060
		$46,514

  Average cost per year: $9,303 (see figure 1)

● Based on an expected 15% increase in records for each of the next five years, Human Resources can save an estimated $560 a year ($2,800 over five years). This benefit is based on the avoidance of the necessity to purchase additional filing equipment (see figure 1).

● The yearly supply cost for paper records may average $100 per year. This cost would be avoided using optical disk technology (see figure 1).

Current system average total cost per year: $10,583

A full stand-alone optical disk system, including an average of one disk per year would average $14,200 - a difference of less than $4,000 a year.

The following benefits appear to be of even higher priority than the space consideration.

BENEFITS

- Security

  Human Resources currently has 229 unique file series. At least one vital file series contains a serious gap. Years 1940-1950 are missing from the Master Roster of Employee files.

  Research has revealed also that pages which should be in all personnel files are missing from some.

  Currently, Human Resources staff has managed to plug the security holes. But this effort is a major cost to the unit in terms of time and productivity.

  Because Human Resources personnel files, both active and terminated have permanent retention, and because the individual volume of paper work per file is increasing about 25% per year, the control process can only become more costly.

  Eventually, control will become a full-time position at $20,000 a year. Even then, when the only copy of a file is removed from the vault security is breached.

- Privacy

  Many file series contain data on individuals which the Federal statutes have defined as Private and in some cases Confidential. This means that access to these files must be severely limited according to the restrictions placed on Public, Private and Confidential data.

  Because Dairyland Power Cooperative is a highly regulated industry it is subject to Federal and State rules regarding data privacy.

  Optical disk is, at the moment, the only image reduction system, the only vital records back up system, the only access-limited system which can provide the data privacy prescribed by law.

  Savings resulting from secured and protected files would be derived from litigation: suits won as well as suits avoided.

- Productivity

  Human Resources staff spend about 15% of their time retrieving files and/or searching for files.

  An optical disk system insures that files cannot get out of order. Retrieval time of a file folder typically is reduced from a few minutes to a few seconds.

  Putting a dollar figure on increased productivity is difficult because the value of work accomplished due to released time (time not spent in searching for files) is unknown at this point. The released time figure is estimated at $20,000 annually.

- Research

  The next five years of State and Federal oversight will undoubtedly require detailed reporting based on accumulated data of many types.

  Searching paper files to accumulate data is a time-consuming and often incomplete task. Optical disk files allow the luxury of browsing thousands of documents in minutes.

  Reviewing original documents in this manner will not only facilitate responses to special and routine reports, it will generate ideas for improved services to Dairyland Power Cooperative employees and provide more accurate and detailed information for department planning.

- Uniformity

  At the moment Human Resources files are on paper and microfilm. The microfilm has not proved to be the effective tool expected. Microfilm has been ruled out as an alternative to paper files.

  Optical disk is a complete system. It will accommodate all the old records as well as those now being created.

  Human Resources staff will have many new problems to cope with in the 90's. Now is the time to organize data, to protect information, and to speed retrieval time. A single system, optical disk, will meet these needs.

ADDITIONAL BENEFITS

- Approximately 76% of current Human Resources records can be placed on the Optical Disk system. This will eliminate the majority of paper filing.

- This system can be operated and maintained at current staff-levels.

- Optical disk supports the integrity of records. Once a document is on the system, it cannot be altered or misfiled.

- The system can be password protected among users, and at specific levels of users.

- Duplication of records virtually can be eliminated.

IMPLEMENTATION ITEMS

Finalize Index, System Downloading, System Design

The overall system design needs to be finalized with the computer
department and in conjunction with Human Resources needs before
the system is implemented. These areas can be addressed with the
computer programmer who will work with the implementation team.

                    Estimated Cost: $3,000

                    Estimated Hours: 40 hours

Conversion Procedures

Coordination of the conversion effort is very important to the
overall system success.   The conversion plan and procedures
should be developed and approved before the conversion takes
place. Everyone involved with the conversion needs to be trained
and given specific procedures.

                    Estimated Cost: $2,000

                    Estimated Hours: 40 hours

Conversion

The conversion itself will consist of scanning and indexing the records onto the system. _____ is available to do
the conversion.

Procedures Manual

A procedures manual is essential to the use and maintenance of
the system. It could be used as a training tool before and
during the time the system becomes operable. It would also
provide consistency in policy and procedures for current staff
and for any person hired in the future.

                    Estimated Cost: $3,000

                    Estimated Hours: 60 hours

ACTION PLAN

Estimated Start Date: April 1, 1989
Estimated System Test: October 1, 1989

Activity/Month	Ø	1	2	3	4	5	--	11
Approvals	———							
Finalize System & Index	——							
Finalize Specs/Bid Process	———*							
Delivery, Training				——				
Additional Programming		——	——					
Training and Procedures (Conversion)			————					
System Loading (Conversion)				——				
System Test				——				
Run System					————			

Index

[Numbers in *italic* refer to actual samples.]